Reluctant Reception

Seeking to understand why host states treat migrants and refugees inclusively, exclusively, or without any direct engagement, Kelsey P. Norman offers this original, comparative analysis of the politics of asylum seeking and migration in the Middle East and North Africa. While current classifications of migrant and refugee engagement in the Global South mistake the absence of formal policy and law for neglect, *Reluctant Reception* proposes the concept of "strategic indifference," where states proclaim to be indifferent toward migrants and refugees, thereby inviting international organizations and local nongovernmental organizations to step in and provide services on the state's behalf.

Using the cases of Egypt, Morocco, and Turkey to develop her theory of "strategic indifference," Norman demonstrates how, by allowing migrants and refugees to integrate locally into large informal economies, and by allowing organizations to provide basic services, host countries receive international credibility while only spending minimal state resources.

KELSEY P. NORMAN is Fellow for the Middle East and Director of the Women's Rights, Human Rights and Refugees program at Rice University's Baker Institute for Public Policy. She holds a PhD in Political Science from the University of California, Irvine.

Reluctant Reception

Refugees, Migration, and Governance in the Middle East and North Africa

KELSEY P. NORMAN
Rice University, Houston

CAMBRIDGE
UNIVERSITY PRESS

University Printing House, Cambridge CB2 8BS, United Kingdom

One Liberty Plaza, 20th Floor, New York, NY 10006, USA

477 Williamstown Road, Port Melbourne, VIC 3207, Australia

314–321, 3rd Floor, Plot 3, Splendor Forum, Jasola District Centre,
New Delhi – 110025, India

79 Anson Road, #06–04/06, Singapore 079906

Cambridge University Press is part of the University of Cambridge.

It furthers the University's mission by disseminating knowledge in the pursuit of
education, learning, and research at the highest international levels of excellence.

www.cambridge.org
Information on this title: www.cambridge.org/9781108842365
DOI: 10.1017/9781108900119

First published 2021

A catalogue record for this publication is available from the British Library.

Library of Congress Cataloging-in-Publication Data
Names: Norman, Kelsey P., author.
Title: Reluctant reception : refugees, migration and governance in the Middle East
and North Africa / Kelsey P. Norman, Rice University, Houston.
Description: Cambridge, United Kingdom ; New York, NY : Cambridge University
Press, 2020. | Includes index.
Identifiers: LCCN 2020019567 (print) | LCCN 2020019568 (ebook) | ISBN
9781108842365 (hardback) | ISBN 9781108900119 (epub)
Subjects: LCSH: Refugees – Egypt. | Refugees – Morocco. | Refugees – Turkey. |
Immigrants – Egypt. | Immigrants – Morocco. | Immigrants – Turkey.
Classification: LCC HV640 .N66 2020 (print) | LCC HV640 (ebook) | DDC
362.870956–dc23
LC record available at https://lccn.loc.gov/2020019567
LC ebook record available at https://lccn.loc.gov/2020019568

ISBN 978-1-108-84236-5 Hardback
ISBN 978-1-108-82047-9 Paperback

Additional resources for this publication at www.cambridge.org/reluctantreception

For Abdoul Raouf

Rationally I know what is right: my attempt at living in this village with these happy people. But mysterious things in my soul and in my blood impel me towards faraway parts that loom up before me and cannot be ignored. How sad it would be if either or both of my sons grew up with the germ of infection in them, the wanderlust.

Tayeb Salih, *Season of Migration to the North*

When our citizenship laws effectively become intertwined with distributing shares in human survival on a global scale – designating some to a life of relative comfort while condemning others to a constant struggle to overcome the basic threats of insecurity, hunger, and destitution – we can no longer silently accept this situation.

Aleyet Shachar, *The Birthright Lottery*

Contents

Figures

Tables

Acronyms

AKP	Turkey's Justice and Development Party (Adalet ve Kalkınma Partisi)
ALECMA	Association for Illuminating Clandestine Emigration to North Africa (Association Lumière sur l'Emigration Clandestine au Maghreb)
AMDH	Moroccan Association for Human Rights (Association Marocaine des Droits Humains)
ANAPEC	Morocco's National Agency for the Promotion of Employment and Competencies (Agence Nationale de Promotion de l'Emploi et des Compétences)
CHP	Turkey's Republican People's Party (Cumhuriyet Halk Partisi)
CNDH	Morocco's National Council for Human Rights (Conseil National des Droits de l'Homme)
DGMM	Turkey's Directorate General of Migration Management (Göç İdaresi Genel Müdürlüğü)
ECtHR	European Court of Human Rights
EGP	Egyptian pound
EU	European Union
EURA	European Union Readmission Agreement
GADEM	Antiracist Group for Accompaniment and Defense of Foreigners and Migrants (Le Groupe Antiraciste de Défense et d'Accompagnement des Étrangers et Migrants)
IGAM	Migration and Asylum Research Center (İltica ve Göç Araştırmaları Merkezi)
INGO	International nongovernmental organization
IO	International organization
IOM	International Organization for Migration
MAD	Moroccan dirham
MENA	Middle East and North Africa

MHP	Turkey's Nationalist Movement Party (Milliyetçi Hareket Partisi)
MOFA	Ministry of Foreign Affairs
MOI	Ministry of the Interior
MOU	Memorandum of understanding
MSF	Doctors Without Borders (Médecins Sans Frontières)
NCCPIM	Egypt's National Coordinating Committee for Combating and Preventing Illegal Migration (al-lajna al-waṭanīya al-tansīqīya li-mukāfaḥa wa-manʿ al-hijra ghayr al-sharʿīya)
NGO	Nongovernmental organization
ODT	Democratic Organization for Work (Organization Démocratique du Travail)
OCHA	United Nations Office for the Coordination of Humanitarian Affairs
NDP	Egypt's National Democratic Party (al-ḥizb al-waṭanī al-dīmqrāṭī)
PJD	Morocco's Justice and Development Party (ḥizb al-ʿadāla wa-l-tanmīya)
RSD	Refugee status determination
TRY	Turkish lira
UN	United Nations
UNDP	United Nations Development Programme
UNHCR	United Nations Refugee Agency

Note on Translation

The transliteration system used in this book is that of IJMES, except where local Egyptian terms are used (e.g. *mugamma*).

Preface

In 2015, several years after the Arab Spring and as Syrians sought refuge in neighboring countries, the migration and refugee "crises" I had been researching suddenly became front-page news in Europe, the United States, and across the world. What had been a niche topic as I was writing proposals, seeking out contacts, and conducting interviews suddenly became front-page news across the globe. Initially this seemed promising; I hoped increased attention would mean increased support in terms of international funding and perhaps even better international cooperation for refugee resettlement. But the momentary global sympathy after the body of three-year-old Aylan Kurdi washed up on a Turkish beach quickly dissipated and was replaced by xenophobic nationalism, anti-immigration platforms, and calls for reinforced borders.

Against this backdrop, the process of writing this book between 2015 and 2019 seemed constantly to evolve. Often, I felt that my efforts would have been better directed toward activism or public engagement that attempted to counter some of the racist and exclusionary rhetoric that had become so prominent. But I persisted in my efforts because I believe that the topic addressed in this study is a critical yet neglected component of the broader contemporary migration picture: the reception of migrants and refugees in the states that are arguably carrying the greatest "burden." As I have written elsewhere, countries in the Middle East and North Africa need to be taken seriously by the international community and donor countries as more than mere migrant- or refugee-hosting vessels. These states and their incentives should be better understood.

While my focus in this study is primarily on the host states, the interviews I conducted with individual migrants and refugees living in Egypt, Morocco, and Turkey formed the backbone of my thinking for this project. I am extremely grateful to everyone who was willing to share his or her story and time so generously because this research would not have been possible without the insight of lived experiences. I am not overly optimistic that the circumstances – lack of economic opportunity, war, and insecurity – driving individuals from their homes will suddenly resolve themselves in the near future, nor am I optimistic that the countries and regions – particularly Europe, North America, and Australia – currently barring these people from access will suddenly change their policies and permit them to enter legally and safely. But as a collective result of the conversations I had with men, women, and families in makeshift homes, tents, and coffee shops, I am optimistic that migrants and refugees will persevere, even in the face of closed and fortified borders and absent meaningful international protection. These individuals are more tenacious and brave than they are ever given credit for by the media, and while many are victims, all are resilient, resourceful, and imaginative, willing to see a future in a new home despite the many obstacles en route.

This research required extensive multicountry and multivisit fieldwork, and I am eternally grateful to the many friends, family members, colleagues, and strangers who assisted me along the way. Thank you to the various foundations and centers that provided financial support for this project, including the Social Sciences and Humanities Research Council; the Carnegie Corporation of New York; Rice University's Baker Institute for Public Policy and the Kelly Day Endowment; the Project on Middle East Political Science at George Washington University; and the Department of Political Science, the Kugelman Center for Citizen Peacebuilding, the Center for Peace and Conflict Studies, and the Center for Research on Immigration, Population, and Public Policy at the University of California, Irvine. Thank you also to the Center for Migration and Refugee Studies at the American University in Cairo and the Center for Migration Research at Istanbul Bilgi University for hosting me while I was in Egypt and Turkey, respectively, and to the Arab American Language in Morocco for providing a home base during my initial trip to Morocco. Finally, thank you to my undergraduate research assistants at the University of California, Irvine – Madison Francescia Avila and Parth Jani – and to Brahim Benyous for research assistance in Rabat, Morocco.

I am extremely grateful for the tireless mentorship of my doctoral advisor, Louis DeSipio, and my committee members, Sara Wallace Goodman and Kamal Sadiq, who were proponents of this project since its inception. In addition, many colleagues graciously read or listened to parts of this book in various forms and provided invaluable feedback. In particular, I would like to thank Yehonatan Abramson, Hannah Alarian, Rawan Arar, Maysa Ayoub, Ibrahim Awad, Çiğdem Benam, Fillipo Dionigi, Antje Ellermann, Ilka Eickhof, Lisel Hintz, James Hollifield, Karen Jacobsen, Michael Kagan, Rana Khoury, Audie Klotz, Maria Koinova, Lev Marder, Erin McGrath, Nicholas Micinski, Dana Moss, Lama Mourad, Harris Mylonas, Carrie Reiling, Craig Damien Smith, Leila Tayeb, Ayelet Shachar, Bertan Tokuzlu, Phil Triadafilopoulos, Gerasimos Tsourapas, and Ayman Zohry. Thank you also to my colleagues at the Sié Chéou-Kang Center for International Security and Diplomacy and the Josef Korbel School for International Studies, including Ahmed Abdrabou, Deborah Avant, Marie Berry, Yolande Bouka, Erica Chenoweth, Rachel Epstein, Nader Hashemi, Cullen Hendrix, Oliver Kaplan, Julia Macdonald, and Katherine Tennis, for their advice and encouragement. Thank you also to my colleagues at the Institute for European Studies at the University of British Columbia and to those at the Baker Institute for Public Policy at Rice University for their encouragement during the final stages of revising this manuscript.

I am also grateful to the organizers and participants of the following workshops: "Forced Displacement in the Middle East" at the Middle East Centre at the London School of Economics; "Regional Security Complexes in the European Union and Its Neighbourhood: A Critical Reflection" at the University of Dundee; "Comparative Responses to Asylum Seeking in Europe, Australia, the US, and Middle East" at the Center for Comparative Immigration Studies at the University of California, San Diego; "The Stakes of the Middle East and North Africa Migration Studies" at the Moise A. Khayrallah Center for Lebanese Diaspora Studies at North Carolina State University; and "Diasporas and Challenges to Statehood in the Middle East and North Africa" at Warwick University. These collegial events provided the opportunity to present early stages of this work. I also thank the participants of the POMEPS Junior Scholars Symposium – in particular, my discussants Fiona Adamson and Laurie Brand and organizers Jason Brownlee, Marc Lynch, Amaney Jamal, Wendy Pearlman, and Jillian Schwedler – who provided me with extensive feedback on the first full version of this manuscript. Finally, thank you to two anonymous reviewers for helpful suggestions, to editors

Maria Marsh and Daniel Brown at Cambridge University Press, and to Kate Sampsell and Cheryl Lenser for assistance with copy editing and indexing.

I am deeply indebted to the family, friends, and colleagues who hosted me between 2012 and 2015, whether for a night, a week, or several months at a time. I could not have done the traveling that I needed to do for this project without your kindness and generosity. Most importantly, my thanks go to my father, Jon Norman, for being a proponent of the PhD endeavor from the get-go (for better or worse) and to my mother, Deborah Norman, for her unwavering confidence in my abilities. And of course, endless thanks go to my husband, Mohammed Ali, who during the course of writing this book became a migrant himself, forced to leave his home of thirty years and start over in the United States. Some of the themes discussed in the following pages – building a life amid uncertainty, contending with onerous legal regimes – thus became deeply personal for our marriage, but his patience, love, and ability always to see the bright side are a testament to the perseverance and fortitude that underlie any migratory journey.

1 | *Introduction*

Migration in the Global North and South

1.1 The Myth of the Transit Country

Sama[1] is a forty-five-year-old woman from Syria who fled to Egypt in 2012 with her husband, her elderly mother-in-law, and her six children. They live together in a two-bedroom flat on the outskirts of Alexandria in a beach community that is populated by Egyptians during the summer but relatively empty throughout the rest of the year. Sama's husband has a stomach ailment that makes it impossible for him to work, and the family subsists on a small stipend paid to them by the United Nations Refugee Agency (UNHCR), formerly known as the United Nations High Commission for Refugees. Many of Sama's neighbors – other Syrians who had been living in Egypt – paid smugglers to be taken by boat to Europe. Sama says she would gladly buy space for all her family members on a smuggler's boat, if only she had the money to afford it.

Abdou is a thirty-year-old migrant from Cameroon. He has lived in Morocco since 2008 and in Tangier, his current home, since 2013. Before that he was in Rabat and Casablanca, but he prefers Tangier because he still hopes to travel to Spain, his initial destination and the reason he chose Morocco. But going to Spain is expensive and dangerous, and he knows that the likelihood of crossing the Strait of Gibraltar or successfully scaling the fences into the Spanish enclave of Melilla or Ceuta is slim. Abdou lives in a Tangier neighborhood called Boukhalef that has a large migrant population, many of whom are, like Abdou, also hoping to eventually reach Europe. For Abdou the problems in his neighborhood are as bad as ever. Primarily, migrants are subject to racism from their Moroccan neighbors, and in some cases young Moroccan men, *shabāb*, will break into and rob migrant houses or assail migrants in the street. Abdou and his neighbors do not feel comfortable going to the police to report these attacks because many do not have legal status in Morocco, leaving them vulnerable to more harassment and possible deportation.

Ibrahim, a twenty-six-year-old Congolese migrant, moved to Turkey because he understood Istanbul to be a large, cosmopolitan city with ample work opportunities and because Congo nationals find Turkish visas relatively easy to obtain. But after one year in Istanbul, Ibrahim has not found any satisfactory work; he is considering moving on to Europe. Ibrahim prefers this prospect to returning home because he wants to make some return on his migratory investment. His family and friends helped him come to Turkey by providing him with funds and assisting in the visa process, so he feels he cannot return to Congo empty-handed. Ibrahim calls this the "African" way; family members help you leave, but then they expect something when you return. Ibrahim thinks that he would probably qualify for refugee status given continued unrest in parts of his country, but he has heard from friends in Istanbul that some refugees have to wait up to five years to be resettled to a third country in Europe or North America, if they are ever resettled at all. He does not want to wait that long and prefers instead to work in Istanbul's informal economy while looking for his chance to move on to Europe.

What Sama, Abdou, and Ibrahim have in common is that they are stuck in countries thought only to be spaces of transit. Many migrants and refugees come to countries like Morocco, Turkey, and Egypt intending to pass through on their way to Europe or other Western states. In reality, however, only a small fraction successfully complete their intended journeys. The majority of migrants and refugees find themselves lingering, perhaps indefinitely, in transit states that are rapidly becoming countries of migrant and refugee settlement (Hoeffler 2013). Some, like Ibrahim, arrive with the intention of staying put. As Philippe Fargues (2009) acknowledges in his study of migration in Middle East and North African (MENA) countries, the number of migrants aiming to end up in countries like Egypt, Morocco, or Turkey is on the rise. This is perhaps because individuals are increasingly aware of the near-impossibility of reaching heavily fortified states within the European Union (EU). This study is not so much concerned with migrant and refugee intentions as with the outcome: states that were previously assumed to be only countries of transit are now hosting semipermanent migrant and refugee populations. This book explores the phenomenon of migrant and refugee settlement in countries not usually thought of as host states from the perspectives of both migrants and refugees themselves as well as from the perspective of receiving countries.

Many countries touted only as transit states are nonetheless fully aware of the migrant and refugee groups residing within their territories and thus unofficially permit migrants' and refugees' continued presence. Through states' inability to successfully prevent migrants and refugees from entering the country and unwillingness to deport the vast majority of them, these countries permit migrants and refugees to remain indefinitely. An unanswered question in current scholarship is, why? What determines whether host states treat migrants and refugees inclusively, exclusively, or with what I call "strategic indifference"?

1.2 Three Assumptions

While it is beginning to change, bias dominates in the academic literature on migration and citizenship regarding the movement of individuals from the Global South[2] to the Global North and the migrant reception policies of Global North host states. This partly reflects the fact that countries of the Global North host a slight majority of the world's migrants (OECD 2010; UN Population Division 2013), yet it neglects the fact that *nearly half* of all international migrants reside in countries of the Global South (UN Population Division 2017). Furthermore, between 2000 and 2017, the number of international migrants residing in Global South countries increased from 40 to 43 percent of the total worldwide (UN Population Division 2017). In 2017, 83 percent of refugees in the world, representing 21 million individuals, lived in a Global South country (UN Population Division 2017). Despite these trends, there is comparatively little information and theorization about how countries in the Global South receive and host migrants and refugees. I argue that several assumptions embedded within the existing academic literature on migration can help account for this discrepancy.

First, the extant literature assumes that migrants and refugees are residing impermanently in host states in the Global South. Residence initially intended to be transitory can easily extend into something more permanent. Instead, much of the extant literature expects that migrants and refugees in transit are only aiming for Western democracies in Europe, North America, or Australia and that countries crossed while en route to the Global North are spaces of temporary residence. While not per se incorrect, this viewpoint represents an incomplete picture that misses many of the nuances underpinning the realities of contemporary migration to and through countries in the Global South. Many individuals may initially set out on a migratory journey with a Global North state in mind as an intended destination, but the difficulties of actually reaching heavily fortified and secured Western democracies mean that both migrants and refugees can spend months and even years in "transit" countries along the way. Furthermore, migrants and refugees are strategic actors who will adapt their travel routes based on the most recent information available (de Haas 2007). If the possibility of reaching destination countries becomes too dangerous or costly, these individuals may amend their plans.

Further underpinning this assumption of impermanence is the idea that forced migratory movements across an international border will eventually reverse themselves once refugees are able to repatriate. In theory, repatriation is just one of three durable solutions available to refugees; the others are integration into a host state and resettlement to a third country (Jacobsen 2001). Yet, beginning in the 1980s, host states in the Global South began to view repatriation as the only viable solution, even when the situation in a refugee's home country remained unresolved (Milner 2009). Michael Barnett (2001) examines how the UNHCR attempted to reconcile states' preference for repatriation with the agency's mission to protect against *refoulement*, the forcible return of a refugee to a life-threatening situation in his or her home state. Previously,

[voluntary repatriation] demanded that the refugee consent to return to a country that in his or her view no longer represented a threat to his or her safety. But UNHCR officials began introducing new concepts like "voluntariness" that meant that refugee consent was no longer necessary and that the home situation need only have appreciably improved or held out the promise of improving. (261)

Many conflicts since the end of the Cold War have been protracted, producing refugees that may not have been willing to return home even when violence subsided due to economic, infrastructural, or property devastation or because of the threat of renewed conflict (Helton 2007).

In the last several decades, refugees from Ethiopia, Sudan, Iraq, and Afghanistan found themselves in circumstances where the conflict that forced them to flee did not end with a secure situation in the refugees' home state. Nonetheless, the UNHCR justified its new practice of returning refugees to less-than-ideal home country environments by arguing that such situations might still be better than camp life (Barnett 2001).

However, the majority of refugees no longer live in camps, a fact that counters the second assumption embedded within the literature on migration and refugees. In the last several decades, migration research has focused heavily on camps as sites of refugee residence, particularly in the sub-Saharan African context (Chan and Loveridge 1987; Hyndman 2000; Agier and Fernbach 2011; Gabiam 2016). As recently as 2014, Phil Orchard (2014) wrote, "[The] long-term encampment of refugees in the developing world [has] become the norm" (206). In fact, more than half of the world's refugees – and all migrants for that matter – live in urban or rural areas outside of camps (Ward 2014). Recognizing this shift, the UNHCR finally developed an urban refugee policy in 2009 (Ward 2014). In the Middle East and North Africa specifically, the vast majority of refugees reside outside of camps in either urban or rural areas (Ward 2014). In Jordan, a country with some of the largest refugee camps in the world, approximately 80 percent of refugees live in urban areas (Achilli 2015). In Turkey, which hosted more than 3 million refugees in 2017, less than 8 percent lived in camps (Erdoğan 2017). This is not to discount the experiences of refugee populations living in camps, including Palestinians in Jordan, Lebanon, and Syria or Sahrawis in Algeria, but to highlight that urban refugees have received less attention from both policy actors and academic researchers, impacting the ways in which these bodies consider possible responses from Global South host states to the presence of refugees. While refugees residing in UN-managed camp situations may have little interaction with a host population or host state officials, refugee and migrant populations living in urban areas are likely to have significant interaction with host-country nationals and, possibly, host state authorities.

The final misconception embedded in the literature on migration within the Global South is that Global South host states lack the ability to respond to the presence of migrants and refugees because of lower state capacities. In his work on global refugee burden sharing between countries of the Global North and South, Alexander Betts (2011) writes, "With relatively porous borders, limited capacity to deport, and a clearly defined legal obligation not to forcibly return refugees to their countries of origin if they face persecution, these neighboring states have little choice but to host refugees" (13). Betts conceives of Global South host states as lacking the capacity, and thus the choice, to respond to refugees, which must accept their position as temporary host countries due to the international norm of burden sharing and pressure from more powerful Global North states. Similarly, James Hollifield (2004) writes, "In Africa and the Middle East, which have high numbers of migrants and refugees, there is a great deal of instability, and states are fluid with little institutional or legal capacity for dealing with international migration" (905). In sum, these authors suggest that the international community should expect very little from countries of the Middle East or Africa in responding to migrants and refugees due to their limited state capacity.

I address these unsubstantiated claims going forward by demonstrating that in and of itself, state capacity is not the most important determinant of state responses to migrants and refugees. Rather, states make calculations based on diplomatic, economic, and security-oriented considerations in deciding when and how to utilize state resources for engaging migrant and refugee populations. Michael Kagan (2012) comes to a similar conclusion when looking broadly at refugee host states in the MENA region. He writes,

With the possible exceptions of Lebanon, Yemen, and post-Baathist Iraq, where central governments are weak, one risks making an incorrect generalization to think that Arab governments are unable to administer refugee policy on their own. It would be more accurate to say that they are unwilling, and there are specific reasons why. (320)

Furthering Kagan's argument, this book proposes a reconceptualization of state engagement choices in Global South countries. Too often, host states in the MENA region, and in the Global South more broadly, are taken as passive actors. It is assumed that they accept migrants and refugees because they cannot keep their borders closed and then allow these groups to remain because they do not have the capacity to do otherwise. I argue that MENA states are instead *strategic* actors when it comes to migration policy. They carefully select the policy most suitable to their domestic and foreign-policy goals while also attempting to utilize as few state resources as possible. In order to make this argument, I redefine the engagement options available to Global South host states.

While existing citizenship and migration scholarship asserts that host countries essentially have two policy options regarding the treatment of migrants and refugees on their territory – a liberal policy that encourages integration or a repressive policy that aims to exclude – I introduce and develop the concept of *strategic indifference*. Aware of the presence of migrant and refugee groups residing semipermanently on its territory, a host state chooses not to directly engage these populations. This proclaimed indifference toward the issue of migration and refugee hosting invites international organizations and nongovernmental organizations (NGOs) to carry out engagement on the state's behalf, yielding tangential benefits for the state. States thus have three options for engaging with migrants and refugees on their territory: a liberal policy, a repressive policy, or an indifferent policy. In Chapters 2, 3, and 4 I show that in the 1990s and the first decade of the 2000s, Egypt, Morocco, and Turkey were able to use strategic indifference to their advantage. By allowing migrants and refugees to integrate locally into large informal economies, and by permitting international and domestic NGOs to provide basic services to these populations, Egypt, Morocco, and Turkey were able to derive international credibility while only dedicating minimal state resources.

I also demonstrate that indifference is unique from a host state doing nothing – or the absence of engagement – in that indifference requires a relationship between a host government and the international organizations and civil society actors that step in to engage with migrants and refugees on the state's behalf. This indirect form of engagement is in contrast to a policy of neglect whereby a state would (1) have no interaction with the migrants and refugees residing on its territory and (2) have no relationship with the international nongovernmental organizations (INGOs) and domestic NGOs that provide services and fill protection gaps. The host countries examined in this study are aware of and have developed relationships with the international and domestic organizations providing services to migrant and refugee populations. They regulate how and whether these organizations can operate, monitor their activities to ensure they do not cross red lines when it comes to security issues and state sovereignty, and encourage the use of international funding to benefit not only migrants and refugees but also host-country nationals.

The next chapter presents the three elements of my theory of strategic indifference. First, it differentiates between a liberal policy, a repressive policy, and an indifferent policy. Second, it explains why a policy of indifference does not indicate an incapable state; rather, a state strategically selects indifference because of the economic and diplomatic benefits this type of policy provides. Third, it presents explanations for why a state might change from a policy of indifference to either a more liberal or repressive policy. To illustrate this theory empirically, this study focuses on a particular type of Global South state – the transit-turned-host country – and examines three cases within the MENA region.

1.3 Transit-Turned-Host States

Part of what necessitates this study of what I call transit-turned-host states is the changing security regimes put in place by Western countries over the last several decades. These means of fortifying territories manifest themselves both physically – such as the United States' amplification of the wall along its southern border with Mexico – and through technological means, including biometric scanning systems or enhanced passports. New methods of immigration control have also extended beyond the state itself, both in concrete forms, such as zones established for policing irregular migrants (those without a proper residency document or visa) within the territory of another state, and through more subtle soft-power mechanisms like coercing or threatening other states to more effectively counter unauthorized migration. David FitzGerald (2019) argues that while these measures are not new – for example, states used instruments of remote border control throughout the twentieth century – international changes in the 1960s for determining who could qualify for refugee protection led states to seek out and amplify means of indiscriminatingly preventing both asylum seekers and migrants from reaching the territory of Western countries.[3] Ruben Andersson (2014) sums up these complex and growing measures of border control under the term *illegality industry*.

In the European context in particular, the EU and its member states have taken various measures to limit and manage both regular and irregular migration (e.g., migrants who arrive with an authorized entry document vs. those who arrive without one). When the EU created the Schengen space – an internal zone of free movement among EU member states – in 1985, it simultaneously began to limit legal access for migrants from non-EU countries and has granted continually fewer visas for non-EU nationals in all immigration categories since that time (Goldschmidt 2006). Part of the reasoning behind this was a backlash against the guest-worker system that fueled much of Europe's migration prior to the 1990s. With the realization that many migrants would not return home following the end of their contracts, Europe began to phase out the guest-worker system (Castles 2006). When it became clear that European states would be unable to "import labor but not people," governments instead sought to limit the number of migrants able to immigrate by formal means (Castles 2006).

Beyond attempting to limit regular migration to Europe, the EU has also engaged in various forms of border externalization through partnerships with countries of its periphery. Since 2005, the Global Approach to Migration and Mobility (GAMM) has served as the overarching framework of the EU's external migration and asylum policy, defining how the EU conducts its policy dialogues and cooperation with non-EU countries, including development cooperation. Bilateral and regional frameworks like the European Neighborhood Policy implement the GAMM (Wolff 2015), and the most elaborated bilateral cooperation frameworks under the GAMM are Mobility Partnerships (MP) and the Common Agendas for Migration and Mobility (CAMM). Both frameworks allow the EU to engage in "comprehensive, enhanced and tailor-made dialogue and cooperation with partner countries ... including a set of targets and commitments as well as a package of specific support measures offered by the EU and interested Member States" (European Commission 2014).

In addition to the GAMM, the Rabat and Khartoum processes – enacted in 2006 and 2013, respectively – are two regional processes that allow for transnational collaboration and negotiation on the issue of migration (Wolff 2015). The Rabat process – also called the Euro-African Dialogue in Migration and Development – addressed the increasing number of migrants attempting to cross the Straits of Gibraltar or to reach the Canary Islands and acknowledged that migration along this route "was not exclusively the responsibility of Morocco and Spain" (ICMPD 2018). The Khartoum process was launched in 2013 to address smuggling and trafficking, particularly for migrants originating from the Horn of

Africa and involving countries of origin, transit, and destination (ICMPD 2018).

Yet Andrew Geddes (2005) acknowledges that while "the language of EU policy development ... has been couched in terms of 'co-operation' and 'migration dialogue,'" in actuality, "policies have tended to reflect EU security concerns without dialogue that takes into account the interest of sending, receiving or transit countries" (278). As part of these partnerships and dialogues, EU governments pressured neighboring Eastern European, Balkan, and North African countries to amplify border control and security efforts in order to prevent irregular migration toward Europe. This strategy was particularly successful in Libya. Beginning in 2003, the EU used the joint incentives of increased trade and the normalization of diplomatic relations to compel the Gaddafi regime to establish Italian–Libyan joint patrols in Libyan and international waters to intercept and apprehend boats carrying migrants (Boubakri 2013). Tunisia and Morocco also conformed their border control practices to the EU's preferences during the same time period. On its eastern border, the EU incentivized Turkey to prevent irregular transit migration through the improvement of border controls and the construction of detention centers with the carrot of eventual EU accession.

Furthermore, the EU has pressured neighboring states into signing readmission agreements. Burden sharing is difficult to enforce in the EU, and non-EU countries can generally not be forced to accept migrants. As such,

in this legal environment, the external dimension of protection becomes one of the pillars of the mechanism, which is designed to shift the responsibility of protection seekers to third countries. Readmission agreements have appeared as a solution to make such rules operable by creating a mechanism capable of forcing transit countries concerned to readmit asylum seekers as well as migrants. (Tokuzlu 2010, 6)

Bertan Tokuzlu (2010) argues that non-EU countries agree to sign readmission agreements if the economic or diplomatic benefits provided by the EU are considered more profitable than the perceived cost of hosting migrants and refugees. While the EU has not yet reached an agreement with Morocco at the time of writing, Morocco has a readmission agreement in place with Spain. Turkey has agreed to various readmission agreements with individual EU countries and with the EU as a whole.

The outcome of these multifaceted forms of European security exter-nalization has been the increasing cost and difficulty for both irregular migrants – individuals lacking documentation – and asylum seekers to successfully reach countries of the EU, leading to the buildup of migrant and refugee populations in surrounding Middle Eastern and North African countries. This book examines the implications of these patterns for state policy in Egypt, Morocco, and Turkey as well as for individual migrants and refugees residing therein.

1.4 Semantics

A brief discussion of the terms *migrant, refugee,* and *asylum seeker* is warranted. In most host states in the Global South, the term *refugee* refers to an individual who has been officially recognized by the UNHCR or by a host state government as having fled from his or her home country for officially approved reasons and who now deserves protection under the 1951 UN Convention on the Status of the Refugee or under subsequent protocols. The term *asylum seeker* refers to an individual who has applied to receive the designation of refugee from the UNHCR or host state government but who has not yet gone through the refugee status determination (RSD) process. An asylum seeker is thus entitled to some protection in a host country under international law, but he or she may not be eligible for UNHCR or host government–funded services or assistance.

The term *migrant* in countries in the Global South is a hold-all term indicating a person who does not fit neatly into other categories. A migrant can be someone who left a home country to seek economic opportunities elsewhere – often labeled as an economic, illegal, or undocumented migrant – as well as a person who fled home to seek refuge but does not meet the legal criteria for official designation as a refugee. Often that person is known as a "rejected refugee applicant" or as a "closed file." The term *transit migrant* is also used to refer to people initially heading for regions farther away – Europe, North America, or the Gulf states – but who never complete their journey because they do not meet visa conditions (Fargues 2009).

Since the 1990s some migration scholars and international migration bodies have advocated for the term *mixed migration* in recognition of the fact that some of the root causes of migration, including conflict and poverty, are difficult to separate (Castles and Van Hear 2011; Betts

2011). *Mixed migration* also recognizes that people will travel via the same routes, use the same smugglers, and be subject to the same dangers regardless of whether they are seeking asylum or economic opportunities (Castles and Van Hear 2011). Furthermore, individuals may switch categories, transitioning from having a regular status in a country to being undocumented or vice versa, as they obtain new information or once they cross an international border (Castles and Van Hear 2011). As of 2020, however, legal international refugee classifications do not recognize twenty-first-century complexities of mixed migration. Defined in the 1951 Convention Relating to the Status of Refugees (hereinafter the 1951 Refugee Convention) or subsequent protocols, refugee status is only available to those who meet a fairly narrow set of parameters: persecution on the basis of race, religion, nationality, membership of a particular social group, or political opinion. Conversely, individuals fleeing poverty, state economic failure, or generalized violence are not recognized as refugees, even if they feel unable to return home (Zolberg et al. 1989; Gammeltoft-Hansen 2011; Hathaway and Foster 2014). Host-government or UNHCR refugee or asylum seeker status is thus not protecting a significant portion of people who migrate.

Recognizing the debate over mixed migration and the complexities of the contemporary global migration landscape, the term *migrant* will be used in this book when speaking generally about those who migrate: refugees, economic or transit migrants, and asylum seekers residing in a host state. If referring only to those who are recognized by the UNHCR or a host state government as either asylum seekers or refugees, and excluding migrants who are not recognized, the term *asylum seeker* or *refugee* will be used, respectively.

An important caveat is that this study does not focus on formally recruited labor, while acknowledging that such forms of migration do exist in the selected host states – Egypt, Morocco, and Turkey. I also recognize that migrants, both regular and irregular, may originate from Western countries. In the migration lexicon these individuals are sometimes referred to as *ex-pats* (from *expatriate*), connoting their privileged status above other migrant groups as they can easily enter, remain and leave Global South countries. As such, they are not the focus of my study.

Instead, this book focuses on migrants who are generally deemed undesired by host states, defined by Christian Joppke (1998a) as individuals seeking asylum or irregular migrants including those who overstay their visas. My study includes individuals with official refugee designation, asylum seekers who have requested status and are awaiting an interview, and migrants who are rejected refugee applicants (closed files) or who never applied for refugee status but consider themselves unable or unwilling to return to their home country. While there is variation even within this population – some refugees or migrants may leave their home country with savings or receive financial support from friends and family members elsewhere – my focus is on vulnerable migrants, refugees and asylum seekers who collectively constitute a marginalized population in each of the host states in question.

1.5 Case Selection, Data Collection, and Analysis

To examine when and why Global South host states select certain engagement strategies, I employ a qualitative case study analysis (George and Bennett 2005). I selected three cases, all of which are from the Middle East and North Africa, which can also be referred to as the Southern and Eastern Mediterranean region in the academic and policy literature on migration. Geographically, this region is of special interest because it has been immediately impacted by Europe's border securitization and externalization efforts over the last three decades as well as conflict-generated migration (Fargues 2009; FitzGerald 2019) that has led to increased patterns of migrant and refugee settlement and the transformation of transit states into host states.

Within this region, I made decisions for case selection based on both exclusion and inclusion criteria. Beginning with exclusionary factors, I removed Iraq, Iran, Libya, Syria, and Yemen due to their inaccessibility and/or dangerous domestic situations at the time of researching. I also chose to exclude all countries that are members of the Gulf Cooperation Council (Bahrain, Kuwait, Oman, Qatar, Saudi Arabia, and the United Arab Emirates) since these oil-rich states operate a specific migrant recruitment scheme – the *kafala* program – that makes them highly dissimilar from other states regarding migration (Ruhs 2013). Second, I wanted to include countries that best capture the transit-turned-destination country phenomenon. Because Jordan and Lebanon have been hosting refugees of various nationalities – most prominently Palestinians – since the 1950s, they do not fit this category. And while Algeria receives migrants from sub-Saharan Africa hoping to transit to Europe, it also hosts approximately 165,000 Sahrawi refugees in camps in its southwest in one of the world's longest protracted refugee situations.

After these exclusions, I was left with four possible cases: Egypt, Morocco, Tunisia, and Turkey. At this point I considered two primary factors for inclusion: countries that maximize variation on the outcome variable – whether a country utilizes an indifferent, liberal, or repressive policy to address migration – and countries that maximize geographic variation *within* the selected MENA region. Ultimately, I selected Turkey, one Mashriq country (Egypt), and one Maghreb country (Morocco).

These three countries are all major receivers of migrants and refugees and have each signed treaties and conventions relating to the protection of refugees and migrants (both regular and irregular) on their territories, including the 1951 Refugee Convention[4] and the 1990 International Convention on the Protection of the Rights of All Migrant Workers and Members of Their Families. All three countries also have a moderate to strong presence of international organizations and NGOs working on human rights and migration issues, but they vary in terms of their official engagement outcomes with migrants and refugees and thus constitute a diverse set of cases (Gerring 2006). As the subsequent chapters will examine, Egypt, Morocco, and Turkey used one type of policy – indifference – to respond to increased patterns of migrant and refugee settlement in the 1990s and 2000s before turning to either a more repressive or more liberal policy in the second decade of the 2000s.

Additionally, Egypt, Morocco, and Turkey are all transit-turned-host countries along three different but popular migration routes leading to Europe, as illustrated in Figure 1.1.

In total I conducted 133 semistructured interviews in these three countries. I conducted initial fieldwork between September 2012 and August 2014 and the bulk of interviews between September 2014 and July 2015 using a two-tiered system.[5] First, I spoke with elite interview subjects, including relevant government ministries, INGOs, local NGOs, and international migration bodies like the UNHCR and the IOM. I asked elite interview subjects questions about their roles in engagement with migrants and refugees in the host state and, if applicable, how each organization interacts with the host state government.[6] In total I conducted fifty-three elite

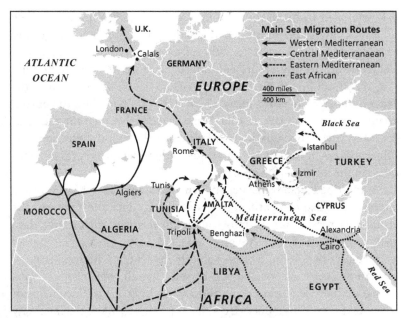

Figure 1.1 Irregular migration routes in the Mediterranean.
Map adapted from: Chwastyk, Matt/National Geographic Creative/NG IMAGE COLLECTION.

interviews. A full list of elite interview subjects is available in Appendix A.

In addition to elites, I conducted interviews with individual migrants and refugees in order to determine if and how interaction occurs between these individuals and state institutions or authorities. I asked migrant and refugee interviewees how they navigated life in the host state on a day-to-day basis: whether they were able to access certain services or employment, whether they were subject to discrimination, and whether and how they interacted with organizations and state authorities. The leaders of community-based organizations (CBOs), which are run by migrants and refugees themselves, were often the initial point of contact for migrant and refugee interview subjects. Yet those organizationally affiliated with NGOs and CBOs tend to be politically and socially active which can present bias. To avoid a biased sample, I used snowball sampling to gain multiple entry points to migrants and refugees who are not affiliated with community organizations.[7]

I attempted to make the sample of migrant and refugee interview subjects as diverse as possible in terms of nationality, gender, age, and years spent in the host state. While I cannot say that the sample is a statistically accurate representation of the migrant/refugee population in each country (for a number of reasons,[8] it is difficult to know the exact number of migrants in each host state), I did my best to approximate representativeness. In total I conducted eighty migrant and refugee interviews. Appendix B provides further details on these interview subjects; Appendix C (www.cambridge.org/reluctantreception) elaborates on the interviewing process.

I transcribed and translated (when necessary) all audio-recorded interviews. I also deidentified any confidential data and prepared the transcripts for uploading into a computer-assisted qualitative data analysis software (CAQDAS) program (ATLAS.ti). Once all interviews were transcribed and interview subjects deidentified (if appropriate), I began a process of open coding by selecting all relevant quotations from each interview subject's responses, resulting in 1,379 segments of coded text. I used an inductive coding approach to allow the interview subjects to speak when identifying themes, which then formed the basis for the analyses presented in the chapters of this book. Undergraduate research assistants helped to create a quantitative data set using the information contained in the migrant and refugee interviews, the purpose of which was to look for patterns between characteristics of migrants and refugees and experiences or treatment in the host state. These data are utilized in Chapter 6, "Differential Treatment by Nationality? Ethnicity, Religion, and Race."

1.6 Chapters and Organization

This book comprises nine chapters. In this chapter I presented the basic logic of my theory of the options that host states in the Global South have for engaging with migrant and refugee populations residing on their territory, introducing the concept of strategic indifference. I also described my methods for case selection, data collection, and data analysis. In Chapter 2, "Host State Engagement in the Middle East and North Africa," I situate my theory of indifference in existing scholarship, drawing on three primary bodies of research: the comparative politics literature on migration and citizenship, the literature on semi-authoritarianism and state capacity with an emphasis on the

Middle East, and the international relations literature on global migration and refugees. I also construct the central arguments of this book: (1) states can strategically use indifference to respond to growing migrant and refugee populations; (2) states in the Global South are capable of making strategic policy choices when it comes to migration; and (3) transit-turned-host states will adopt more liberal migration and refugee policies to avoid international shaming and if they perceive a combination of economic and diplomatic benefits from doing so or turn to a repressive policy if the topic of migration becomes highly politicized or securitized.

Chapter 3, "Egypt: From Indifference to Postrevolutionary Repression," is the first empirical chapter and introduces the case of Egypt. Readers meet Deng, an asylum seeker residing in Cairo, the country's capital, for four-and-a-half years at the time I spoke with him. Through Deng's story, the chapter introduces Egypt's indifferent approach toward engagement with its migrant and refugee population and the consequences of this policy choice for individuals residing semipermanently in the host state. It also analyzes how indifference in Egypt gave way to a more repressive policy following the Arab Spring and the 2013 military coup.

Chapter 4, "Morocco: From Raids and Roundups to a New Politics of Migration," presents the case of Morocco, introducing the country through the story of Amadu, a migrant from Senegal living in Sale, near Rabat. Amadu was unable to utilize his professional training as a mechanic upon arriving in Morocco but scraped together a livelihood by selling SIM cards along the street in Rabat. He learned the informal rules of his host state and managed to integrate in a de facto sense despite not having formal residency. The chapter moves on to examine Morocco's migratory history and its securitized engagement approach up until 2013 when King Mohammed VI introduced a major policy reform. The chapter provides an analysis of the events preceding and following the reform, offers an explanation for the state's intention behind the new policy, and examines the outcomes of policy change for individual migrants and refugees. In some sense, the reform changed the situation for the country's migrant and refugee populations, yet the day-to-day lives of individual migrants and refugees like Amadu were not drastically altered, and many continue to eke out an existence through informal means, with the help of community ties, and by understanding the country's norms. Chapter 4 also asks why international shaming over the issue of migration – one of the explanations behind policy reform in Morocco – was successful in Morocco but not in Egypt, arguing that Morocco is more sensitive to foreign aid conditionality.

Chapter 5, "Turkey: From Indifference to Institutionalized Control," introduces the case of Turkey through the story of Youssef and Noora, the only two Syrian employees at a Turkish-owned *künefe* restaurant in Gaziantep. Both Youssef and Noora survive in Turkey without any assistance from the Turkish government, despite Turkey's 2013 policy reform. Although the host government touts its spending on refugees to international partners, many individuals do not receive aid. As with the other case studies, Chapter 5 examines Turkey's history as an emigration, immigration, and transit country and assesses the government's use of indifference to manage increasing migrant and refugee arrivals in the 1980s, 1990s, and 2000s. It also examines the reasons for Turkey's 2013 policy change, contrasts them with those behind Morocco's reform, and considers the implications of change for domestic politics, international relations, and individual migrants and refugees residing in the country.

Chapter 6, "Differential Treatment by Nationality? Ethnicity, Religion, and Race," switches views to approach the question of state engagement from the perspective of individual migrants and refugees and to address the alternative explanation of host state culture playing a determinative role in engagement policy decisions. Looking primarily at Egypt and Morocco and using quantitative data collected from migrant and refugee interviews, Chapter 6 explores whether migrants and refugees experience differential treatment from the authorities of their respective host states based on nationality. Research suggests that the perception of a migrant or refugee as being a co-cultural can have a bearing on integration outcomes in some instances, but in general other factors better explain the treatment incurred by individuals of different nationalities, namely, the length of time individuals spend in the host state and whether or not they have legal status. Furthermore, I demonstrate that any privileging of co-cultural migrants or refugees may actually emanate primarily from the state's diplomatic and political interests rather than as a result of cultural factors.

Chapter 7, "The Domestic Influence of International Actors: UNHCR and IOM's Role in Host State Policy Outcomes," focuses on assessing whether the role of international actors like the UNHCR and IOM can explain host state engagement decisions. This chapter details the history of the UNHCR and IOM presence in Egypt, Morocco, and Turkey to determine what impact, if any, these institutions – as well as the donor states funding them – have on host state policy choices. International migration organizations like the UNHCR and IOM have been key actors and facilitators between European states and countries of origin or transit post–World War II, but it is unclear to what extent international organizations operating in the region are able to convince host state governments to carry out the agendas or preferences of Global North states. The chapter argues that international actors have been able to influence host state policy outcomes to varying degrees depending on historical experiences with migration and international aid, the leverage international organizations can offer host state governments and populations, and the extent to which the topic of migration has been politicized in the host state, ultimately concluding that host state preferences are priorities over the interests of international organizations.

Chapter 8, "The Post-2015 Migration Paradigm in the Mediterranean," zooms out to examine migration policy, diplomacy, and security in the Mediterranean region as a whole. While the bulk of the research for this study was conducted between 2012 and 2015, this chapter draws upon recent academic studies, policy documents, and nongovernmental reports in the wake of the 2015 European refugee "crisis". It provides insight into what a new Mediterranean paradigm means for MENA host states regarding economic, diplomatic, and security concerns, as well as the consequences for individual migrants and refugees at the heart of a new migration management environment. It argues that all host states in the Mediterranean region and states farther afield in sub-Saharan Africa benefited from Europe's post-2015 political crisis and used migration diplomacy to extract more concessions from the EU than they were able to previously. Of course, those benefiting least from this new diplomacy paradigm are migrants and refugees themselves.

Last, Chapter 9 concludes with an examination of the scope conditions of the argument herein and its potential applicability to other regions – Asia or South America – undergoing similar migratory transformations. It also argues in favor of an ethnographic sensibility in conducting research on state policy and considers the findings of this book in light of the 2018 Global Compact for Safe, Orderly, and Regular Migration and other multilateral attempts to manage migration in the Mediterranean region and elsewhere.

2 | Host State Engagement in the Middle East and North Africa

2.1 Migration Policies in the Global North and Global South

The political science, sociology, and anthropology literature on migration in the Middle East tends to operate around two themes. First, there is a fairly extensive and continually growing literature on the role of Middle East and North African sending states in facilitating the movement of, capitalizing on, and sometimes repressing their nationals abroad (Brand 2006; Iskander 2010; Pearlman 2014; Moss 2016; Tsourapas 2019a; Adamson 2019). Second there is an abundant literature examining the experiences of refugees and migrants in the Middle East, but it tends to focus on the role of Palestinians as *fedayeen* or so-called refugee warriors in the Arab–Israeli conflict (Zolberg et al. 1989; Nasr 1997), the governance and lived experiences of Palestinians in camps (Chatty 2010; Hanafi and Long 2010; Ramadan and Fregonese 2017; Gabiam 2016; Feldman 2015, 2017; Davis 2012), and more recently migrants who arrive in Gulf states under the *kafala* system (Vora 2013; Babar 2014; Babar et al. 2019). What has received comparatively less attention is the reception policies of host states. Examinations of why states choose to adopt welcoming versus exclusionary policies toward the admittance and subsequent engagement of migrants and refugees are infrequent.[1] For answers to questions about host state decision-making in this area, I instead look to the comparative politics literature on migration and citizenship.

Neoinstitutionalism is the idea that states adopt liberal migration policies when migrants are able to mobilize within a host state and utilize state institutions to their advantage, first proposed by Mark Miller (1981), James Hollifield (1992), and Christian Joppke (1999a). In this neoinstitutionalist approach, migrants gained the support of civil society actors, business-oriented organizations like trade unions, and active judiciaries that were willing to assist in advancing their rights claims. Looking specifically at France, Switzerland, and Germany in the 1970s, Miller (1981) asserts that migrant political advocacy coupled with extraparliamentary opposition and support from state institutions and civil society led to a liberalization of migration-related policies. Studies purporting neoinsitutionalism ultimately argued that if migrants could form alliances with rights-based groups and domestic economic actors like trade unions, states would be forced to adopt more inclusive laws (Hollifield 1992).

Postnationalists have also asserted that the influence of international norms explains why Western states converged in the ways they address migration. Proponents of this theory argue that because many noncitizen residents of Western states like those in Europe and North America currently enjoy the same rights and privileges as citizens, human rights have become globally sanctioned norms that supersede the rights granted by nation-states (Soysal 1994). Postnationalist norms take on a domestic presence through international organizations, treaties, and conventions that pressure states and domestic actors to adopt these norms (Sassen 2002). This process is also helped along by the actions of civil society and NGOs that campaign against discrimination toward migrants.

States also seek to strike a balance between the economic need for migrants and security interests in considering migration policy (Freeman 1995; Hollifield et al. 2014; Adamson 2006). In the period following World War II, Western states became increasingly open to cross-border trade, yet cross-border migration imposes security risks on states that sometimes lead to symbolic policies that serve to bolster an image of control (Rudolph 2003). In regard to refugees, where Western states once saw ideological value in admitting refugees during the Cold War period, they began in the 1990s to see security threats and the possibility of conflict spilling over into their own territories, which led to a preference for refugee containment in neighboring states rather than admittance (Helton 2007). And, beginning in the 1980s, European states moved purview over many migration-related matters to the supranational level, thereby circumventing liberal-leaning influences – such as civil society actors and judiciaries – that might otherwise have blocked more security-oriented, restrictive migration policies (Guiraudon 2000; FitzGerald 2019). Western states are still somewhat limited in their ability to fully close off to migration or to enact wholly restrictive policies toward migrants and refugees already present within a country's borders. This is either due to the economic need for continued migration – the "liberal paradox" (Hollifield 2004) – or due to norms that are codified in constitutions and legislation, which can be used by migrants and active judiciaries to counter exclusionary policies (Joppke 1998).

However, these competing explanations for migration policy decisions are derived from the experiences of Western migrant-receiving states and come with certain embedded assumptions. In considering whether these explanations for host state reception will transfer to the Global South, researchers need to account for the potentially different historical and current relations between minority and majority groups in non-Western, postcolonial contexts. For example, in Arab countries the idea of "protection of minorities," (whether nationals or non-nationals), particularly where it involves potential appeal to international actors, is not necessarily seen as a legitimate or normal form of domestic political contestation (Kymlicka and Pföstl 2014). Instead, protection of minorities can be viewed as a geopolitical threat to state security as a result of the region's experience with colonization (Kymlicka and Pföstl 2014) and the dissolution of the Ottoman millet system, under which there had been relative multiculturalism and religious pluralism (Chatty 2010). Other cultural legacies may also influence the treatment of non-national residents. In the case of Arab host states, this could be a result of Islamic identity or notions of pan-Arabism (Abu-Sahlieh 1996; Davis 2000), meaning that co-ethnic migrants and refugees from other Arab states or co-religious migrants who are also Muslim might be given preferential treatment.

Several studies from the last decade have made significant headway in addressing whether immigration theories derived from Europe and North America transfer to Global South contexts. While not primarily concerned with state policy per se, all elucidate states in which migration is more informal, less state-controlled, and in which Western understandings of immigrant integration and citizenship acquisition are challenged (Adida 2014; Onoma 2013; Sadiq 2009). Claire Adida (2014) looks at three West African migrant-receiving states – Benin, Ghana, and Niger – to question whether theories of immigrant assimilation derived from the experiences of Western democracies also provide insight into the phenomenon of assimilation in a South–South migration context. Adida concludes that immigrants with co-ethnic ties to the host population in these three countries are *less* likely to assimilate. This counterintuitive finding challenges extant theories in the immigration and citizenship literature in which immigrants with religious or ethnic similarities (high-overlap immigrants) are more likely to assimilate and experience stronger socioeconomic outcomes. Adida argues that the reason for this contradictory finding is that in West African countries, where integration occurs in the absence of any formal policies or state structures, migrants organize around informal leaders who resist assimilation on behalf of their constituents in order to preserve their own power and prominence.

Also examining three states in sub-Saharan Africa, Ato Kwamena Onoma (2013) examines various refugee settlements in Guinea – and to a lesser extent Uganda and the Democratic Republic of the Congo – to understand the conditions under which a local population will carry out acts of antirefugee violence when called on by state officials to do so. He finds that when refugees settled in local areas that "privilege indigeneity in the area of rights," and where refugees must perform symbolic acts of subjugation and the frequent exchange of gifts with hosts, local leaders protected refugees and prevented antirefugee violence. Conversely, refugees who settled in areas autonomous of local leaders were not protected when government leaders called on citizens to carry out acts of violence targeting refugees. Autonomy from local leaders meant that refugees were viewed as unknown outsiders, making it easier for those leaders to participate in the demonization of refugees instigated by national elites.

In the Asian context, Kamal Sadiq (2009) assesses irregular migration to three states – India, Pakistan, and Malaysia – where migrants managed to obtain "citizenship from below," conferred through the accumulation of documents like ration cards, high school matriculation certificates, national identity cards and, eventually, passports. This process was facilitated by "networks of complicity," comprising co-ethnic bureaucrats and administrators who facilitate the entry, settlement, and socioeconomic and political participation of migrants. Sadiq argues, "Documentary citizenship … is a response from below to citizenship from above. Documentary citizenship is an informal device, a back channel, to many of the benefits associated with the narrower and more difficult path to legal citizenship" (109). While Sadiq argues that this phenomenon is partly a result of "poor countries with incomplete state formation" (34), he also acknowledges that state officials are likely involved in this process, and that states have an interest in suppressing information about the presence and inclusion of irregular migrants. The states examined in forthcoming chapters are similarly viewed as weak states, but nonetheless possess an impressive ability to monitor and sometimes intervene in migration affairs should they deem it necessary. As one interviewee in Egypt involved in the migration and refugee protection sector aptly stated, "a security state is very aware of its borders" (Elite Interviewee S).

Admittedly, state policy is not the primary focus of these three studies. In turn, they focus on explaining co-ethnic relations as an impediment to immigrant integration, antirefugee violence and its absence, and the process through which irregular migrants are able to obtain documentary citizenship. Yet they are helpful in setting the scene in that they all speak to immigration and integration in the Global South occurring as a local-level, informal process that is largely shaped by interactions with community organizations, informal employers, international organizations, and, in some instances, host-country authorities rather than through official government policy.

Conversely, for Audie Klotz (2013), state policy is a central focus of her historic and present-day examination of immigration policy-making in South Africa. In an assessment of whether Hollifield's (1992) neoinstitutionalist thesis applies to South Africa, she argues that the country is missing a critical coalition of rights advocates and labor forces – such as trade unions and businesses – to advocate for nonprotectionist, inclusive policies toward migrants. While rights groups saw some judicial victories in the post-apartheid era, "as under apartheid, political advocates for greater flexibility in the labor market have been coopted (the mines), placated (farmers), or divided (industry)" (222), leading to, on the whole, exclusionary policies toward refugees and low-skilled foreign workers. However, a key difference from this book's focus is that Klotz's study of South Africa examines immigration policy-making within an, albeit imperfect, democracy, where the rule of law is upheld and where domestic courts are willing to rule in favor of rights protections. It is not clear how migrants, refugees, or their civil society advocates might seek rights in a nondemocratic context where the rule of law is not always upheld.

A second implicit assumption embedded in the migration and citizenship literature derived from the Global North is that immigration is occurring in the context of a liberal democratic state. Many states in the Global South, and particularly in the Middle East and North Africa, are classified as varying degrees of being illiberal, including hybrid regimes that are neither fully democratic nor fully authoritarian (Levitsky and Way 2010), characterized by an uneven application of the rule of law (Olcot and Ottaway 1999), and by regime leaders that have the capability to impose rules that may be arbitrary or not evenly applied to all groups or individuals (Brown 2011). Furthermore, judiciaries may be inhibited from ruling against the party in power or charismatic leader through bribery, extortion, and other mechanisms of co-optation (Levitsky and Way 2002).

The backdrop of a semi-authoritarian state has important implications in terms of the types of recourse that non-nationals might have for obtaining rights in a host state. Although in South Africa rights groups were able to obtain some protections for refugees through court rulings – even without establishing a coalition with business advocates – migrants or refugees and their partners in semi-authoritarian countries attempting to seek recourse may not be protected by constitutional norms and may face unresponsive or co-opted judiciaries unwilling to rule in their favor. Chapters 4 and 5 looking at Morocco and Turkey demonstrate that in the context of semi-authoritarian states that are geographically positioned between powerful countries to the North and key sending states to the South, migrants, refugees, and rights groups are more likely to succeed by bringing their claims to the international level (Keck and Sikkink 1998). However, this tactic of international shaming has not been enough on its own to force a state to adopt a more liberal policy; a state must also perceive that it will be rewarded diplomatically or economically for doing so. This dynamic is further explored in Section 2.4 and empirically in Chapters 4 and 5.

Two recent studies of host state migration and refugee policy – one of sub-Saharan Africa and one of the Middle East – best complement the questions I seek to address in this book.[2] First, James Milner (2009) challenges the idea that states of the Global South, and specifically those of sub-Saharan Africa, are weak and incapable of responding to refugees. Examining the asylum policies of Kenya, Tanzania, and Guinea, Milner argues that political factors unrelated to the presence of refugees – such as domestic pressures on a governing regime as well as a state's regional and international diplomatic relations – often play a dominant role in the development of asylum policies. States incorporate decisions on asylum into their broader political calculus. To demonstrate the temporal and geographic variance of host state responses, Milner assesses the regional politics of these states in the 1960s and 1970s when asylum policies were understood to be more open and inclusive as well as shifts in domestic politics and refugee-related security concerns in Africa following the Cold War.

Sophia Hoffmann (2016) examines the response of the Syrian state, as well as the response of international organizations including the UNHCR, to the arrival of Iraqi refugees in the first decade of the 2000s. While Iraqis were confronted with the same instability and threat of violence as Syrian citizens, Hoffman argues that they also experienced "opportunit[ies] for integration and success in spite of official rules" (16). In this sense, Hoffman argues that the Syrian state was relatively open and liberal in its hosting of Iraqis in comparison to systematically restrictive migration contexts in European and North American states. The Syrian regime viewed the arrival of Iraqis as a means through which to bolster its international image and open its doors to international assistance in the form of humanitarian aid. By refraining from interfering with the local integration of Iraqis and by allowing international aid organizations into the country to assist and provide services to the population, the Syrian state was able to utilize its image of a generous refugee host state to gain favor with Western countries and donor states. The Syrian government "reaped international praise for its protection of Iraqis while the oppression and impoverishment of Syrians continued unabated" (184). Similarly, I demonstrate that states under consideration in this study are capable of choosing migration and refugee policies that best fit their strategic aims. Second, I show that when doing so, they consider both domestic political constituents and diplomatic relations with sending countries in the Global South and powerful states in the Global North as an extension of Robert Putnam's (1988) two-level game. The expansive literature on migration and refugees in the field of international relations is instructive in this regard.

One segment of this literature examines how and under what circumstances states cooperate in the international refugee regime.[3] While responding to refugees represents a collective action problem that is in the interest of all states to address, the vast majority of refugees reside in countries of the Global South. Consequently, "the commitment of Northern states to support the majority of the world's refugees who remain in the South through financial support or resettlement is discretionary, subject to their own priorities and political interests" (Betts

2008, 159). While the principle of *non-refoulement* is accepted globally as a fundamental legal and normative tenet of the refugee regime, meaning that no state should forcibly deport a refugee, "the structural imbalance creates a perverse incentive for Northern states to allocate far more resources toward exclusion and deterrence policies than toward support for refugee protection in regions of origin" (159). Mariano-Florentino Cuéller (2006) terms this unequal hosting situation the "grand compromise" between Global North states and host states in the Global South. Since the 1950s, the UNHCR has served as the intermediary attempting to negotiate this impasse, convincing countries of the Global North to provide further funding to meet the needs of Global South host states (Loescher 2003), often using issue linkages to other substantive areas like security and trade (Betts 2009). While the North–South power asymmetry is well addressed in this literature, states in the Global South come across as relatively devoid of agency and incapable of autonomy in their decision-making. Although not dismissing the hierarchical nature of the international refugee regime, this study shows that states like Egypt, Morocco, and Turkey have been willing to comply with some requests emanating from the Global North and from international organizations like the UNHCR but have denied others. This discerning behavior demonstrates that Global South states are not merely the policy recipients of more powerful states but instead strategically consider both domestic and international priorities when making migration and refugee policy decisions.

   Kelly Greenhill's (2010) work on coercive migration is helpful in this corrective. Building off the theoretical insights of Myron Weiner (1985) and Michael Teitelbaum (1984), who recognized that sending states can use migrants as a resource, Greenhill (2010) examines how relatively weak states can create or exploit migration and refugee crises to extract resources from more powerful countries, especially targeting western liberal democracies. The power of such threats is enhanced by what she terms "hypocrisy costs," or "symbolic political costs that can be imposed when there exists a real or perceived disparity between a professed commitment to liberal values and norms and demonstrated actions that contravene such a commitment" (6). All three states under examination in this study – Egypt, Morocco, and Turkey – recognized the importance of their role in hosting migrants and refugees in the first and second decades of the 2000s. While they have not instigated refugee crises – though Turkish president Recep Tayyip Erodğan did threaten to do so in 2016 – these three countries nonetheless effectively used diplomacy, whether persuasive or coercive, to achieve trade deals, visa liberalization for their own citizens, or development aid. Greenhill's theory is particularly applicable to the post-2015 environment, whereby host states across the Middle East and North Africa renegotiated the stakes of the grand compromise to achieve even more concessions than they were able to previously, as will be explored in Chapter 8.

2.2 Strategic Indifference

The argument presented in this book is threefold. Current classifications of migrant and refugee engagement in Global South host states mistake the absence of formal policy and law for neglect. Classifications in the existing literature tend to describe engagement in a dichotomous manner – states are either inclusionary or exclusionary toward migrants and refugees – leaving no room for the possibility of state *indifference* as a policy choice by itself. Instead, host states have three affirmative policy options: liberalism, repression, and indifference. With a liberal policy, a host employs mechanisms such as education, employment, or legal structures in an effort to bring migrants into the national system (Kymlicka and Norman 2000). A repressive policy constitutes exclusionary measures that aim to remove migrants or refugees from the state and is characterized by high levels of policing, arrest, detention, and possibly deportation (Mylonas 2012). However, a policy of indifference means that a host state refrains from directly engaging with or providing services to migrants and refugees and instead relies on international organizations and NGOs to carry out engagement on its behalf, which has tangential benefits for the host state.

Indifference allows civil society and international actors to step in and provide services to migrants and refugees which alleviates the state from having to expend its own resources to do so. The host state must utilize some resources to monitor and regulate the activities of the organizations providing services, as well as the activities of migrants and refugees, but the reputational and economic benefits it receives from a policy of indifference outweigh these costs. Specifically, a policy of indifference garners international credibility for the host state while

Table 2.1 *Engagement strategy by policy area*

| | Policy area | | |
Strategy	*Residency and membership*	*Access to services*	*Access to employment*
Liberal	General access	Provided directly	Permitted
Repressive	Highly regulated/ exclusionary	Not provided	No access
Indifferent	Short term/unregulated	Provided indirectly	Informal access

it procures economic benefits through the participation of migrants and refugees in informal economies and through development aid channeled through international organizations and NGOs, aid that also benefits host-country nationals. Table 2.1 describes the parameters of a liberal, a repressive, and an indifferent policy, although these categories represent ideal types and a state may not fall perfectly into all three parameters of each strategy.

A state employing a liberal policy will permit residency and membership (though perhaps not citizenship) for regular migrants and refugees because it aims to include these groups in the national system and permit their legal presence. The state may also provide regularization processes for irregular migrants. Regarding services, the state will take primary responsibility for basic service provision (health, education for children, and possibly housing) and will provide these services directly as opposed to leaving the responsibility up to international organizations or civil society actors. States generally permit and encourage employment in the formal economy, as the goal is to facilitate the economic participation of migrants or refugees in the national system.

A repressive strategy will make it very difficult for migrants to obtain residency or membership because its goal is to exclude them from participation in the national system, despite simultaneously seeking gains from their labor. Similarly, the state will refrain from providing services to migrants or refugees directly and will also make it difficult for international organizations or NGOs to do so. Employment will be legally prohibited, and informal employment will be illicit, strictly monitored, and punished.

An indifferent strategy may make it difficult for migrants to obtain residency, but either (a) this only has mild implications because residency permits are not frequently checked by authorities, or (b) residency is permitted but only for a short period of time that requires permits to be frequently renewed. The state will not provide services directly to migrants or refugees but will allow the operation of international bodies and NGOs that provide services on its behalf. This alleviates the responsibility of the host state while still ensuring that migrants and refugees are not excluded from basic services. Last, states will not permit employment in the formal economy under most circumstances, but are aware that employment in the informal economy is widely pervasive and choose not to police this practice.

While indifference can appear to be state inaction or characterized as doing nothing at face value, this seeming nonresponse is actually strategic. The difficulty in demonstrating the strategy behind indifference is related to the difficulty of demonstrating intention behind state nonresponses more generally (Bishara 2015; McConnell and 't Hart 2019). To build the concept of indifference and to differentiate it from the perception of doing nothing, I look to other policy areas in which states are understood as accommodating, tolerating, ignoring, or demonstrating forbearance as a policy response. Recent work on the responses of semi-authoritarian governments to popular protests is particularly insightful in this regard.

In the Chinese context, Yang Su and Xin He (2010) argue that when protests appear seemingly spontaneous, the state is likely to take an *accommodating* approach to diffuse the conflict, rather than responding with overtly repressive measures (177). In the Middle Eastern context, Dana Moss (2014) describes how the Jordanian government has used *disattention* – defined as an instance when state institutions selectively withhold recognition of activists who are attempting to elicit a response from a governmental department or high-level state representative – to repress protests and deter future activism. Similarly, Dina Bishara (2015) proposes the concept of *ignoring* to understand instances in which Egyptian government officials have appeared dismissive – either through inaction or contempt – of popular mobilization. Albeit on a very different topic, another useful study for thinking about strategic state inaction is Alisha Holland's (2017) study of certain Latin American states' restraint in enforcing laws against squatting and street vending. Holland finds that in poor areas where formal welfare provision is minimal, politicians are able to garner votes by practicing or promising to practice *forbearance*.

In all of these studies, the state in question is highly likely to be aware of the presence and actions of protestors or the activities of squatters and street vendors but chooses not to respond or to withhold attention. Nonetheless, scholars cannot say with absolute certainty that the state is *choosing* not to respond. Scholars also acknowledge that focusing solely on state intentionality can be problematic because sometimes elite state actors may be highly conscientious of a policy or strategy and at other times not (Stern and O'Brien 2012). Instead, these scholars choose to focus on the actions *set in motion* by the state utilizing tolerance, actively ignoring, or exercising forbearance. In the context of protest movements, scholars examine how activists to whom these state strategies are directed consider the state policies intentional, and how they subsequently act based on that assumption (Moss 2014; Bishara 2015). As Moss (2014) states,

ironically, the frequent high-level attention given to activist leaders and organizations distinguishes disattention from their otherwise routine access to political elites and the security apparatus. As such, respondents logically did not believe that disattention stems simply from a lack of state capacity to recognize their requests. (269)

Similarly, while one cannot say with absolute certainty that indifference is a deliberate state strategy relative to doing nothing, one can analyze the effects of an indifferent policy and compare those to what complete inaction or neglect would look like.[4]

Egypt, Morocco, and Turkey utilized a strategy of indifference in the 1990s and the first decade of the 2000s to manage the social and political implications of their new inward migration. Because these states refrained from direct engagement, international organizations and domestic organizations intervened to provide essential services, and migrants and refugees found ways to integrate into large informal economies. The issue of migration was also not so highly politicized that it gained prolonged traction in media or among the national population during this period, making indifference a highly feasible and cost-effective policy. By allowing migrants and refugees to participate in the host state – although not actively encouraging integration in the sense of a liberal policy – and by permitting international and domestic organizations to operate and provide primary services, these host states derived international credibility while only exerting minimal state resources.

2.3 State Capacity

There is an implicit assumption in the literature on global migration that host states in regions such as the Middle East and sub-Saharan Africa lack the capacity to engage with migrants and refugees (Hollifield 2004; Betts 2011). In this thinking, states with low or minimal capacity are unable to enact a resource-intensive engagement strategy and instead resort to indifference. Only when states gain more capacity will they able to put in place a policy that requires greater institutional output. While state capacity is one factor that should be considered in seeking to understand state decision-making, I argue that geostrategic imperatives and international perceptions drive engagement decisions *at least as much as* the capacity of each host state.

It is true that illiberal states, characterized by power consolidated in a small, political elite and often lacking an even application of law, are generally considered to be *weak* or *low-capacity* states. In theory, illiberal states should be highly competent and efficient at taking on infrastructural projects and making unilateral decisions since they are less constrained in their actions than liberal democratic countries. In practice though, the inverse is true. Autocratic regimes are most often associated with weak state capacity and low economic development (Hall and Ikenberry 1989). As John Hall and John Ikenberry (1989) explain,

the notion of state capacity is not straightforward: above all it is an error to equate the strength or autonomy of the state with the ability of state elites to ignore other social actors or to impose their will in any simple manner on society. If this were the case, totalitarian states, which seek to suppress the independence of other social actors, would be most capable of realizing state goals and of promoting larger social purposes. (95)

Looking at the Arab state specifically, Nazih Ayubi (1996) argues that while governments in the region may be "fierce" in terms of their coercive capacity, they are nonetheless weak in terms of infrastructural power. For Michael Mann (1988) an important element of capacity is predicated on the state's infrastructural power to "penetrate and centrally coordinate civil society through its own infrastructure" (7). In this sense, states in the Middle East have also generally been considered weak (Dorman 2007). Crucially, however, this infrastructural weakness does not imply a lack of strategic decision-making, or an unwillingness to expend state resources *when the incentives are in place.*

For example, Egypt's move toward a more repressive strategy post-2013 required active policing. To carry out this strategy the Egyptian state chose to redeploy resources for the purpose of (negatively) engaging with migrants and refugees through policing, detention, and deportation. Furthermore, Morocco and Turkey implemented major migration policy changes in 2013, not because their state capacities suddenly changed but because these states decided to move away from indifference and actively redeployed state funding and resources to the institutions that deal with migrants and refugees as a result of perceived political gains from doing so. In the case of all three host states – Egypt, Morocco, and Turkey – changes in migration policy were driven by geostrategic imperatives rather than changes to state capacity. Capacity is therefore not only an empirical reality based on a state's GDP or its ability to "penetrate society" (Mann 1988). States also use the perception of capacity to serve strategic domestic or diplomatic purposes, and this influences the choices that host states make regarding which type of engagement strategy to use and under what circumstances.

This research thus has important implications for our understanding of state capacity in semi-authoritarian settings, which coincides with a renewed focus in political science on practices of informality (Helmke and Levitsky 2004). Recent scholarship has argued that informality does not necessarily result from low state capacity; instead, states may choose to refrain from interference, regulation, and engagement when they perceive benefits from restraint (Moss 2014; Holland 2017; Gallien 2019). Even when states have the legal or institutional authority to regulate populations, "it may not always be in the state's interest to do so, depending on whether such actions may undermine its governing capacity or legitimacy more generally" (Davis 2018, 372). In the case of de facto integration for migrants and refugees, host states may actually permit and even encourage economic and social integration, even as they publicly decry such practices (Hovil 2014). This may not be because they lack the capacity to police or prevent such practices but because states recognize the benefit of refraining from direct engagement. Through this analysis of the willingness of the Egyptian, Moroccan, and Turkish states to engage – either directly or indirectly – with migrants and refugees on their territory, I problematize rigid understandings of state capacity as they apply to Middle East host states and demonstrate the strategic use of migration policy choices.

Related to the issue of state capacity, a plausible alternative explanation for host state engagement choice has to do with the size of a state's migrant or refugee population. Perhaps host states only decide to enact a liberal or repressive strategy once the size of the migrant population has reached a critical capacity. Otherwise, these groups fly under the government's radar and the state does not react to them. Alternatively, perhaps a state instigates a repressive policy once a migrant or refugee population becomes large enough that the state deems it a security threat. Regardless of these explanations, whether and how states choose to engage directly with migrants and refugees – as opposed to leaving the task to domestic and international actors – is in fact more likely to depend on the origin of the migrants or refugees themselves rather than the sheer number of migrants or refugees present in a host state.

For example, even though Syrians outnumbered other nationalities in Egypt and Turkey at the time of interviewing, these states supported Syrian refugees because doing so promised international gains, whereas these host states did not derive the same benefit from other refugee populations. For Turkey, despite any known limitations to its newly created migration system following the implementation of its policy change in 2014, Turkey's ruling party wanted to project the image of Turkey as a high-capacity state in its relations with Europe. Erdoğan continuously emphasized Turkey's capability throughout the 2016 negotiations over the EU–Turkey deal in order to demonstrate the country's ability to host Syrians and to emphasize that the EU needed to further assist Turkey in the name of burden sharing. In Egypt, under former President Mohammed Morsi, Syrians who arrived in 2011 and 2012 received access to state services, which was a policy departure from Egypt's indifferent approach to its other refugee populations. However, domestic political events – as opposed to any increase or decrease in the number of Syrians in the country – caused this treatment to change drastically. After Morsi fell, Syrians were arrested, detained and, in some cases, deported. This selective support is also true for Morocco and sub-Saharan migrants, even though the number of migrants in Morocco is not particularly large. Because Morocco wanted to position itself as a leader in West Africa in order to encourage trade and gain regional political clout, supporting these populations was beneficial.

Overall, the analysis in this book shows that geopolitical factors are more determinative in driving engagement decisions than the capacity of each host state or the number of migrants and refugees present, in as much as certain nationalities of migrants and refugees can provide diplomatic advantages to a host country.

2.4 Toward Liberalization and Repression

The third prong of this argument explains what happens when a policy of indifference becomes untenable. As discussed earlier in this chapter, the migration literature has several theories that explain why liberal democratic states adopt inclusive policies toward migrants (Miller 1981; Hollifield 1992; Joppke 1999b; Soysal 1994; Sassen 2002). But how can we understand why reform might occur in countries like Egypt, Turkey, and Morocco with semi-authoritarian governmental systems?[5] In semi-authoritarian regimes, pressures exist that prevent these governments from sliding completely into authoritarianism, including global human rights norms, transnational advocacy networks, funders that promote democracy, and/or media that is not fully censored (Olcot and Ottaway 1999). While fully authoritarian governments are unlikely to respond to external pressure from international actors, semi-authoritarian governments are still concerned with upholding their image and playing by the rules of the international system. In practice, this means that other states or international actors may have the ability to influence or incentivize semi-authoritarian governments to adopt certain practices or policies.

In the context of a semi-authoritarian state, we can understand host state policy liberalization through two incentives. First, host states will employ a liberal policy when doing so allows them to avoid international shaming or co-opt domestic civil society critics. This explanation requires a brief look at the function of civil society in illiberal environments. While scholarship links an active civil society with democratization and assumes that civil society actors provide a check against authoritarian governance (Durac 2015), Michael Foley and Bob Edwards (1996) argue that the role that organized groups play in civil society depends critically on the larger political setting. Where the state is unresponsive and its institutions illiberal, the parameters in which civil society actors can operate will be decidedly different than under a strong and democratic system (Foley and Edwards 1996).

Looking at MENA states in particular, Amy Hawthorne (2004) cites several reasons for the ineffectiveness of civil society organizations: repression, precarious funding, and weak management. Fragmentation of civil society across the Arab world hinders the ability of these actors to unite groups of citizens around common goals in a way that might generate pressure on regimes. Hawthorne claims that while Arab leaders will often support service-oriented civil society groups – which tend to fill a gap created by the adoption of neoliberal state policies – they see activist groups as adversaries: "Indeed, when Arab leaders boast of their countries' burgeoning civil societies, as they often do, they are referring to service NGOs and similar organizations that are carrying out their own national development agenda" (12).

In fact, the increase in civil society activism in Arab states since the end of the Cold War may be seen as reflecting state-led processes of controlled political liberalization rather than the expression of autonomous associational activity on the part of citizens (Durac 2015). In many regimes, civil society actors are co-opted by the state in a corporatist civil society–state arrangement, thereby limiting their ability to defy the regime (Deane 2013). By inviting civil society actors to the table regarding the implementation of reform processes and by undertaking periodic consultations with them, the government reduces the risk of criticism that could hurt a state's reputation internationally. Frederic Vairel (2013) describes this process as the state "modifying its form of domination" (47).

In the case of migration reform, a state facing pressure from activist civil society groups (INGOs, local NGOs, or migrant community groups) may choose to control these actors by bringing them on board rather than allowing them to openly defy the state. A state may implement a liberal engagement strategy and invite civil society groups to participate in the implementation of the policy in order to alleviate domestic pressure and strengthen a regime's stronghold over the issue of migration. In other words, by elevating the importance of the issue and inviting migrants, refugees, and rights groups to actively participate in the implementation of a new practice or policy, the regime also co-opts civil society actors and limits their ability to defy the state.

This explanation is related to the neoinstitutionalist and the post-nationalist hypotheses, but with a realist twist that accounts for the differing political and institutional context of the type of state in question. The state is responding to domestic civil society actors that enact pressure (in a neoinstitutionalist sense) and is incentivized to enact reform because of potential international shaming regarding human rights norms (postnationalism). Ultimately though, the state does so as part of a strategic plan that allows the state to retain control over an issue (in this case, migration). However, the need to co-opt domestic critics on its own is not a sufficient explanation for the enactment of a liberal strategy. I argue that a host state must also perceive tangible economic or diplomatic benefits in order to do so. In other words, this is a necessary but insufficient condition for liberalization.

The second factor determining whether a host state will enact a liberal strategy is if doing so will reap economic or diplomatic benefits from either a powerful neighboring state or a geostrategically important sending state. This draws on the idea that a state can use migration policy as a bargaining chip to bolster its economic or diplomatic standing and project international influence (Teitelbaum 1984; Cornelius and Rosenblum 2005; Tsourapas 2019a). Marc Rosenblum (2004) finds that states may be able to employ migration as a foreign-policy tool by linking cooperation on visa and residency access to other dimensions of bilateral relations, such as trade, investment, and security relations. Therefore, Global South host states can use their own domestic migration policy – and specifically policy liberalization – as a tool in bilateral negotiations.

In the case of MENA host states in particular, this tool can be directed toward the EU and its member states. One mechanism for this is through the European Neighborhood Policy (ENP) framework, which governs the way that the EU approaches and hopes to influence the countries of its periphery. Established in 2003, the ENP aims to influence the political association and economic integration of neighboring countries through the fostering of shared values, including rule of law, democracy, human rights, and social cohesion. It consists of a series of bilateral agreements and regional frameworks through which the EU offers financial aid, market access, and visa facilitation to neighboring countries in exchange for the conduct of domestic reforms in the political, economic, and administrative spheres (Lavenex 2008). External borders and migration controls have been a clear priority for the EU over the last several decades, and this priority is reflected in the bilateral agreements negotiated as part of the ENP (Lavenex and Schimmelfennig 2009). Thus, if a Global South host state is willing to conform its policies to meet EU migration and asylum standards (i.e., employ a liberal strategy), this may mean potential accession or enhanced association for the host state. While the countries of Europe's southern and eastern neighborhood are often framed as the unwilling recipients of European policy choices (Geddes 2005), MENA host states should rather be understood as strategic actors who make calculations about when and whether to comply with European demands regarding migration engagement and policy reform.

As mentioned earlier, the use of migration policy as an instrument of diplomacy can also be directed toward sending states. This is certainly true in the case of European receiving states and migrant source countries (Lavenex and Schimmelfennig 2009). This is also the case for a Global South host state and its desire to influence the behavior of a country of origin. For example, a Global South host state may employ a liberal policy toward migrants residing on its territory in order to bolster economic or political relations with the source country of those migrant groups. In other words, if a Global South host state wishes to project influence toward a source country or region, then it needs a more liberal policy to welcome migrants who originate from there.

The mechanism at work in this hypothesis is derived from recent scholarship on sending-state governance of diasporas, which suggests that sending states are becoming less concerned with the circulation and return of migrants and increasingly focused on dispersion as a resource (Ragazzi 2009; Gamlen 2014). While a Global South host state's reason for implementing a liberal policy may be related to projecting geopolitical or economic influence, the goal for sending states is the ease with which their migrants can work, travel back and forth, and "act as 'lobbyists' and extensions of the state's foreign policy" (Ragazzi 2009, 390). As such, source countries may also benefit from a Global South host state putting a liberal policy in place and may be willing to negotiate economic or political deals. Together with the co-optation of civil society, diplomatic and economic interests are a necessary condition – and together these two factors are sufficient – for a host state to enact a liberal policy.

Conversely, a host state will move toward repression from indifference if the issue of hosting migrants and refugees becomes securitized or politicized. Under such circumstances, a state may be willing to exert the additional resources required to engage directly with migrants and refugees through actions such as policing, detaining, or, in extreme cases, deporting individuals. A repressive state may also choose to interfere with or limit the work of organizations attempting to provide services to migrants and refugees if it deems that such organizations constitute a security threat or have crossed a line. For example, the changing political environment of postcoup Egypt in 2013 led to a securitization of the topic of migration, whereby the state moved from a policy of indifference to a more repressive policy, which required greater expenditures on the part of the state. The Egyptian state deemed this expensive change in approach necessary as security concerns outweighed the benefits that Egypt received under an indifferent approach. Furthermore, at the time of finalizing edits for this book in 2019, Turkey moved toward a repressive policy that involved the active policing, detention, and deportation of Syrian nationals to Northeastern Syria in response to the increasing politicization of refugees by voters and opposition parties in addition to domestic economic concerns.

2.5 Competing Explanations

Together, these three arguments make up the core of this book. In Chapters 6 and 7, I also address two competing hypotheses. The first suggests that cultural factors could be the primary determinant behind host state engagement choices. For example, in a recent book focusing on Syria as a state that has historically welcomed refugees, Dawn Chatty (2018) argues that providing hospitality or asylum in the Middle East region is customary, and that the "moral positioning to treat the stranger as a guest does not require national legislation to be implemented" (208). As long as guests or strangers behave correctly and respectfully, and do not "raise their head[s] above the parapet" (207), they are treated with the same rights as nationals. While not dismissing the concept of *karam* – or generosity – as a principle that can guide the actions of individuals and potentially governments, this explanation is unsubstantiated. Explanations for state policy based in national tradition relate to the hypothesis purported by Rogers Brubaker (1992), claiming that a host state's cultural foundations influence its migrant engagement policy choices. In the case of MENA states, the most influential cultural legacies are likely to be Islam, former rule under the Ottoman Empire, and notions of pan-Arabism (Abu-Sahlieh 1996). This could mean that co-ethnic migrants from other Arab states or co-religious migrants who are also Muslim would be given preferential treatment by host states in the region. For example, some Arab countries give preference in terms of naturalization to those who adhere to Islam, and some, such as Egypt, provide special rules for co-ethnics, or other Arabs (Parolin 2009). I address this explanation by examining policies toward migrants and refugees at the group-level (i.e., Syrians residing in Egypt or Nigerians in Morocco) to assess whether host state strategies vary by nationality. I also separate migrant and refugee treatment into its de jure and de facto components, determining that while de jure policies can vary by nationality – often as a result of bilateral agreements that host states have with sending states – de facto treatment is not primarily determined by an individual's nationality or whether they are considered co-ethnic but by other factors such as how long a migrant or refugee has lived in a host state or whether an individual has legal status.

A second alternative explanation regards the role of international organizations – particularly the UNHCR and IOM – in influencing host state decision-making. Perhaps states are primarily influenced by the norms propagated by international migration organizations (Scheel and Ratfisch 2014), or perhaps they are directly responding to incentives offered by powerful donor states, specifically those of the EU (Kilberg 2014). The role that lobbying efforts of migration-focused international organizations such as the UNHCR and IOM played in Egypt, Turkey, and Morocco over the last several decades cannot explain the *timing* of migration reform in Turkey or Morocco or Egypt's move to a more repressive policy in 2013. While the UNHCR and IOM have subsequently been involved in a high-profile way in the rolling out of new policies in Morocco and Turkey (and were involved in the drafting of new legislation in Turkey), both governments – ministerial bureaucrats in Turkey and the Moroccan monarch – strategically decided to reform. These governments recognized the geostrategic positions of their countries and the role that migration would come to play in diplomacy going forward. To overemphasize the role played by the UNHCR and IOM is to underestimate the capabilities and calculations of domestic actors.

Ultimately, the host state is an autonomous actor that makes decisions about the most beneficial policy to pursue. As such, these states are not driven by essentialist notions of culture or religion, nor are they mere recipients of the policy choices of more powerful states or international organizations. Instead, they make strategic decisions about how best to allot resources and enact strategies. Denying the agency of Global South states is a form of colonial thinking in a postcolonial world.

3 | *Egypt*

From Strategic Indifference
to Postrevolutionary Repression

3.1 Introduction

Deng is a twenty-eight-year-old asylum seeker originally from Abyei, a contested border region between Sudan and South Sudan. In 2014, Deng had lived in Cairo for four-and-a-half years. He left his home for two reasons: the ongoing war and the lack of opportunities for higher education. He holds a yellow card, meaning that shortly after he arrived in Cairo he approached the UNHCR and underwent an initial interview. In order to receive a blue card and become an official refugee, he will have to go through a more thorough interview process. When we spoke at the end of 2014, he was still waiting for an appointment date for the blue card interview.

With his yellow card, Deng is able to obtain residency from the Egyptian government. Every six months he has to visit the *mugamma*, a government building in central Cairo, to renew his residency permit. While he had trouble obtaining the card on his initial visit, he has not had much difficulty since then. Deng has not had to visit a hospital during his time in Egypt, for which he is very thankful; he has heard from friends that the public hospitals that asylum seekers are able to access at no cost are unsanitary and unhelpful. Plus, he tells me, "only the easy problems are free. If you have something simple, then it's for free. But if you have diabetes or a problem with your heart, then you have to pay. And if you have to go to a private hospital, it'll cost a lot more. Sometimes the UN and Caritas [an international NGO] will help you pay for that, but it's a long process with paperwork."

Deng has not had any difficulty with the Egyptian authorities. He lives in a remote part of Cairo, a planned district called 6th of October city, which can be a thirty-minute or a two-hour microbus ride away from the center of Cairo, depending on the city's notorious traffic. He has not encountered checkpoints or policing in his part of the city and says that those types of state monitoring only happen in "important places and the wealthy places." This is helpful, since Deng travels regularly for his current job as a psychosocial officer with an NGO in Cairo that assists migrants and refugees who are struggling with trauma and other mental health difficulties. His job is to respond to any urgent calls for psychosocial assistance among members of the South Sudanese community, no matter the time of day or night, and sometimes he finds himself working twelve straight hours. One evening as we are taking a microbus from al-Hosawri Square in 6th of October city back to central Cairo, Deng gets a call from someone he does not know telling him about a potentially urgent case that he needs to follow up with the next morning. "It's supposed to be my day off," he tells me gloomily.

Somehow Deng still finds time to stay involved with members of his home region who have formed a community-based organization (CBO) in Cairo. The group's center is located in Abbassia, a busy neighborhood in central Cairo marked most prominently by Ain Shams University. The community center is a ten-minute walk from the main metro station and located on the second floor of a building that looks like it may be on the verge of collapsing. The office is musky smelling, and the walls are littered with posters containing political slogans about Abyei joining South Sudan and pictures of community leaders. The center hosts a variety of activities, including prayer group meetings, classes for women and children, and political meetings about home country politics and the possibility of liberating Abyei.

Like many refugees and migrants in Egypt, Deng exists in relative anonymity, subsumed within the sprawling metropolis of Cairo. By virtue of his relationships with co-nationals, his ability to find informal employment, and the occasional help of an international organization or NGO, he has managed to integrate, in a de facto sense, within his host country. He has not interacted much with Egyptian authorities, but he must still obtain a residence permit on a bi-monthly basis, making his presence legible to the Egyptian state.

This chapter explores Egypt's recent history as a host country for individuals like Deng, members of a marginalized migrant and refugee population. When Egypt began to see this population grow in the 1990s and 2000s, it utilized a policy of *strategic indifference* to mitigate the effects of migrants staying in Egypt over the medium to long term. The Egyptian state allowed international organizations and NGOs to offer services to these populations, carefully monitoring their activities and ensuring that organizations, as well as migrants and refugees themselves, did not engage in political activity or challenge the state. Yet following the 2011 revolution and the 2013 military coup, the Egyptian government took a more proactive, securitized, and repressive approach to its migrant and refugee population, expending further state resources in order to police and detain migrants. The following sections examine each of these periods in turn, beginning with an overview of migration to Egypt.

3.2 Migration Patterns and Demographics

While academic literature focusing on migration has tended to regard Egypt as either a sender of migrants abroad or as a country of transit, Egypt has a long history as a receiver of migrants. For example, ethnic Greeks resided in Egypt from the Hellenistic period until many were forced to leave after the 1952 revolution that overthrew the monarchy and established a republic (Zohry 2003; Mylona 2018). Egypt also has a long and intertwined history with the geographic area now covered by Sudan and South Sudan, and up until 1995, Sudanese nationals enjoyed relative ease of travel to and residence in Egypt. Additionally, individuals that would now be referred to as refugees fled to Egypt after the Bolshevik revolution in Russia in 1917, the Armenian massacres in Turkey in the 1920s, and during both world wars (Zohry 2003; Mylona 2018). Several tens of thousands of Palestinian refugees arrived between 1948 and 1967, welcomed by former President Gamal Abdel Nasser and permitted to hold Egyptian travel documents until 1978 (El Abed 2004).[1]

In the early 1990s, however, Egypt began receiving new forms of immigration from both sub-Saharan Africa and other MENA countries. Migrants and refugees arrived from the Horn of Africa, most predominantly from Sudan but also from Eritrea, Ethiopia, and Somalia (Kagan 2002). In the 2000s, Egypt experienced migrants and refugees arriving from other Arab states: first Iraq, followed by Libya, and then Syria. For many individuals arriving as asylum seekers, Egypt is thought of as a jumping off point for another destination, a transit country. Egypt hosts a relatively large resettlement program operated by the UNHCR in conjunction with private sponsorship programs run by countries such as Canada, Australia, and the United States (Grabska

2006). International organizations have expressed concern that the existence of generous resettlement opportunities might be acting as a pull factor that draws asylum seekers to Egypt in increasing numbers (Sperl 2001). While the system may constitute an incentive for those hoping to be resettled, the number of refugees actually selected for resettlement is quite small: an average of only 3,000 per year (Kagan 2011). Other migrants and asylum seekers arrive in Egypt looking for opportunities to be smuggled to Europe via Egypt's north coast or through Libya. And, in the mid-2000s, some migrants and asylum seekers arrived in Egypt hoping to afterward cross into Israel, although this route was closed in 2013 after the construction of a separation barrier between Israel and Egypt and the use of aggressive and violent policing tactics (Judell and Brücker 2015).

Other migrants arrive with Egypt as an intended destination. Cairo's economy can be a draw for migrants from the Horn of Africa, and as the director of one of the fifty-seven refugee schools located in Cairo explained, "they come to Egypt because it's a big city, a big economy. Maybe eventually they'd like to go elsewhere, but in comparison to African countries, Egypt looks pretty good" (Elite Interviewee T). Asylum seekers may also choose Egypt for its relative affordability. Usama, a Syrian man living in 6th of October on the outskirts of Cairo, explained that he would rather be in Egypt than in Jordan, Lebanon, or Turkey, the other countries hosting large numbers of Syrians. I asked him, "Even Turkey?" And he replied, "Yes, Turkey is too expensive. It's better in Egypt where things are cheap."

The size of Egypt's migrant and refugee population is uncertain and contentious. President Abdel Fattah el-Sisi claimed in 2016 that Egypt hosts 5 million migrants and refugees, but this estimate – if accurate – includes several million Sudanese migrants who were able to reside in Egypt for generations without a residency permit prior to 1995 (Karasapan 2016). While 5 million migrants may be an overestimate, the number of refugees officially registered with the UNHCR is widely understood to be an underestimate. For example, while the UNHCR cited 250,000 Syrians registered with their office in late 2014 at the time of interviewing for this project, the Egyptian Ministry of Foreign Affairs estimated that 100,000 Syrians remained unregistered yet residing in the country (Elite Interviewee AY).

The distinction between refugees and migrants is not always very clear in practice. Refugees who arrive in Egypt and approach the

UNHCR are initially given a yellow card – the card that Deng holds – which connotes that they are asylum seekers and under temporary protection until they undergo refugee status determination (RSD). At the time of interviewing in 2014, RSD interview dates were being given to asylum seekers for 2019, meaning that would-be refugees would have to wait five years before potentially receiving a blue card, connoting that they hold official refugee status (Norman 2016c). However, some individuals who would likely have qualified as refugees were unaware of the UNHCR registration procedure and remained in Egypt as migrants rather than asylum seekers or confirmed refugees. Kareem, a refugee from Central African Republic, explained that he lived in Egypt for more than two years before learning that he could approach the UNHCR to apply for status. Eventually he obtained a yellow card and later officially qualified as a refugee.

3.3 The 1990s and 2000s: Indifference

Most refugees and migrants reside in Egypt's capital, Cairo, although other coastal cities such as Alexandria and Damietta have become popular locations for migrants and refugees hoping to be smuggled to Europe by boat and for Syrians due to historical connections between Syrian and Egyptian merchants in the area. Egyptian landlords are known to capitalize on the presence of migrants and refugees in urban locations by charging them inflated rental prices. As the director of one of Cairo's refugee schools noted, "for landowners it's a great opportunity to make more money because a lot of the Egyptians are under the old Nasser system where they're paying fifteen pounds a month [in rent]" (Elite Interviewee T). Ahmed, a refugee from Darfur in Sudan, explained that Egyptian *samāsira*, or housing brokers, will size up migrants or refugees based on nationality and show them neighborhoods accordingly. Alluding to this informal system, he explained, "They know each type of customer, they know how much they have in their pocket." A representative from the IOM confirmed this, saying, "I remember it starting with the Sudanese when I was living here in 2003 or 2004. There's lots of demand anyway, and there's a shortage of housing. So, with increasing numbers of Sudanese refugees the rent kept increasing" (Elite Interviewee E).

To afford inflated rental prices in Egypt, most migrants and refugees find work in the country's informal economy. Egypt adopted the 1951

Refugee Convention with careful restrictions related to the right of refugees to search for formal employment (Zohry and Harrell-Bond 2003).[2] While refugees technically have the same right to employment as other foreigners living in Egypt, the individual job seeker must prove that an Egyptian national is not more qualified for the same job, which is an onerous if not impossible requirement for most refugees. However, migrants and refugees, like many Egyptian nationals, have been able to secure employment without authorization in agricultural, industrial, artisanal, and service sectors, in addition to domestic work in wealthy Egyptian households. The UNHCR and other international migration bodies are aware and understanding of this practice. As one representative stated:

I'm not calling them refugees because they are not registered with the UNHCR, but for many reasons they are in the country. They are migrants. So, Egypt is welcoming for this migrant population. They are integrated somehow. They are not integrated to the extent of taking the nationality, but they can find their livelihoods, they can reside in the country. (Elite Interviewee A)

Responding to a question about whether refugees work informally, another UNHCR official stated, "Naturally, how else would they survive since the UNHCR cannot support all of them? We do not have enough money. There are some areas that have boosted with small business[es] and many restaurants. They do informal work to survive. It is beneficial for the host country and the refugees" (Elite Interviewee B).

Kareem from Central African Republic explained how he sees the Egyptian economy benefiting from the presence of migrants and refugees. "Some groups that maybe benefit are . . . Egyptian middle and upper-class families because a lot of refugees find work in households as maids. Some men even. But mostly for men finding work is hard, and if they find work it's maybe in one of the factories. They have a lot [of factories] out in 6th of October." Of course, informal work can lead to exploitation. Ahmed, a refugee from Sudan, described his experience working in a factory:

For one month I worked at a factory in Cairo. The Egyptians in the same job would make 150 EGP a day. But the Sudanese, for example, would make 70 or 50 for the same job. And working from eight in the morning until eight at night. Twelve hours. So, for the month I'd make 1,200 EGP, but apartments are expensive, and gas is expensive, and the salary isn't enough.

Migrants and refugees also face long working hours and exploitation in other sectors. Fathi, a Syrian refugee working informally at a juice shop in 6th of October city, explained, "In my country I also worked in a juice shop but nicer than this one. There were seven people working there, and the hours were good. Here I work eleven or twelve hours a day, unless the electricity goes like it did yesterday. Then I get an hour or two off, maybe." Nonetheless, many individuals like Fathi will put up with unfavorable working conditions in order to support themselves and their families.

International migration organizations like the UNHCR and IOM, in addition to smaller migration-focused international NGOs, serve as the primary service providers for refugees and, in some cases, irregular migrants. From the perspective of the Egyptian government, these organizations also bring in international funding that translates into development funding for the broader Egyptian populace. For example, the UNHCR provided the Egyptian government with US$1.4 million in 2014 for rehabilitating Egyptian schools, which some nationalities of refugees are also able to attend (Elite Interviewee A). The organizations also provide essential services for migrants and refugees that the Egyptian government might otherwise have to provide itself.[3] As the interim director of a refugee school noted, "all the international money goes to the UNHCR. But in a sense, it's like this is going to Egypt, because it's money that Egypt doesn't have to spend on refugees and migrants" (Elite Interviewee S).

In regard to education, refugee children of specific nationalities – Sudanese and Syrian – were permitted to attend Egyptian primary school at no financial cost at the time of interviewing. In the case of Sudanese children, this was due to the Four Freedoms Agreement signed in 2004,[4] and in the case of Syrians, an exceptional decree was issued by the Egyptian Ministry of Education in 2012 under former President Mohammed Morsi and upheld by the subsequent regime (Elite Interviewee A). For other nationalities, refugee children have the option to either attend NGO-funded community schools, often affiliated with churches or mosques, or private Egyptian schools. If an individual with children has refugee or asylum seeker status, the family can apply via Catholic Relief Services (CRS) for funding to attend a community school or private school. According to a field office manager for CRS, of the 2,500 students served by the organization in 2013, 60 percent attended community schools, and 40 percent attended either public or private schools. Of that 40 percent, only about 10 percent went to private schools (Elite Interviewee AN).

At the time of interviewing in 2014, there were fifty-seven community schools in Cairo alone (Elite Interviewee T). The cost of attending a community school varies, but one Sudanese woman, Hiba, explained that all of her children were in a community school for refugees in Maadi, a relatively wealthy neighborhood in the south of Cairo. According to Hiba, "the school costs 800 EGP a year per child, if you don't have a [UNHCR] card. With a card, CRS pays half, so then I have to pay 400 EGP. They only pay half." Even for individuals with their children enrolled in Egyptian public schools, there are additional costs. Sama, a Syrian refugee living in Alexandria, explained that with all four of her children in public school, "I had to buy everything. I bought pens, I bought notebooks, I bought books, I had to buy everything. [I spend] maybe 2,000 [EGP] every year. For each child. Notebooks, and books, and teachers."

Regarding health care, all emergency admittance to public hospitals for migrants and refugees is covered by the Egyptian government regardless of an individual's status. According to a UNHCR representative, "for the first twenty-four hours, it's a life-saving intervention, and it's for free. After that, if they continue to be in the hospital, they need to secure [funding]" (Elite Interviewee A). Jemal, a refugee from Eritrea, confirmed this policy: "Any refugee can use the hospital for twenty-four hours, only. And after that you have to pay."

For nonemergency services, individuals with asylum seeker or refugee status must contend with a bureaucratic system run primarily by Caritas, an international NGO that receives funding from the UNHCR. Caritas has its own doctors on staff and may also cover a percentage of a medical bill for an operation, treatment, or prescription. Individuals wishing to make an appointment with Caritas must do so in person, and each time I visited the Cairo office located in the neighborhood of Garden City in 2014, there was an enormous queue winding out of the building and stretching down the street. Abdelrahman, an asylum seeker from South Sudan who needed a minor operation described the process, saying, "So I went to Caritas to take a paper and to pay the percentage I have to pay, but now I'll take the paper to the hospital and not have to pay there, *inshallah*. Before Caritas I had to go to the UNHCR to make an interview. In total the process is taking about six weeks."

For those without asylum seeker or refugee status, accessing health care is difficult. The IOM provides some direct assistance through an organization called Refuge Egypt (Elite Interviewee C). Munira, a migrant from Sudan, informed me that a Catholic church in the wealthy Cairo neighborhood of Zamalek provides minimal assistance (EGP 150 or about US$25 at the time of interviewing) to help with the cost of giving birth. Additionally, the system is not straightforward and the amount that an individual has to pay for health care can sometimes depend on the doctor or hospital they visit. Raoul, a refugee from Congo, speculated that his hospital visit had a satisfactory outcome only because "I know how to communicate with Egyptians. Not just language; it's about knowing how to get things and which people to talk to." Others, like Kedija from Eritrea, complained of having to pay more than Egyptian nationals:

Yes, I've gone to the hospital. I didn't have help paying though, I had to pay. I went to the public hospital because the private ones are too expensive. At the public hospital the service depends on how much you pay. If you can pay a lot, it's good service. You have to pay more than Egyptians though. For example, my mom went, and the service would have been about five or ten [EGP] pounds for an Egyptian, but she had to pay [EGP] 30.

Some individuals, regardless of whether they have status, will opt to visit private Egyptian hospitals or clinics because they fear the quality of care at Egyptian public hospitals. Fathi, a refugee from Syria, relayed a tragic story of losing his unborn child because he was not able to afford the cost of private care:

I lost my third child last month. It wasn't born yet. My wife had a problem, she was almost due, and we had to go to the hospital suddenly, at nine o'clock at night. We went to one hospital in 6th of October first and they wanted EGP 3,000. I said I could pay EGP 500 right away and pay the rest later, but they wanted it all right away. We went to another hospital and they wanted a lot too. After that it was too late and we lost the baby .... This was a private hospital. You don't go to public hospitals here unless you want to die.

Some operations are also not possible in Egypt, or doctors are reluctant to perform them. Nizar, a Syrian man living in Alexandria, lamented, "I have a problem with my stomach. I went to Caritas. I need an operation, but the doctor told me it's not possible in Egypt. The doctor is a state doctor, from Alexandria University. The doctor says the operation isn't possible in Egypt, so I have to live with the problem, or I have to travel outside [Egypt]."

Despite complaints from refugees over the lack of funding and access to health services, the UNHCR and its partner organizations consider this type of funding and service-provision model to be a major, unsustainable expense. They continue to push for further host state responsibility on the part of the Egyptian government. For example, at the time of interviewing in 2014, the UNHCR had recently signed a memorandum of understanding (MOU) with the Egyptian Ministry of Health and was piloting a primary health care plan for refugees that would be operationalized through existing government health care services. Previously refugees were required to go directly to Caritas, which has centers in Cairo and Alexandria, to receive health services. Beginning in 2014 Syrian refugees in Alexandria were instead told to go directly to government hospitals for primary health care services, which would then make a referral for secondary or tertiary care. According to the UNHCR, after implementing this system for Syrian refugees in Alexandria, Caritas's caseload went down by 70 percent (Elite Interviewee F).

Based on this success, the UNHCR and the Egyptian government planned to eventually apply this model to all refugee nationalities in both Alexandria and Cairo. A representative of the UNHCR in Alexandria viewed this change as a positive example of the Egyptian government taking on some of its rightful responsibility for refugees. In his view, health care is

a responsibility we would like to share with the [Egyptian] government, because the government has all these facilities in the country .... And we're also trying to build their capacity by having some trainings. We have started organizing that. And we are also trying to help them with some medicines, some infrastructures through UNICEF. So, our aim is to capacitate those services that exist, rather than creating a parallel system. Because there is no sustainable parallel system. (Elite Interviewee F)

Yet even in pushing for greater host-government responsibility, the UNHCR continues to include the host community of Egyptian citizens in its service provision, by providing, for example, "all the vaccinations, some infrastructure, some medicines through UNICEF and UNHCR" (Elite Interviewee F). In other words, there is an ongoing negotiation between international organizations and the Egyptian government regarding financial responsibility for refugees and migrants, as well as generating tangential benefits for Egyptian nationals.

To fill the gap between migrant and refugee needs and the services provided by international organizations (or, in limited cases, the Egyptian government), many migrants and refugees in Cairo have formed CBOs. These organizations often provide a physical location for gatherings as well as services like language training, aid for those experiencing difficulty in obtaining health or educational services, legal counseling, and community activities for children or mothers, as depicted in Figure 3.1.

There are also CBOs that work specifically on the issue of community organizing. The Psychosocial Training Institute of Cairo – PISTIC – trains members of various refugee communities over several months, preparing them to work in schools, with other organizations, and within their respective Cairo neighborhoods, where they are expected to provide various mental health services – such as suicide prevention, child protection, counseling, and therapy – to their constituencies. Another CBO, Tadamon (*taḍāmun*, or "solidarity" in

Figure 3.1 A community gathering for migrant and refugee children in Ard el-Lewa, Cairo.
Photo credit: Kelsey P. Norman, 2013

Arabic), has six locations across Cairo, each of them run by a member of the local migrant or refugee community. They provide language and computer classes, assistance in finding work or obtaining status, and activities for children. Although CBOs have come to fill an essential role in brokering the space between individual migrants and refugees and NGO and INGO service providers, these organizations have generally not taken an overly political stance or engaged in advocacy. This may be partly due to the fragmented nature of the CBO network; each organization is usually focused primarily on supporting the individual members of their national communities (e.g., Sudanese, Eritrean) rather than pushing for better policies toward migrants and refugees as a whole. Alternatively, it may be due to the institutional memory among members of Cairo's migrant and refugee community of a particular attempt at advocacy that ended in violence and death.

In late 2005, Egyptian security forces killed twenty-six Sudanese refugees after they refused to disband their three-month long peaceful sit-in outside the UNHCR office in the upper-class Cairo neighborhood of Mohandessin (Salih 2006). The protest was organized in objection to the UNHCR's decision to suspend refugee status determination procedures for Sudanese in Egypt after peace talks in Khartoum the previous year (Judell and Brücker 2015). Following the violent crackdown on Sudanese protestors by Egyptian authorities, the Egyptian government requested that the UNHCR move its offices to 6th of October in order to deter any future protests or confrontations. The Sudanese director of an Egyptian-based NGO that works on migrant and refugee issues recalled:

I was there [at the protest]. Lots of people died, and lots of people went missing as well .... And since then we haven't seen any protests like this, because that was the setting up of refugees. It was naïve as well, because demonstrations can't get them anything, but they take a lot. (Elite Interviewee R)

The superintendent of a community school for refugees echoed this statement, stating, "I think most of the refugees have taken the attitude of 'we want to stay low. We don't want to raise attention to ourselves'" (Elite Interviewee T).

Even while refugees deal primarily with nongovernmental actors and community-based organizations for basic services, support, and international protection, they must still go directly to Egyptian authorities to obtain legal residence in the country as described in Deng's story. When conducting interviews in Egypt in 2014, refugees of all nationalities described the increasing difficulty of completing this process. According to Yonas, an Eritrean refugee, "before the revolution [the permit] was for one year or even more, but after the revolution it's always for six months." Aside from needing a residence permit to protect against arbitrary arrest and possible deportation, service provision in Egypt is also linked to having residency. One difficulty complicating this arrangement is that processing times for obtaining a residency permit are unreliable. As a program officer with Catholic Relief Services (CRS) in Cairo explained, obtaining a permit from the *mugamma* can take "forever, and they keep saying, next week, next week" (Elite Interviewee AN). The education projects for refugees run by CRS are funded by the UNHCR, and as such, no refugee can obtain an education grant without both a refugee card and a residence permit issued by the government.

A representative of the Ministry of Foreign Affairs claimed that the government would be unlikely to consider lengthening the duration of residency offered to refugees (Elite Interviewee AY). In the government's view, doing so could jeopardize international funding that Egypt receives to manage its refugee population. According to the official, "extending [residency] toward one year or more means that the government may be responsible for normalizing the situation of refugees without being equipped by international help in this regard" (Elite Interviewee AY). This coincides with what Kagan (2012) identifies as the "perverse incentive" facing Middle Eastern host states for making refugees on their territory as vulnerable as possible. Kagan notes, "If refugees are able to support themselves, it will appear that they are on the road to integration, a policy opposed by host governments which seek to share costs with the international community in hosting refugees" (Kagan 2012, 335). If Egypt takes steps toward officially integrating refugees, this could mean that it receives less aid from Western donor countries (Norman 2016a). Many refugees will end up spending five to ten years in Egypt, yet the government is not willing to consider formal integration as a policy solution, continuing to insist that refugees will be resettled to a third country. The Ministry of Foreign Affairs representative affirmed, "It's what governs us ... that they stay here on a temporary basis with renewal until

their situation has changed over time" (Elite Interviewee AY).
Consequently, refugees must renew their residency permit every two
to six months, which can prove to be a long and harrowing bureaucratic process.

Even as Egypt receives economic benefits from hosting refugees and
migrants, it may simultaneously use an indifferent approach as
a subtle means of deterrence, hoping to encourage individuals to
move onward or return home over the long term. One representative
at the IOM office in Cairo posited that the government uses its lack of
direct service provision and absence of integration measures to deter,
saying:

[The government does not] want them here, they don't want to be here. It's
fine. And so how do I make it difficult for them to stay? As I mentioned,
administratively, a lack of integration, etc. ... I'm not doing anything for
them, so therefore they will end up going. You know what I mean? (Elite
Interviewee C)

This coincides with deterrence measures used in other host-country
contexts – primarily western liberal democracies – whereby states make
accessing legal or social benefits difficult (Hassan 2000). In the existing
literature, these policies can include the use of detention, denial or
limitation of welfare, economic rights, and health care, reduced access
to the court system, and the extension of temporary protection or
residence rather than permanent protection (Morris 1998; Hassan
2000; Minderhound 1999).

In public statements and even in private conversations, the Egyptian
government most often decries its refugee and migrant hosting responsibilities. Ambassador Naela Gabr, chairperson of the National
Coordinating Committee for Combating and Preventing Illegal
Migration [NCCPIM][5] – a governmental body formed in 2014 to
draft a law criminalizing smuggling in Egypt – expressed her indifference toward the issue of migrants and refugees, stating,

[We are] not so much concerned [with] the people coming, the infiltrators or
illegal migrants; it's not my primary concern. I can tackle it with cooperation
with the African Union. And we are working with the African Union in that
regard. We don't love having extra people in detention. We don't like this; it's
costly, it's a headache, a responsibility with human rights and anything can
happen to the detainees, so we'll be having additional problems. (Elite
Interviewee AW)

For Gabr and for other government officials, this positioning of Egypt as a country that is indifferent to the presence of migrants and refugees is beneficial. It sends a message to Western donor states that Egypt is an overburdened country that has too many political and social challenges on its plate. If these countries want Egypt to directly engage with and manage its migrant and refugee population, they need to pay for it. As James Milner (2009) acknowledges in the context of sub-Saharan Africa, host states may see advantages in downplaying the benefits of hosting refugees as part of a broader effort to address external pressures from donor states.

The Egyptian state permits migrants and refugees to remain – and refrains from directly engaging with them – because of the economic and reputational benefits it receives from utilizing a policy of indifference. An individual at the Ministry of the Interior stated bluntly, "Of course we know about [migrants and refugees]. We let them stay. Even those without papers or who come illegally" (Elite Interviewee AV). Migrants and refugees, and the organizations working with them, are also aware of the Egyptian state's capacity to document and track their presence. As the director of an NGO in Cairo who is originally from Sudan told me, "the Ministry of the Interior knows. They know everyone who passes through the border" (Elite Interviewee R). By allowing international organizations and NGOs that receive international funding to manage service provision for these populations, the Egyptian state derives credibility from Western donor countries while simultaneously receiving funding that tangentially benefits its own national population. A representative at the Ministry of Foreign Affairs explained:

We prefer that the IOs help us in enhancing the infrastructure of the local communities that receive refugees and immigrants. That way, in the sense of building new schools, building new hospitals, you're benefiting the local society, so you're killing or you're undermining the xenophobic tendencies that exist naturally in any society toward the arrival of refugees or illegal immigrants. And you're benefiting both the refugees and the local communities at the same time. And you're assisting the government in alleviating part of the challenges that it is facing in dealing with the issues. (Elite Interviewee AY)

However, a policy of strategic indifference can give way to repression if the government decides that its security concerns outweigh the benefits it receives from an indifferent approach.

3.4 Toward Repression

The acting director of one of Cairo's refugee schools summarized the indifferent approach detailed in the previous section, saying, "The Egyptian government's not going to do anything with refugees and migrants – good or bad – unless it considers them a security threat. And if it considers you a security threat, it doesn't matter if you have a yellow card or a blue card. Nothing comes before security" (Elite Interviewee S). Prior to 2011 security officials generally did not actively seek out irregular migrants or refugees without identification and did not intentionally police communities or neighborhoods known to house these groups.[6] As an individual at a local NGO who specializes in detention issues explained:

In general, there's no policing of refugees and migrants. There was one incident maybe, where some Somalis were arrested, and the police went after them, but they were looking for particular individuals regarding a crime. Those who end up in detention centers and who are arrested were either trying to cross the border into Sinai or by sea, or they were trying to enter Egypt from Sudan. (Elite Interviewee AP)

This laissez-faire policing began to change after 2011 following the Egyptian Revolution. On January 25, 2011, which is also a national holiday celebrating the Egyptian police force, activists spread calls for protest via social media and asked citizens to take to the streets in objection to the wide-ranging police brutality of civilians, although demands of protestors grew to include bread, freedom, social justice, an end to the state of emergency that had been in place on and off since the 1950s, and the resignation of then President Hosni Mubarak. Mubarak first came to power in Egypt in 1980 after the assassination of former President Anwar Sadat, subsequently legitimizing his presidency through a referendum in the majlis al-nuwāb (People's Assembly) and remaining in power for more than three decades.

After initial protests on January 25, millions of protestors from a range of socioeconomic and religious backgrounds gathered in public squares in Cairo and across other cities in Egypt for eighteen days. They faced armed riot police, plain-clothed police officers, and tanks. On February 11, 2011, Vice President Omar Suleiman announced that Hosni Mubarak would resign as president and turn over power to the

Supreme Council of the Armed Forces (SCAF), who maintained power until presidential elections could be held the following year.

The Egyptian Revolution created a temporary security vacuum during which various factions – leftists and revolutionaries, Muslim Brotherhood supporters, and those who supported the former Mubarak regime – vied for the ability to shape Egypt's political and social future. Mohammed Morsi, representing the Muslim Brotherhood, was elected to power on June 30, 2012, although he was ousted from office just over one year later in a military coup that had wide-ranging popular support. Following the coup and the rise of current President Abdel Fattah el-Sisi, power was once again consolidated under a military-backed regime.

The period following the coup also saw a securitization of migration (Buzan et al. 1998). The topic became associated with threats to state security including terrorism, border regulation, and smuggling. In 2014, I was advised by a representative at the IOM regional office in Cairo not to mention the phrase "border security" in my interviews with government officials. "If they know you are inquiring about border security, don't be surprised if you are kicked out of the country," the individual warned me (Elite Interviewee D). This noticeable shift in the government's approach to migration began shortly after the 2013 coup and was initially directed specifically toward Syrian refugees. When Syrians began arriving in large numbers in Egypt in 2012, former President Mohamed Morsi announced an uncharacteristically welcoming policy toward them, reminiscent of Nasser's initially warm reception toward Palestinians in the 1960s and 1970s. Morsi decreed that all Syrian children were allowed to enroll in public schools, even if they did not yet have official UNHCR status, all Syrians could access Egyptian public hospitals free of charge, and all Syrians were eligible for the same food and energy subsidies as Egyptian nationals. However, as a direct result of this special treatment for Syrians and the affiliation with former President Mohammed Morsi, Syrians became the target of a government-organized media campaign that painted them as terrorists that supported the Muslim Brotherhood (Elite Interviewee A).

While the privileges – health care and access to primary education – extended to Syrian refugees under former President Mohamed Morsi were technically upheld by the subsequent military government, the de facto treatment of Syrians changed dramatically. Hady, a Syrian refugee living in Cairo, relayed a story from this time period:

I had two friends who were driving with a taxi and when the driver heard them speaking in the Syrian dialect, he took them in front of the Ministry of the Interior and started yelling "I have Syrians here!" It's not as bad as that now. But it's still worse than it was under Morsi when I first came here as a refugee. Last year [2013] I got stopped twice while coming back late at night. They were checking everyone, but I felt like they were targeting me more than the [Egyptians]. Luckily, I had the residency document. But if I didn't have it, I don't know what would have happened. I don't know what people who don't have documents do.

Human Rights Watch documented over 1,500 cases of prolonged detainment of Syrian refugees between July and December 2013, as well as hundreds of cases of coerced *refoulement* to Syria (Human Rights Watch 2013). As a result of the rapidly deteriorating protection environment for Syrians, Amnesty International also documented a sharp increase in the number of Syrian refugees attempting to travel irregularly from Egypt's north coast to Europe in mid-to-late 2013 (Amnesty International 2013). Between January and August 2013, an estimated 6,000 Syrian refugees managed to reach Italy by boat from Egypt, but between September and mid-October 2013 alone, more than 3,000 Syrians departed from Egypt to Italy. Syrians also had difficulty renewing their passports during this time period in Egypt. Refugees need a valid passport that is not close to expiring in order to obtain residency, but at the time of interviewing many Syrians were fearful of approaching their embassy to make a renewal. Mohammed, a young Syrian man living in Cairo, explained:

I have a yellow card. I waited for several months though after I got here to go to the UN. I didn't feel comfortable, I was scared. And now, my passport will expire in four months, and the UN says just, "Don't worry, it'll be fine. You have the yellow card." But a yellow card isn't a passport. They don't recognize the card here. I will be stateless.

The situation was further complicated for Palestinian Refugees from Syria (PRS). According to Human Rights Watch, the Palestinian Embassy in Cairo registered 6,834 Palestinian Refugees from Syria who arrived in Egypt between December 2012 and October 31, 2013. Some of these individuals were born in Syria and had never lived in Palestine but were legally treated as Palestinians both within Syria and once they fled to a third country. As Palestinian Refugees from Syria residing in Egypt they were not only stateless but were also without any international body to assist them. The UNHCR is unable to formally register them as they fall under the purview of the United Nations Relief and Works Agency (UNRWA), a body that specifically registers and provides services to Palestinians, but which does not do so in Egypt.

Egyptian authorities refused to allow the UNHCR to register Palestinian Refugees from Syria, citing article 1D of the Refugee Convention, which excludes these individuals from the UNHCR's mandate in areas where UNRWA provides services, such as in Syria. While Palestinian Refugees from Syria should fall under UNHCR's protection mandate because UNRWA does not provide services in Egypt, the Egyptian government chose to disallow this. The Deputy Chief of the Palestinian Consulate in Alexandria attempted to step in to assist Palestinian Refugees from Syria (in addition to their long-standing Palestinian caseload), but explained,

We cannot do everything. The income here in Egypt is not enough for covering expenses. If you find a job, you cannot get enough to live here with your family. And Palestinians cannot take a residency permit even if they have children in school. So, an Egyptian with a shop is not going to hire a Palestinian without a residency permit. It means that a Palestinian will have to start his own shop or his own market, so he needs a lot of money. It's difficult. (Elite Interviewee AX)

The unwillingness to assist Palestinian Refugees from Syria may be related to alleged connections between Palestinian refugees, Hamas (an acronym for the Islamic Resistance Movement or ḥarakat al-muqāwama al-islāmīya), and the Muslim Brotherhood. This alleged connection was used by the military leadership following the 2013 coup to discredit former President Mohammed Morsi, and one of the criminal charges he faced after his removal from the presidency was disloyalty to Egypt through collaboration with Hamas.

By 2014, state concerns over terrorism and its alleged links with migration in Egypt spread to all migrant and refugee nationalities. In November 2014, a representative from the Egyptian Ministry of Foreign Affairs affirmed that the alleged association between migration and possible terrorist activities had become a priority for the government. He explained, "And let me say that for us now, from a governmental perspective, there is a link between terrorism, illegal migration, and human trafficking. The networks are connecting together" (Elite Interviewee AY). Organizations attempting to advocate on behalf of migrants and refugees observed this new prioritization and the securitization of migration firsthand. An activist at the Egyptian Initiative for Personal Rights who focuses on the issue of migrant and refugee rights stated,

Nowadays it's the first time that the Egyptian intelligence [is] involved with the migrant situation. There are 113 migrants arrested in Abu al-Kheir, west of Alexandria. They're always detained in some police station or some detention place, and after that national security searches their papers. [Last week is] the first time that the intelligence [*mukhābarāt*] searched their papers, not the national security. (Elite Interviewee X)

The elevation of the issue of migrant detainees to the purview of state intelligence signals that migration became a stronger priority for the post-2013 military-backed regime, specifically as the topic related to state security.

Organizations attempting to conduct advocacy on the issue of migrant or refugee rights found the post-2013 environment debilitating. Generally, organizations providing services to migrants and refugees in Egypt do not have any direct interference or difficulty from state authorities in regard to their work, if they have any interaction with the government at all. However, the government still actively monitors the presence and activities of migrant and refugee-focused organizations, even if it does not directly liaise with them. The director of one of Cairo's fifty-seven refugee community schools relayed an ominous story that illustrates this dynamic. In August 2013, shortly after former President Mohammed Morsi was ousted from power, security forces were used to disband a protest of Muslim Brotherhood supporters in Rabaa al-Adawiya Square killing at least 817 individuals in a devastatingly violent use of state force (Human Rights Watch 2014). The morning of the attack, before the security forces moved in, the school director received a phone call from a representative at the Egyptian Ministry of the Interior politely warning him not to open the community school that day due to anticipated unrest. The community school was not registered with the government, and the Egyptian authorities had never previously contacted the director. "I laughed," the director said, "because I had actually been overseas, and I had just changed my phone number only three days earlier, but they managed to get straight to me, on my mobile" (Elite Interviewee T). While the director had never directly interacted with the ministry previously, it had clearly been monitoring the activities of his school.

The Egyptian government only adopts a hands-off approach toward organizations directly providing services to migrants and refugees, rather than organizations conducting advocacy. An official from the Ministry of Foreign Affairs articulated this distinction clearly, stating, "We differentiate between political organizations that deal with human rights, solely human rights, and organizations that deal with social welfare and economic prosperity for migrants and refugees" (Elite Interviewee AY). The UNHCR is also willing to defend its service-providing partner organizations in meetings with the Egyptian government, reinforcing the distinction between service-providing and advocacy-oriented organizations. A UNHCR representative stated:

Actually, in our discussions with the Ministry of Social Solidarity, we always advocate for NGOs working with the UNHCR, and we always tell them that these organizations, they do emergency assistance, they do the type of activities that are sometimes life-saving, and we cannot afford blocking activities because of bureaucracy. (Elite Interviewee A)

Organizations that attempted to engage in advocacy, rather than provide services, faced an extremely challenging operating environment after 2013.

Technically, NGOs in Egypt must register with the Ministry of Social Solidarity, although adherence to this law was not strictly enforced prior to the 2011 revolution (Elite Interviewee R). In fall 2014 all unregistered organizations were issued a mandate requiring them to register with the Ministry of Social Solidarity, which would then have the right to approve all organizational activities and funding in advance. The crackdown on unregistered NGOs eventually culminated in a draft law in 2017 and a revised draft law in 2019, leaving NGOs in Egypt in a space of legal limbo and contributing to a "climate of uncertainty, fear, and self-censorship" (TIMEP 2019). Members of Egypt's parliament justified the introduction of the new NGO law on the grounds that it was necessary to protect national security (Aboulenein 2017).

In the context of the 2014 crackdown on NGOs, the president of the Egyptian Foundation for Refugee Rights explained that he was taking precautions in his work not to cross the line from providing legal aid for detained migrants and refugees to conducting advocacy. He explained, "With this campaign against the NGOs in Egypt, I think they will not be focused so much on the people working in development or service organizations. They care about the people who work on election observing, democracy, human rights" (Elite Interviewee U). Representatives from the Egyptian Initiative for Personal Rights also noted that public perceptions toward NGOs due to the rhetoric of state-owned media made their work both difficult and dangerous. One activist reported:

It's ridiculous. Sometimes you can't tell them that you're a human rights defender; you have to tell them something else. It's not safe on the streets. And the other part of our work, making campaigns, it's very hard because of the media. Not one voice in the media is talking about [migrant detention], so we can't deal with the media. Sometimes journalists come and make reports about some [detention] case, and when they go back, they can't publish it because of the police and the newspapers. (Elite Interviewee W)

Those trying to raise awareness about the plight of Syrian or other refugee groups also came under scrutiny in the post-2013 period. One activist from the Refugees Solidarity Movement (ḥarakat al-taḍāmun maʿa al-lāji'īn) described the climate:

At the beginning [in 2011] it was easier than now, because the authorities back then were not paying much attention to us; they were concentrating on what was happening on the streets, and they were giving us more room to be involved with the refugees. We didn't have many problems like we have now. It was something new for them, so they were trying to lift the burden off their shoulders, [saying] "If you can do something, do something. Don't give us a headache, *ya'ni*." But now it's different. (Elite Interviewee Y)

Again, migrants and refugees themselves are also reluctant to engage in overt advocacy or mobilization. This reluctance predates the 2011 revolution but was reinforced in the politically uncertain and securitized post-2011 period. Of the thirty-three migrants and refugees interviewed in Egypt, only three stated that they participated in political activities directed at the Egyptian government. For those three individuals, political activities did not involve overt protests or demonstrations. Instead, migrants and refugees mentioned speaking with a journalist or writing an article in conjunction with an NGO. Many migrants and refugees were still involved in political advocacy directed at their home country governments but were reluctant or unable to participate in political actions directed at their host state.

Ahmed, an asylum seeker from Sudan explained, "In Sudan I was a member of the Sudan People Liberation Movement. But now that I'm here, I'm an artist. No more politics, only in Sudan." Kamal, a refugee from a contested region between North and South Sudan, stated, "I used to do a lot of advocacy back in Sudan, but I can't here. The Egyptian government won't let us." Some migrants and refugees were not aware of any opportunities to engage politically, and some did not feel they had time, but others were fearful of Egyptian security forces and *mukhābarāt*, or state intelligence. Yonas, a refugee from Eritrea, expressed his fear, stating, "It's hard. Within twenty-four hours, they'll take you. Here, sometimes the UNHCR will not take people from the prison, because the UNHCR has no right to enter the prison. So, if you enter the prison, forget it" (Eritrean Migrant A).

Some Egyptian advocacy organizations also warned migrants and refugees against protesting, fearing that lawyers may not be able to intervene should they be detained. A representative of the Egyptian Initiative for Personal Rights explained:

We don't advise them to [protest]. Some Syrians think about some kind of protests, but we advise them not to .... Some of them were thinking to protest against UNHCR, but we advised them not to do [so], because then they may get arrested. (Elite Interviewee W)

One activist described the case of a Syrian man who was accused of participating in a demonstration. He was arrested, held in detention for two months, and even after he was found innocent he was still deported (Elite Interviewee Y). The securitized atmosphere of post-2013 Egypt where even Egyptian nationals are barred from organized protest[7] meant that opportunities for overt political actions on the part of migrants and refugees were limited, although more subtle forms of political participation – such as community gatherings, cultural activities, writing articles, or speaking to journalists – were deemed innocuous enough to be permissible by the Egyptian state.

3.5 Conclusion

This chapter illustrated Egypt's strategically indifferent approach toward its role as a receiver of migrants and refugees, the benefits it derives from such a policy, as well as the consequences for individual migrants and refugees residing semipermanently on its territory as the political landscape changed. In general, the Egyptian state refrains from direct engagement with migrants and refugees, explained primarily by the economic and reputational benefits it receives from this type of approach. Yet once migrants and refugees were considered a security threat by domestic actors, the state did not hesitate to expend the additional state resources required to police, detain, and in some cases deport migrants and refugees. In the post-2013 space in particular, Egypt moved toward a more repressive policy that required additional policing of migrants and refugees as well as active interference in the activities of organizations attempting to challenge its policy choice. The use of such resources was considered necessary to construct and uphold the regime's security state, whereby the issue of migration became coupled with other security concerns, including terrorism, trafficking, and smuggling.

Under a policy of indifference, migrants and refugees were relatively free to participate in the informal economy, organize community meetings, and send their children to school (depending on legal status). This informality and absence of state involvement had both benefits and drawbacks for migrants and refugees. They were allowed relative freedom of movement and are able to piece together small livelihoods, regardless of legal status, yet were left in a precarious position when the state suddenly considered them a security threat, as was the case for Syrians in mid-2013 and for other migrant and refugee groups in 2014. Furthermore, overt political action or advocacy directed at the Egyptian state was disallowed, and the threat of the *mukhābarāt* or being stopped at a checkpoint by Egyptian security forces was ever present.

In the next chapter, I contrast the case of migrants and refugees in Egypt with that of Morocco. I argue that Morocco and Egypt looked fairly similar in terms of their use of strategic indifference during the 1990s and 2000s, and Morocco also changed its approach in 2013. Unlike Egypt, however, Morocco moved from indifference toward a more hands-on, direct form of engagement and a liberal domestic legal framework.

4 Morocco

From Raids and Roundups to a New Politics of Migration

4.1 Introduction

Amadu arrived in Morocco from Dakar, Senegal two years ago. He speaks French fluently, but he also speaks Arabic, since he grew up reading the Koran and studied in Saudi Arabia briefly as an adult. He lives in Sale, a city just opposite Rabat located northwest across the Bou Regreg river, where he and four other migrants rent an apartment for MAD 300 (about US$30) per month. To make a living, Amadu sells cell phone SIM cards along Avenue du Grande Maghreb, one of the main thoroughfares that divides Rabat's new city (*al-madīna al-jadīda*) from the old (*al-madīna al-qadīma*). Technically foreigners must purchase a SIM card from one of Morocco's official vendors using their passport, but SIM cards in Rabat are widely available via informal means, and migrants like Amadu are often the vendors.

Amadu left Senegal not because of any political problems but because he heard from friends that opportunities for work and advancement are better in Morocco. In Senegal Amadu worked as a mechanic, but he has not been able to find a job in Morocco without a *carte de séjour*, or residency permit. Individuals from Senegal, Tunisia, and Algeria can apply for work in Morocco without having established residency, but most employers want to hire migrants that already have a *carte de séjour*. For now, Amadu sells SIM cards along the street.

In his usual location along Avenue du Grande Maghreb, various friends of Amadu also sell an assortment of items – cell phones, clothes, earbuds – either placed on foldable wooden tables or on top of a blanket spread out on the ground. Amadu explains that the men and women selling items on this street are mostly from Senegal, but some are from Ghana and other West African countries, and some are

Moroccan nationals. At one point a friend of Amadu comes by to offer us what he calls "Senegalese coffee" in small plastic cups poured from a thermos. As we drink our coffee and Amadu shows me photos of himself on Facebook, a Moroccan police officer approaches us. The police officer suddenly grabbed Amadu's phone from his hand and it seems for a moment that Amadu might be arrested. But then both he and the police officer burst out laughing and begin joking around in Moroccan Arabic.

Amadu introduces me to the officer, Driss, and they continue to joke for several minutes until the police officer meanders up the street. Perplexed by this interaction, I ask Amadu why the police officer is not bothered by Amadu selling SIM cards informally along the street. Amadu reassures me that there is nothing to worry about (*"lā, ma fī mushkil, ma fī mushkil"*) and goes back to showing me pictures on his phone.

Then, just a few minutes later, the entire street of informal merchants suddenly begins packing up their goods. I look down the road and see several men in police uniform walking slowly in our direction, members of Morocco's general security (*sûreté nationale* or *al-'amn al-waṭanī*). "Ah, *contrôle*," Amadu says, packing up his goods in response. The group of four police officers walks slowly past us, casting serious, somewhat menacing looks in our direction, which makes quite a change from Driss and his jovial, laughing expression.

Amadu has learned the informal rules of his host state. He knows when to joke and laugh with a particular police officer but also when to pack up his goods and leave. He is not legally permitted to work in Morocco without a residency permit but has been able to scrape together a livelihood through participation in the country's bustling informal economy. As this chapter will explore, Morocco underwent a major policy reform in 2013, which in some sense altered the situation for the country's migrant and refugee populations. Yet the day-to-day lives of individual migrants and refugees like Amadu were not drastically changed, and many continue to eke out an existence through informal means, with the help of community ties, and by understanding the country's norms.

4.2 Migration Patterns and Demographics

Like Egypt, Morocco has a long history of immigration, although recent literature has tended to focus on its role as a sender of migrants abroad (Brand 2006; Iskander 2010). Arab invasions beginning in the seventh century led to the Islamization of Saharan Berbers and of the southern Sahel region, through both military conquests and nonviolent contact including trade, teaching, and intermarriage (El Hamel 2012). In the 1200s, the ruling Marinid dynasty increased the use of sub-Saharan slaves brought forcibly from West Africa, an institution that was not abolished in Morocco until the end of the nineteenth century (El Hamel 2012). One of the lasting consequences of this is the presence of certain groups descended from freed West African slaves, such as the Gnawa (El Hamel 2012). The Franco-Spanish protectorate in Morocco was established in 1912, whereby France controlled the central portion of the country while Spain controlled what is now Western Sahara and the northern Rif mountains (de Haas 2005). During the colonial period that lasted until Morocco's independence in 1956, a large French community immigrated to Morocco, with tens of thousands of French nationals continuing to reside in the country presently.

Beginning in the late 1980s, Morocco also began serving as the penultimate stop for migrants from sub-Saharan Africa hoping to reach Europe, particularly for individuals from West Africa.[1] Before the year 2000, migrants were able to travel more easily by sea via the route through Tangier or via the Spanish enclaves of Ceuta and Melilla on the northern coast of Morocco. This began to change between 2003 and 2005 when the EU successfully convinced Morocco to adopt enhanced policing policies toward irregular migrants, making it more difficult, costly, and dangerous to transit through Morocco to Spain. In 2002, the EU provided €70 million for the development of northern Morocco to encourage European Union Readmission Agreement negotiations in addition to several other financial incentives (Wolff 2014). Shortly thereafter, in 2003, Morocco produced its first law on irregular migration, Law 02–03, which criminalized irregular migration, established strict sanctions for support of irregular migration, and increased human and technological control capacities at Morocco's borders with Algeria and Spain (Natter 2015).

This new immigration law also translated into violent policing measures toward migrants as well as refugees, particularly near Ceuta and Melilla. Beginning in 1993 – but amplified between 2000 and 2006 – Spanish authorities enhanced border fortifications between Morocco and the Spanish enclaves with the intention of making it more difficult to cross from Morocco to mainland Europe (Goldschmidt 2006).

Spain's Guardia Civil, in conjunction with Frontex – the EU's border agency – also collaborated in 2006 to launch unprecedented antimigration sea patrols along African coasts, which cut off further migratory routes (Andersson 2014). Fearing arrest by Moroccan authorities, migrants still hoping to cross into Ceuta and Melilla began living clandestinely in a forest outside the Moroccan city of Nador (MSF 2013). In 2005, in response to coordinated attempts by migrants to scale the fences bordering Ceuta and Melilla, Moroccan authorities raided the migrant camps and arrested individuals they found living there. Authorities would also periodically raid urban locations known to be housing migrants in Morocco's major cities – primarily Casablanca, Rabat, and Tangier. Once arrested, migrants were often taken to Oujda, a Moroccan town on the eastern border of the county, and then forcibly deported into the no-man's land separating Morocco and Algeria (MSF 2013).

The securitization of Morocco's northern borders with Spain in 2005 helped to decrease the arrival of migrants and asylum seekers in Spain via the Western Mediterranean migration route. The result was that many migrants chose – or were forced to choose – to remain in Morocco (de Haas 2007). By the mid-2000s and into the 2010s, sub-Saharan Africans constituted one of the most prominent, politicized, and racialized groups of migrants in Morocco (Peraldi 2011; Niang 2017), of whom most did not qualify for official refugee status. According to a 2010 study, 76 percent of the total number of sub-Saharan migrants residing in Morocco at the time – approximately 30,000 individuals – were irregular (Khachani 2010). It may be the case that not all would-be refugees were able to successfully file their claims for status. For example, Francis, a migrant from Cameroon, informed me that when he arrived in Morocco in 2010 he attempted to approach the UNHCR office in Rabat, but because the office is only able to see a small number of individuals each day, he eventually gave up on the process. He explained the problem:

We had to wake up at 4:00 AM to leave from the tent to be the first person to get to the UNHCR. There were two groups: the Francophones and the Anglophones. There was a lot of violence. When you go to the organization, you can't even enter. You need a number and they only give out ten numbers. To get a number there is a lot of pushing and struggling.

Regardless of whether an individual left his or her home state due to violence and persecution or because of a lack of economic opportunities, migrants and refugees who found themselves stuck in Morocco during this period often remained for extended periods of time. For some individuals, the price of a return journey was too high, while for others the situation in Morocco was marginally better than what they left behind.

4.3 The Years 1990–2013: Indifference and Policing

Both migrants and refugees live throughout the country, either in major cities (primarily Rabat, Casablanca, Tangier, Oujda, Fez, and Marrakesh) or in remote areas such as the forests near Melilla. In cities, migrants tend to reside in traditionally low-income areas otherwise populated by poorer Moroccans. One such neighborhood is Taqadum in Rabat, depicted in Figure 4.1, a bustling area of the city that is packed with markets where customers haggle over fresh produce and others transit through to surrounding neighborhoods. As Daniel, a migrant from Cameroon, explained, "Taqadum is the area where you'll see all the African nationalities. We live there because it's cheap

Figure 4.1 Taqadum neighborhood in Rabat.
Photo credit: Kelsey P. Norman, 2015

and it gives the migrants the opportunity to sleep five, six, ten to one room."

One house I visited in Taqadum was divided into three apartments; more than fifty migrants (mostly men, but also several women) lived in the building in total. The house was damp and dark, and on the bottom floor there were three bedrooms and a so-called kitchen – a space next to the stairs with a large pot resting above an open fire. On the top floor, fifteen young men shared two bedrooms. In most of the bedrooms, men sat three to a mattress pad on the floor, lounging, listening to music with earbuds, or sitting quietly next to each other. Issa, a resident from Mali, explained that most people choose to spend all of their time outside of the house because they do not want to be at home with so many other people and so little space. Adama, another resident from Senegal, said that he had had trouble with the Moroccan police multiple times while living in Rabat and that the police visited the house on three separate occasions: once in 2007, again in 2008, and a final time in 2012. On all occasions the police unexpectedly barged in and demanded documents, leaving the house's residents feeling vulnerable and apprehensive. Hachim, another migrant from Senegal, recalled this period:

At that time, police could come to a house, open the door, take people. In some places in Taqadum, or G-5 [another Rabat neighborhood], or where I was living, people were scared because they were in Rabat just for a temporary time, to have the money to pay the guys to go to Spain .... Sometimes they take them from Rabat and they take them to the desert, and then they come back by foot to Rabat.

Employers take advantage of the presence and precarious status of migrants living in areas like Taqadum or G5. On the central street running through Taqadum migrants know to line up early in the morning, and employers in trucks drive through to select migrants for a day's labor in construction or agriculture. The head of migration-focused advocacy at the Association Marocaine des Droits Humains (AMDH) explained how this practice constitutes exploitation:

[Migrants] can do some work, for example in food markets, in construction, domestic work. But it's very difficult, sometimes they don't pay them .... Every morning they take twenty or ten people; they work for them for two or three or four days of the week, and then the next week, they take other people [s]o that they don't have to do work papers for them. (Elite Interviewee Z)

Morocco has a high rate of unemployment that hovers around 10 percent, but this is particularly pronounced for young people with degrees (Schwenk 2019). The Secretary General of L'Organization Démocratique du Travail (ODT), which has a sub-section devoted to migrants' rights, explained that sub-Saharan African migrants are often filling the types of demanding, low-paying jobs that Moroccan youth no longer want. An official explained:

Morocco has economic difficulties: poverty and unemployment. But Moroccan youth has changed. The ones who were living in [the] countryside moved to cities and refused to do some types of work. They don't want to work in agriculture anymore. They don't want to work in construction anymore. Many young people don't want to work in building anymore. Why? The salary given by the employer is low. They refuse it. They prefer to buy things and sell them, and be free, sitting in coffee shops and other things. But work that is hard, difficult like building or agriculture, sun and heat. This is the kind of work that Africans search for. And now Africans work in construction and agriculture. Because Moroccans don't want to work in that anymore, and even if they choose to work, they will ask for a high salary. That's the difference. (Elite Interviewee AA)

The Moroccan government is aware of the pervasiveness of migrants employed in the country's informal economy. The Head of the Department of Immigrants at the Ministère Chargé des Marocains Résidant à l'Etranger et des Affaires de la Migration [hereinafter Ministry of Migration Affairs] stated, "The young people who come now from Africa and other areas, many of them are overqualified and all of them work .... They work with hard conditions in the nonformal sector" (Elite Interviewee BA). As in all countries, migrants who work in Morocco without formal authorization and without a valid residency permit, a *carte de séjour*, can be exploited.

Lacking a residency permit can also mean that migrants have little recourse in terms of reporting theft, exploitation, or harassment by the police. Daniel, a migrant from Cameroon, explained how harassment from Moroccan nationals in Taqadum in particular had been an ongoing problem, prompting him to create the organization Association Lumière sur l'Emigration Clandestine au Maghreb (ALECMA) in 2012. According to Daniel, ALECMA had 600 members at the end of 2014 as well as 30 organizers – 16 of whom were located in Rabat – working to sensitize Moroccan citizens to the presence of migrants from sub-Saharan Africa and elsewhere.

However, the difficulty of obtaining legal status and formal employment does not apply equally to all sub-Saharan African migrants. Morocco operates student exchange programs with West African countries, and some migrants arrive as students and are able to find formal work once their academic programs are complete, particularly in Moroccan call centers, although others who choose to stay in Morocco without formal employment end up in an irregular position (Natter 2015). Also, Senegalese, Algerians, and Tunisians are able to apply for employment in the formal economy without first obtaining a residency permit. Nationals of these three countries do not need to demonstrate that they are more qualified than a Moroccan national for a position and are exempt from a process run by L'Agence Nationale de Promotion de l'Emploi et des Compétences (ANAPEC) that normally verifies this requirement.

Still, most sub-Saharan African migrants are only able to access informal jobs and do not receive assistance from the Moroccan government. Instead, a network of international and domestic NGOs developed in the 2000s to provide basic services to migrants and refugees when increasing numbers began to stay in the country. The director and founder of an NGO that offers legal aid and other services to migrants reflected on this time period for migrants in Oujda, the city closest to Morocco's border with Algeria:

Before 2005 Melilla was easier to access and migrants coming from Algeria would just pass through here. They would just rest in Oujda for a week or so, but then they would move on. But afterward it became difficult to cross and migrants had to stay in Oujda longer, so we started to see problems of homelessness, health. And there weren't any organizations for migrants in Oujda then. We were the first. (Elite Interviewee AD)

Caritas, Médecins Sans Frontières (MSF),[2] Association Action Urgence, Médecins du Monde, and Terre des Homes also began offering health services to migrants in various locations throughout the country. Some of these organizations receive support from the UNHCR and the IOM, but others are funded by private foundations or foreign and supranational governments such as the EU. For example, as of 2015, Caritas, which served as the primary provider of health care for migrants from sub-Saharan Africa, had only one central office in Rabat and two smaller offices in Casablanca and Tangier. While Caritas cannot always cover the full cost of an individual's needed care, it subsidizes the cost of doctor visits, prescriptions, and sometimes hospitalization at a public Moroccan hospital for migrants that approach its office (Elite Interviewee AT).

Migrants themselves also established CBOs like the Conseil des Migrants Sub-Sahariens au Maroc or the Collectif des Communautés Subsahariens au Maroc. These organizations often provide a community space for members to meet, but unlike community-based organizations in Egypt, many CBOs in Morocco are outwardly political, actively advocating for more rights in the country. Many of the politically focused CBOs were created in response to the horrific deaths of at least fifteen migrants killed by Spanish and Moroccan authorities while attempting to scale the fences separating Morocco from Melilla and Ceuta in 2005 (Goldschmidt 2006). The Counseil des Immigrants was one of the first organizations created that year in response to the violence, which Boubacar, the current president, described as "the first sub-Saharan organization to defend the rights of migrants in Morocco." Boubacar explained, "The council was created after 2005 when the Moroccan police killed some migrants trying to go to Spain. That's why the council was created. For example, I was in jail for two weeks because I wrote an article and gave it to the AMDH [Association Marocaine des Droits Humains] about the suffering" (Goldschmidt 2006). Both migrants and refugees are involved with the Counseil des Immigrants, which lobbies for better policies toward noncitizens in Morocco in general. One member of the council, Francis, stated that he and other members participate in politics and advocacy by "giving [the government] suggestions of the position of migrants here in Morocco." Francis elaborated, saying that the council does this

in front of the parliament with protests. But always by respecting Moroccan law .... We take authorization. We work with [AMDH]. We protest on the first of May. Every first of May. This is the way we contribute to Moroccan politics.

The same year that the council was created, an organization called Le Groupe Antiraciste de Défense et d'Accompagnement des Étrangers et Migrants (GADEM) was formed to advocate for the rights of foreigners and migrants in Morocco. The following year, a forum was held to bring the disparate community-based organizations and NGOs together. The vice president of the Counseil des Immigrants, Arafa, explained how a network formed in 2006:

I became involved after the problems in 2005. [The president of the Counseil des Immigrants] was militant in the forests in 2005, and I met him in 2006. There was a forum … with all the groups that wanted to battle Frontex. And all the Moroccan civils society organizations that attended were on our side. All of them. GADEM, AMDH, ABCDS.

In 2009, this forum coalesced into a "Platform for Protection" led by GADEM, Caritas, La Fondation Orient-Occident – a Rabat-based organization providing educational services and trainings for migrants – and other NGOs (Elite Interviewee AB). The platform continued to develop in subsequent years despite an indifferent response from the Moroccan government and continued violence toward migrants perpetrated by Moroccan authorities.

In 2012, L'Organization Démocratique du Travail (ODT), which advocates for the rights of Moroccan workers, decided to allow migrants to create a special subsection of the organization devoted to the issue of migrant employment rights. The organization's secretary general had originally declined requests from migrants to join the union following several incidents in which migrants were injured or killed while working informally for Moroccan companies. But after the secretary general returned from meetings with labor unions in France and the United States where he learned that labor groups had been active in helping migrants to gain working rights, he reconsidered the migrants' request (Elite Interviewee AA). The secretary general explained his reassessment:

For immigrants, we had chosen to defend immigrants in Morocco, with or without jobs. Why? It's because we found that these sub-Saharan immigrants had escaped from their home countries due to wars, famine, and ethnic wars. They escaped. They came from the Sahara in Algeria and they entered from Algeria's borders to Morocco. When they came here to Morocco, they remained in cities or they went to forests waiting to go to Europe, because their goal, it's to go to Europe. But when they find in Morocco a certain stability, they start to search for work here in Morocco, because Europe has closed the doors. To go to Europe, it's very difficult, with the crisis, it's very difficult. They now want to stay in Morocco, and their number is rising, maybe 30,000 just for sub-Saharans. Some of them work, some of them are unemployed, some beg for money. The most important thing is that they are here in Morocco and their situation is difficult. (Elite Interviewee AA)

The new migrant section of the ODT is run by an elected leader from the migrant community. Patrice, the secretary general for migrant affairs at the time of interviewing in 2015, saw the ODT's willingness to form a migrant section as critical to the fight for migrant employment rights:

The immigrants were working in many sectors but in a black market. In fishing and agriculture and construction. So, the ODT found that they need to defend them, their rights, because in the black market they don't have rights. They can work in very bad conditions, [and] they work in these sectors without papers. So, we decided to search for a solution, for the defense and the protection of all immigrants.

Along with other CBOs and NGOs, the ODT and its migrant section were highly involved in advocacy that would come to fruition with a major policy reform in 2013.

4.4 Morocco's New Politics of Migration

In mid-2013, GADEM, with input from other NGOs affiliated with the Platform for Protection, wrote a lengthy report that described the state of rights and protection for migrants in Morocco, condemning many of the government's violent actions toward migrants (GADEM 2013). The NGOs that authored the report decided to use an international platform to amplify the report's message. In 1993, Morocco signed onto the International Convention on the Protection of the Rights of All Migrant Workers and Members of Their Families, after which it was required to report to the convention's Implementation Monitoring Committee every five years. Knowing that a Moroccan delegation was due to meet with the committee in September 2013, GADEM and the other NGOs delivered their report to the committee, which then used the report to generate questions for the Moroccan delegation during its review (Elite Interviewee AB).

At the same time, back in Morocco, the Conseil National des Droits de l'Homme (CNDH)[3] used GADEM's report as the basis for a more condensed publication that offered policy recommendations and reforms and was delivered to King Mohammed VI during a closed session (CNDH 2013). According to a representative at GADEM, the

king decided to adopt the CNDH's recommendations because it feared
that its delegation in Geneva would be humiliated, tarnishing
Morocco's international image in front of important Western counter-
parts. The very next day, September 10, 2013, King Mohammed
announced a major migration policy reform. The representative from
GADEM explained the timeline:

We were just two organizations from this collective, and we went to Geneva
and the beginning of the review, on the 9th of September. On the same day,
the CNDH gave its own report to the king. Because there was a lot of
pressure, they realized that their report was [nonsense] and that the delegation was just not prepared, and they would be killed in front of the
Committee, and Morocco hates that, to have a really bad face at the international level. They can really not have it .... [They] need to just have
something new to show the Committee that [they] want to improve the
situation, so they gave this report. And the day after, on the 10th of
September, the king says we will just implement all the conclusions and
recommendations of the National Human Rights Council. So that's what
happened. So, everything is linked. What happened in Geneva and what
happened here: it's really linked. (Elite Interviewee AB)

The head of the Program for Migrants and Refugees at the CNDH
confirmed this timeline of events, stating, "[The reform] coincided
with Morocco's session for the Committee on the Rights of
Migrant Workers. So, it all occurred at the same time. Morocco
had to present their report and they were going to get feedback
from the Committee. I'm pretty sure they're linked as well, because
of how Morocco was then exposed for the human rights situation"
(Elite Interviewee AZ).

   The new policy had three central elements. First, the king announced
the introduction of a regularization process for irregular migrants
living in the country. Second, the Moroccan government planned to
take on responsibility for assessing the claims of asylum seekers, which
the UNHCR had been handling up until that point. A ministry that had
previously only been responsible for managing the affairs of
Moroccans living abroad – Le Ministère Chargé des Marocains
Résidant à l'Etranger et des Affaires de la Migration – was also given
purview over immigration to the country. Third, the government
intended to draft and introduce three new domestic laws on immigration, asylum, and human trafficking.

After the announcement, various Moroccan ministries and the CNDH were handed the task of developing an implementation plan for the unfolding of the regularization process. These groups established a timeline for the process – beginning in January 2014 and running for one year – as well as conditions under which migrants could be regularized. In total the government established six criteria – such as being able to provide proof of having resided in Morocco for five years or being married to a Moroccan national – that migrants had to meet in order to be eligible. Between January and December 2014, the government received 27,332 applications for regularization; Senegalese, Syrians, and Nigerians were the top three nationalities to apply. Ultimately the government committee approved 17,916 – or 65 percent – of all applications submitted in the one-year period (MAP 2015).[4] While the government touted the success of the regularization process domestically and internationally, some of the individuals I spoke with in February 2015 were still waiting for the result of their applications, and others who received a negative decision had filed appeals with the CNDH. GADEM and other members of civil society were critical of the ambiguity of the appeals process as well as some of the overly strict documentation requirements needed for a successful application (Elite Interviewee AB; Faris 2015).

In conjunction with the regularization process, the government actively consulted civil society and community-based organizations on the development of an integration strategy for the country. This was a stark contrast to the pre-2013 period. The secretary general of the ODT emphasized, "We are present now at all the conferences and meetings with CNDH, and we work with the Ministry of Migration Affairs" (Elite Interviewee AA). Migrant community groups noticed this change in approach as well. Arafa, the head of the Voix des Femmes – the only female-focused CBO in Morocco – stated,

Yes [we work] with them, the Ministry [of Migration Affairs], and with the International Delegation of Human Rights. And with CNDH .... They're very receptive. They're very agreeable. They work with us after the announcement for the new law; in 2013, when the king made the announcement.

In the postreform period, the main work of the Counseil des Immigrants was altered to focus on "sensitization." According to the Counseil's President Boubacar, "the primary objective is to sensitize the Moroccan authorities [to the fact] that the [migrants] have many problems." The Counseil was also highly involved in the rolling out of the regularization campaign and in assisting migrants attempting to appeal a negative decision on their application. Boubacar explained, "For example, with the regularization, we've gone to all the places in Morocco to tell migrants how to get regularization." When I asked whether migrants want to be regularized and remain in Morocco, he assured me that while many do, others have reservations:

There are some people who say that even with the card we have nothing. We want to go from Morocco. They say, "they kill migrants here and we have no rights here." We have to tell them, yes, they need to take the card. They should have the cards, even if they don't want to stay in Morocco. But it's difficult to convince them to get regularization because the police can attack migrants, and they have nothing, even with the card. It's like in Tangier. The Moroccan population has attacked migrants and the police were there and they didn't do anything .... I can't give hope to someone to live in a place like that. Right now, there is no justice.

Overall, reactions to the unfolding of the regularization process and hopes about the future of integration in Morocco were mixed.

On the whole, however, migrants and their civil society partners noticed a clear decrease in state violence following the 2013 announcement and the 2014 regularization campaign. Rachid, a migrant from Burkina Faso living in Oujda, explained:

Before 2013 it was bad. I live over near the university, and they would come in and demand papers and sometimes they would deport you to the border and you'd have to walk back. But then after 2013, it's calm. The police don't come and do that anymore.

Kwaku, a migrant from Ghana living in Tangier, confirmed:

Back in 2000, 2010, 2013, it was very bad. But after 2013 everything changed for migrants. Before police would come everywhere – houses, restaurants, but now they don't bother you, unless you're near the border.

And yet in February 2015, just two months after the conclusion of the regularization process, Moroccan security forces carried out a mass raid of migrant camps on Morocco's northern coast near Melilla, arresting 1,200 migrants residing in the area (Associated Press 2015; CCSM-GADEM 2015).

This raid was alarming to the civil society actors still attempting to assist migrants who had not yet received the result of their regularization application. A representative from GADEM expressed her frustration, saying, "Now, they did what they did. They arrested these people. We consider that the regularization is not done yet. Even though the year 2014 is over, there are still people who did not get any answer. And there are people who could not appeal a negative [decision]" (Elite Interviewee AB). When asked about the return to raids on migrant camps, a representative from CNDH hypothesized,

I would think that it [has] to do with the fact that we've regularized people, and now the people that have not been regularized .... Okay, we haven't seen deportations as such, but they try to get them as far away from the Spanish border as possible. Because that's where they were arrested, in Nador that's right next to Melilla. And the Gurugu forest, they kind of ... cleared the whole forest, burnt down tents. (Elite Interviewee AZ)

The director of Caritas described how migrants captured and beaten during the raid were afterward forcibly brought to Rabat and deposited in front of the Caritas office:

The migrants who were caught [after the raids], now they are coming to the center. So [the government] promised them that they would enact the regularization, but it's just that – a promise. And they are coming, and we are managing and supporting them as we can, but really we don't know the situation. We don't know what will happen in one month or in one week. (Elite Interviewee AT)

Caritas was forced to temporarily close its Rabat operation after state officials continued to deposit arrested migrants in front of its office. The director explained that while the decision to temporarily close its office was difficult, it sent a necessary message to Moroccan authorities that the organization did not condone the use of state violence against migrants.

In addition to the government's return to raid-and-arrest policies on the northern coast in early 2015, another criticism from civil society was that the government was not taking the integration aspect of the migration reform seriously. If accepted for regularization, migrants were issued a *carte de séjour* good for the duration of one year. In order to renew the permit, migrants had to show that they had successfully integrated into Morocco through documentation such as a formal employment contract or an apartment lease. The founder of ABCDS in Oujda argued that if the Moroccan government wanted migrants to successfully integrate and to succeed in obtaining formal work and housing, it should have been proactive about sensitizing Moroccans to the presence of migrants immediately after the reform announcement.

The Ministry likes to talk a lot, but it doesn't take integration seriously. If it did it would have started offering integration right away, not a year after it issued residency permits. By now most people's residency cards have expired; they were only good for one year. So now migrants have to go to the offices and renew them, and do you know what they want? They want proof of a life – a work contract or a housing contract. But migrants can't get these things because the Moroccan people aren't sensitized to migrants yet. So, the regularization needed to also be accompanied by a sensitization process. (Elite Interviewee AD)

Patrice, a migrant from Democratic Republic of the Congo, decried the one-year timeline as well, stating, "The process of integration has already begun, and it will last for one year. But one year is still not enough; they need longer in order for the migrants to learn the language and to work. And there's [*sic*] other problems, like the education of children. One year is not enough." Kojo, another migrant from Ghana, acknowledged the difficulty of the residency renewal requirement but remained hopeful that the process would change in the future, explaining, "You can renew [the residency permit], but . . . you have to have the work [contract] before they'll give it to you a second time. I know as time goes on, things will change."

In regard to other aspects of integration promised by the reform – specifically education and health care – progress has been slow. Following the king's 2013 announcement, the Ministry of Education issued a memo stating that the children of all regularized sub-Saharan migrants would be allowed to enter Moroccan public schools (Cherti and Collyer 2015), yet with individuals still waiting for the result of their regularization applications two years later, general access to public education for all migrant children had not yet occurred. Most interviewees I spoke with in 2015 did not have children or had left children with relatives in their home country, but those individuals who did have children sent them to informal schools run by NGOs such as Caritas or La Fondation Orient-Occident and otherwise paid out-of-pocket for education at a private school.

In 2015, the Moroccan government agreed to allow regularized migrants to access the Régime d'Assistance Médicale (RAMED), a public health insurance system created in 2012 for Moroccans of lower socioeconomic backgrounds. RAMED gives recipients access to Moroccan public health facilities, which includes health centers and some hospitals in the case of emergencies. Of course, access to RAMED depends on whether one is able to obtain and maintain residency in Morocco, and a 2016 survey found that even for regularized migrants, most were unaware of the program and their potential access to it (Mourji et al. 2016). Ninety-five percent of the nearly 800 migrants in the study's sample were not aware of RAMED, even though 56 percent of those in the sample filed for regularization, indicating that the program had not been successfully publicized or communicated to beneficiaries. In the absence of access to the Moroccan public health-care system, migrants resorted to the same strategies for accessing health care as in the pre-2013 period: looking to NGOs for assistance or coupling together fees to access to private care with the help of friends and family. Hachim, a migrant from Senegal, lived in a small town between Rabat and Casablanca. He explained,

Now, there [are] migrants in Morocco [who] have medical problems but they don't know how to get to the hospital or how to treat the infection. Sometimes they don't know; sometimes they're scared because the police can come everywhere in the street, in the hospital, the police ... come and take you. And sometimes [migrants] don't have the money.

In this sense, access to primary services like health care felt as informal and difficult for migrants as in the prereform era.

While many civil society actors were skeptical of the reform implementation process, some individuals were cynical about the government's motives more generally. A representative from the Association Marocaine des Droits Humains saw the reform and the regularization process as political posturing toward Europe. He argued that "the reform is a way of appeasing European countries, which can then claim that migrants have no need to travel to Europe when integration possibilities exist in Morocco" (Elite Interviewee Z). In other words, European countries will face less pushback for returning irregular migrants or asylum seekers to Morocco if the country has inclusive domestic policies in place.

In support of this hypothesis, Morocco signed a mobility partnership with the EU in June 2013, just three months prior to the announcement of the reform (European Commission 2014). This partnership affirms Morocco's commitment to preventing irregular migration to Europe and also commits Morocco to eventually signing a readmission agreement with the EU in exchange for visa liberalization for Moroccan nationals (Wolff 2014). Morocco later agreed to relaunch negotiations of the readmission agreement in 2015 (*La Cimade* 2017). This continued commitment to border security and combating irregular migration toward Europe suggests that the EU's securitization preferences are still influential in determining Morocco's actions toward migrants.

Some migrant-focused groups and CBOs were also skeptical of partnering with the Moroccan government due to its history of co-opting civil society elements in order to minimize dissent and criticism. The previous monarch, King Hassan II, ruled Morocco between 1961 and 1987. During this period, referred to as the "years of lead," thousands of Moroccan opposition members – including leftists, Islamists, proponents of Western Sahara's independence, and military personnel implicated in several unsuccessful coup attempts – were jailed, killed, exiled, or forcibly disappeared for opposing the regime (Ottaway and Riley 2008). In the final years of his reign, Hassan II embarked on a path of top-down reform, allowing opposition parties into government after the 1997 parliamentary elections – notably, a section of Morocco's Islamist movement[5] – and permitting members of civil society to speak openly about issues such as corruption (Willis 1999), but his rule is still remembered for its severity.

After King Mohammed VI ascended the throne in 1999, he sought to distance himself from the harsh rule of his father Hassan II by taking measures such as releasing political prisoners and establishing a truth and reconciliation commission to address human rights abuses (El Amrani 2012). Reform policies introduced in the 1990s and early 2000s were not sweeping democratic transformations but targeted very specific policy areas (Ottaway and Riley 2008). As Frederic Vairel (2013) argues, Mohammed VI's succession reinvented methods for minimizing dissent rather than opening opportunities for opposition.

Specifically, Mohammed VI has found ways to co-opt civil society actors by elevating certain issues and bringing actors on board to assist with the implementation of new policies, thereby limiting their ability to defy the state. For example, one tactic has been the establishment of quasi-governmental institutions, such as the Conseil Consultatif des Droits de l'Homme (CCDH), the CNDH's precursor.[6] By giving civil society actors more visibility through integration into government, the monarchy's stronghold over issues such as human rights or women's rights was simultaneously strengthened and associative activism was tied to state authority (Sater 2010; Bono 2010). Vairel (2013) argues that Moroccan civil society organizations "paid a heavy price" by choosing to participate in government-led processes rather than engage in more overt advocacy such as mobilization and street activities (43).

The Moroccan government attempted to frame the 2013 migration reform process as instigated by and inclusive of civil society actors. A representative from the Ministry of Migration Affairs interviewed in 2015 asserted, "There has never been a public policy like this [in Morocco] executed with such a high level of coordination with civil society. We do nothing without coordination with civil society" (Elite Interviewee BA). According to the government narrative, migrants and migrant-focused civil society organizations successfully demanded their rights from the government. Yet civil society organizations were aware of the government's political motives behind the reform. Daniel, a migrant from Cameroon affiliated with the community-based organization ALECMA, expressed his frustration with what he perceived to be only superficial engagement from the government. He felt that outreach from Moroccan officials was only for the sake of publicity, stating,

If it's an international forum, I think they use the association of migrants just to show the world. The problem is not to call me, give me [a] chair, [and] tell [them] something. No, the problem is to contribute to do something, to give some opportunities. Discuss, discuss, discuss. No! [They] have to do something.

The fact that the three new laws attached to the policy reform had still not been passed at the time of interviewing in 2015 also led to doubts among civil society actors (Elite Interviewee AB). Alluding to the suspected ulterior motives of the government, a representative from GADEM asked, "The question is now, was it really, did it really have the intention to change the situation or was it just a big communication event to show the international community that Morocco is doing something new?" (Elite Interviewee AB). Even a representative from

CNDH, which is a quasi-governmental body, acknowledged that domestic politics and Morocco's international reputation played a role in the decision to enact reform, stating,

It just happened so quickly, and once it happened there [was] a willingness . . . to change things, and to see so many organizations and NGOs involved. And also, to see NGOs that were involved before that royal speech. But there is also [the] political aspect to it as well. And making sure that Morocco respects its international obligations. (Elite Interviewee AZ)

Ultimately, migrants and the organizations advocating on their behalf wanted to know if the new law and the regularization process was only for show, allowing the government to co-opt civil society actors and avoid international shaming, or whether 2013 constituted a real change in the government's mentality.

Some individuals were hopeful. Kwaku, a migrant from Ghana who had lived in Morocco for fifteen years when we spoke in 2015, was planning to start his own import/export business in the Tangier *madīna* but explained that he needed a positive outcome on his *carte de séjour* application before he could do so legally. Despite this holdup, he explained that life in Morocco was relatively good. He previously lived in other North African states including Algeria, and this was the only country where he felt migrants – whether regular or irregular – were not bothered by the police, "unless you're near [the] border." Kwaku felt everything changed for migrants after 2013, stating, "Now, there is an opportunity to get the residency, and you can make a life [in Morocco]." Others were disappointed by the state of affairs in 2015 but hoped that all the promised changes would eventually come to fruition. Boubacar, a migrant from Guinea, explained that the regularization process, and reform in general, promised a better future in Morocco despite many faults, saying, "Yes, yes. I think it's a good thing because all the things that have happened in history have happened with steps. In the United States, for example, Obama could not have been president, but now he's president. Maybe we don't have anything now but in five, ten, or fifteen years, maybe we can have something."

4.5 Conclusion

This chapter explored Morocco's change from a strategy of indifference, with repressive use of policing and deportation in parts of the country, to a more liberal strategy in the post-2013 space. In this new approach, the Moroccan government decided to allow access to residency for irregular migrants, to permit access to the formal labor market – at least in theory – and to take on responsibility for refugees. Thousands of migrants were regularized in 2014, but they were only given access to short-term permits and still faced de facto barriers to accessing the labor market, forcing most individuals to participate in the informal economy. Thus, Morocco's strategy remains indifferent in terms of policy outcomes for migrants. Whether this is due to implementation failure or state intention is difficult to say with certainty, but for individual migrants and refugees hoping to establish a more formal presence in Morocco, this distinction is important. Francis, a migrant from Cameroon, expressed his frustration, saying, "Because if there's integration, the people who died trying to go to Spain, to Europe, they will not try and go. They go there to find integration, to find work, to become independent economically. So, if there is integration here, there will be no problem." A survey of sub-Saharan migrants conducted in five cities in 2016 confirmed that most migrants were not satisfied with their employment situation in Morocco despite the 2013 regularization campaign, a second regularization campaign in 2016, and the government's proposed measures for integration and sensitization (Mourji et al. 2016).

Many migrants in Morocco still hope to continue their journey to Europe, and view their time in Morocco as temporary, even when it consists of years rather than months. Others have changed their mentality. Hachim, a migrant from Senegal who had lived in Morocco for fourteen years, explained:

I think that now most people . . . when you talk to people, you don't think that they just want to go to Europe. You think that they just want to have a better life, here or in Europe. Or just to stay here. Because everyone knows what is happening in Europe now; Europe is in crisis. You can go there to find a better life, but you have to be strong. You have to innovate. And here in Morocco, we still have many things to build up, the economy, and social [relationships], things like that. Morocco is a country of opportunity. It's a Global South country and people, they like it. They know it. You still have people who want to go to Europe, but if I can't go, I can stay here to make a better life.

Armand, a migrant from the Democratic Republic of Congo who tried to go to Spain in 2010 but was arrested and released in Morocco, stated, "For the moment, I'm here. I want to stay here."

This chapter also explored the timing and incentives behind the 2013 policy change. While the government narrative puts civil society and migrant mobilization at the center of the reform, this explanation does not fully account for the timing of the 2013 changes, since routine protest, the organizing of platforms for change, and lobbying of the government were ongoing for years prior to the top-down reform decision (Norman 2016b). Sustained civil society pressure and the development of a pro-migrant rights network was important for bringing the issue of migration policy reform to the attention of the CNDH, but it was international shaming led by transnational advocacy networks that ultimately forced the government to take action.

An explanation based around international shaming encompasses a combination of postnationalist (Soysal 1994; Sassen 2002) and neoinstitutionist (Hollifield 1992; Miller 1981) factors; international shaming is effective within the context of a top-down international normative environment (postnationalist), yet it was civil society actors that brought the topic to international attention (neoinstitutionalist). Shaming also highlights the role that transnational advocacy networks can play, especially in nondemocratic contexts or where state actors are unresponsive (Keck and Sikkink 1998). Without an appeal at the international level, it is not clear that the king would have decided to reform the policy in 2013, if at all. Finally, this finding builds on the work of Laurie Brand (2006) in understanding the Moroccan government's tendency to fear and avoid international humiliation. Brand examines how the Moroccan government has used *amicales*, or workers' organizations, in Europe to monitor and intimidate Moroccan emigrants, noting that the government is "concerned about the image of the country abroad, which could affect worker recruitment" and has sought to "limit agitation among its expatriates" (72).

With the announcement of its new policy in 2013, the Moroccan state managed to accomplish several aims simultaneously. The first is the co-optation of domestic human rights actors, international migrant-focused organizations, and migrant community organizations. By inviting these actors to the table of the reform process and by undertaking periodic consultations with them, the government – in particular the newly expanded Ministry for Migration Affairs – reduced the risk of criticism that could, and has, hurt Morocco's reputation internationally. At the same time, Morocco wanted to uphold its commitments to the EU, particularly Spain, by returning to its raid-and-arrest police tactics in the north of the country. A potential third motive explaining the timing of the policy reform is related to Morocco's diplomatic and economic interests in West Africa, which will be further explored in Chapter 6.

The analysis of Morocco's changing engagement strategy presented in this chapter raises an important issue: International shaming is an effective tactic for incentivizing policy liberalization in Morocco while Egypt seems relatively immune. While Morocco's economic and diplomatic connections to the EU mean that Morocco is reluctant to receive any bad press from key EU members, most notably France, the Egyptian regime is much less concerned about outside opinion and criticism. One possible consideration to explain this discrepancy is the relative sensitivity of each country to foreign aid.

While the United States' approach to assisting Morocco has been on a comparatively small scale and has generally been directed at building local capacity, the European approach to aiding Morocco has tended to be directed more toward promoting social change, including democratizing governance practices, building infrastructure, and shoring up macroeconomic indicators (Malka and Alterman 2006). Prior to the Arab Spring, direct government assistance to Morocco was regularly in the tens of millions of dollars for the United States and in the hundreds of millions of euros for European countries (Malka and Alterman 2006). The EU itself was donating on average nearly ten times the amount of money to Morocco as the United States, not including the donations of individual European countries (Malka and Alterman 2006). France's contribution was more than US$300 million annually, exceeding that of the EU by more than 60 percent (Malka and Alterman 2006). In 2014, EU bilateral assistance under the European Neighborhood Instrument (ENI) – the key financial instrument supporting Europe's cooperation with Morocco – amounted to €218 million (European Commission 2016b).

Comparatively, the vast majority of international aid to Egypt issues from the United States. While EU bilateral funding through the ENI to Egypt amounted to €105 million in 2015 and €100 million in 2016 (European Commission 2016a), the United States contributes US$1.5 billion to Egypt annually on average (Plumer 2013). American aid to Egypt, including both military and economic assistance, increased dramatically following the Egyptian-Israel Peace Treaty in 1979, eventually stabilizing at US$1.3 billion annually for military assistance and US$150 million per year for economic assistance (Dunne 2017).

While the United States has periodically threatened to cut aid to Egypt, the country's perceived importance to regional stability has meant that most of these threats have been hollow or symbolic. In 2012, the US Congress made aid to Egypt conditional on the secretary of state certifying that Egypt was "supporting human rights and democratic values," but then-Secretary of State Hillary Clinton waived the certification requirements after the Obama administration claimed that there was no way to ensure such provisions were met (Dunne 2017). In 2013, White House officials refrained from referring to the removal of former President Mohamed Morsi as a military coup because doing so would have prohibited the United States from providing Egypt with military equipment (Dunne 2017). Finally, in August 2017, the United States cut tens of millions of dollars in aid from Egypt citing the country's failure to make progress on human rights and democratic reforms, but considering the average annual aid dispersal, this measure was largely symbolic (Dunne 2017). Ultimately, Egypt's domestic stability and strategic importance is deemed too valuable to US interests, making the Egyptian regime relatively immune to serious foreign aid cuts, and allowing the el-Sisi regime to be brazen in its rejection of any criticism of its human rights record from outside actors.

This analysis potentially explains why the Moroccan regime is more susceptible to international shaming than its Egyptian counterpart, although the aid Morocco receives from the EU is still relatively small in comparison to the country's GDP or even to the budgets of individual ministries, such as the Ministry of Interior (El Qadim 2015, 2019). It may be that the Moroccan government perceives EU migration management funding as a sign of political will and partnership, which can carry more weight than financial incentives alone (El Qadim 2015, 2019). Furthermore, even in a case such as Morocco that may be more susceptible to international shaming, development aid can strengthen authoritarian structures by, for example, tying civil society actors more tightly to state power and making them more narrowly focused and apolitical (Khakee 2017). Following the 2013 reform, the co-optation of migrant community-based organizations and civil society actors in advancing the new politics of migration in

Morocco resembles patterns that the Mohammed IV regime undertook previously with both political parties and civil society groups. Given how co-optation has often led to authoritarian retrenchment, rather than democratization, the path toward continued liberalization in the area of migrant rights may not be linear.

However, others argue that instead of co-optation, bringing civil society actors on board in Morocco can be viewed as these groups using political opportunities to their advantage. As Emanuela Dalmasso (2012) states, "Moroccan civil society activism is more and more the sum of narrow interests that do not question the system as a whole but, on the contrary, takes advantage of the opportunities provided by an authoritarian regime" (229). With this more optimistic view, migrant and refugee leaders and their civil society partners who choose to work with the government may be able to incrementally achieve concessions or further rights for their constituencies, so long as these groups do not threaten the regime's legitimacy.

Morocco's decision to enact legal and policy reforms to its migration engagement strategy will be contrasted in the next chapter with Turkey's 2013 migration policy change. In both cases, I suggest that reform was driven by international shaming and perceived diplomatic and economic benefits, rather than by a truly bottom-up process, which has important consequences for the incentives of these states to follow through on implementing more liberal and inclusive engagement strategies.

5 | Turkey
From Strategic Indifference to Institutionalized Control

5.1 Introduction

Youssef and Noora are the only two Syrian employees at a Turkish-owned *künefe* restaurant near the university in central Gaziantep. The restaurant – a large space with tall ceilings, a shiny metal interior, and booth-style seating – is one of the many shops selling freshly baked *künefe* and *baklava* in the area. Gaziantep has gained notoriety in recent years as the final stop in Turkey for foreign fighters en route to Syria to join ISIS. While the border between Turkey and Syria is officially closed, smuggling operations are still up and running. The city has also become the main base for Syrian cross-border humanitarian operations led by the UN and other INGOs. But aside from this, Gaziantep, also called Antep, is one of the world's oldest continually inhabited cities. Its proximity to Aleppo, Syria gives Gaziantep a different feel than many other parts of Turkey, reflected in the food, language, and architecture. And it is Turkey's leading producer of *baklava*, with more than 100 shops in the city supplying 90 percent of the country's *baklava* consumption.

Noora came to Gaziantep from Aleppo three years ago with her husband Ahmed, her two sons and one daughter, and their spouses and children, all of whom live together in one apartment – thirteen people in total. She lives about an hour walk from the *künefe* restaurant. "You don't take a bus?" I ask her. "You always walk?" I raise my eyebrows, knowing that it is at least several kilometers. "Yes," she tells me resignedly, "an hour to work and an hour back." In Syria, Noora's husband supported the family, but in Turkey she has to contribute to the household income as well. At every opportunity Noora tells me how much she prefers Aleppo to Gaziantep. "Here is like Europe," she says. "It's completely different, even though it is only sixty kilometers away." She returned to Aleppo a few months ago to visit her parents while the border was still open. "Is it safe?" I ask her. "Not so safe, but it's okay," she says, trying to smile but looking distraught.

Youssef, also from Aleppo, had only been in Turkey for nine months when we spoke in 2015. In Syria he worked as a jeweler in his father's shop, primarily as a goldsmith, but in Gaziantep he cleans floors and does other odd jobs around the *künefe* restaurant. While Noora works seven-hour days, Youssef works twelve hours, six days a week. The restaurant where he and Noora are employed has four shops in Gaziantep, and part of his job is to travel the city by bus each morning dropping off *künefe* dough at each shop. I make these rounds with him one morning, and after we step off the bus, he asks me, "Did you see how all the people in the bus were quiet when I was around? People here are scared of Syrians. And people move away from me on the street. They can tell I'm Syrian just by looking at me."

Youssef, his wife, their six-month-old daughter, his brother, his brother's wife, and two other Syrians share a one room apartment, for which they pay an exorbitant TRY1,000 per month in rent. He could pay less elsewhere in the city, but Youssef wants to live near the university, where "at least it's safe there for my wife and baby." Almost all of his income from the restaurant goes toward covering this cost. He explains, "You come here and you're looking for housing, and the landlord says, okay, 1,000 lira for this apartment that's horrible. And you say, no, I won't pay that. And they say, okay, so sleep on the street then. So, you have to take the apartment."

I ask Youssef about the rest of his family, and he says that his parents are still in Syria with his two sisters. They cannot come to Gaziantep because he cannot afford to pay for them, and they do not have enough money to come on their own. "Are you able to talk with them often?" I ask. Every week for about an hour, he says, but the Internet in Aleppo is not very reliable, and power is often cut.

Noora tells me that she thinks Turks have started to turn against Syrians. "In the beginning it was different," she explains. "They were happy to have us here. But now they don't want us anymore." Youssef agrees, saying, "In the beginning, you and me [he points at me] are friends. But now you say, 'I'm tired of being friends. I don't want this friendship anymore. You should go now.' But where can we go?" he asks, shrugging his shoulders.

He uses another example: "Let's say you have a baby in your house, and the baby is crying. Someone comes to the house with the police and they say that if the baby doesn't shut up, it's going to be out on the streets. It's either be quiet, or you have to go out on the street." Turks think that Syrians should not complain, Youssef explains. They need to be quiet and accept this hospitality.

As this chapter will show, Turkey transformed its migration and refugee policy from one of indifference during the 1980s, 1990s, and first decade of the 2000s toward a more liberal framework in 2013 with the adoption of Law No. 6458 on Foreigners and International Protection. While a common narrative asserts that the new law is tied to the EU accession process, which began after the EU recognized Turkey as a candidate country in 1999, the decision to reform the country's domestic migration and asylum policies was a political calculation on the part of the Turkish government. Recognizing Turkey's strategic geographic position and understanding that migration would be an increasingly critical issue going forward, a faction of government officials pushed for reform.

The implications this has had for the daily lives of individual migrants and refugees, however, is minimal. Many, like Youssef and Noora, continue to be largely self-reliant, informally integrating into the Turkish economy and relying on services provided by NGOs when available. The civil war in Syria and subsequent arrival of Syrian refugees in Turkey, the 2015 European refugee "crisis", and the 2016 EU–Turkey deal all hindered Turkey's ability to implement the liberal framework adopted in 2013.

5.2 Migration Patterns and Demographics

Much of the academic research on migration examines Turkey's role as a country of emigration, in particular focusing on Turkish nationals who arrived in Europe in the 1960s and 1970s through guest-worker programs and family reunification processes.[1] Yet like Egypt and Morocco, Turkey has a long history as a country of immigration. During the eighteenth, nineteenth, and twentieth centuries, the Ottoman Empire permitted the immigration of Muslims from lands surrounding Anatolia that had been conquered or reconquered (Kale 2014). After the dissolution of the Ottoman Empire, Turkey's leaders sought to encourage the migration of ethnic Turks from surrounding countries in order to cultivate a new Turkish nationalism that empha-sized the alleged homogeneity of the Turkish population (İçduygu and Kirisci 2009). Specifically, the Law of Settlement (Law No. 1934) gave preferential treatment to immigrants of Turkish descent, and nearly 2 million immigrants of Turkish background settled in various parts of the country between 1923 and 2005 (İçduygu 2007). The Treaty of Lausanne also called for a population exchange of ethnic Turks and Greeks, and between 1922 and 1924, 1.3 million Anatolian Greeks were exchanged for 500,000 Muslims in Greece (Hirschon 2003).

In the 1980s and increasingly after the end of the Cold War, Turkey began receiving increasing numbers of refugees from neigh-boring Middle East states as well as irregular and transit migrants from a variety of regions, including Eastern Europe, Asia, the Middle East and sub-Saharan Africa (İçduygu and Kirisci 2009). According to Ahmet İçduygu (2009), Turkey hosts as many as 1 million irregular and transit migrants, which include circular migrants and laborers informally recruited from Iraq, Iran, Eastern Europe, and former USSR states. Turkey has also hosted refugees from Syria since 2011, with estimates of close to 4 million Syrian nationals living in Turkey at the time of writing in 2019. Some individuals that come to Turkey may not qualify as refugees but choose instead to remain in the country as migrants, hoping to eventually pass onto Europe. Ibrahim, a young man from Congo living in Istanbul, explained to me, "I could probably get refugee status, but I know of people that had to wait years to get it. One of my friends waited five years, and he is only just now being resettled to the US. I don't want to wait that long. Maybe I'll stay one more year and then try to go onto Greece. But I need money, and I need connections. And smugglers only take euros."

While some migrants arrive in Turkey hoping to travel onward to the EU, others are attracted by opportunities for trade in Turkey's large, cosmopolitan cities. As of 2007, Turkey had a very liberal entry policy and citizens of more than forty countries were not required to obtain a visa prior to arrival (İçduygu 2007). For example, Turkey allows nationals of Iran, the former Soviet Union, and the Balkans to enter the country either without visas or with visas that can easily be obtained at airports and other entry points, making Turkey fairly accessible. Consequently, migrants may come as tourists or students and then overstay their visas, finding work in the informal economy to support their continued stay in Turkey (İçduygu and Kirisci 2009), while others arrive irregularly using smugglers (Toksöz et al. 2012).

Until the new law was adopted in 2013, Turkey's engagement with migrants and refugees was governed by the outdated Turkish Passport Law (Law No. 1764) and the Law on the Residence and Travel of Foreigners in Turkey (Law No. 5683) (Açıkgöz and Ariner 2014; İçduygu 2007). The Passport Law regulated which nationals could enter Turkey and what type of visa they were entitled to, while the Law on the Residence and Travel of Foreigners determined an individual's ability to access residence status and a working permit, as well as their maximum length of stay (İçduygu 2007). Turkey also signed the 1951 Refugee Convention in 1960 but did not enact any domestic legislation regarding international protection until 1994. Instead, the issue of asylum was regulated through secondary legislation and periodic administrative regulations (Açıkgöz and Ariner 2014).

After Turkey signed the 1951 Convention, the UNHCR opened an office in the early 1960s, taking over the protection role that the Catholic NGO International Catholic Migration Commission (ICMC) had been playing up until that time (Elite Interviewee AM). Prior to 1978 and the Iranian Revolution, Turkey primarily received refugees from Europe, most of whom were Cold War defectors, and the UNHCR managed to resettle refugees within a short period of time (Elite Interviewee AM). Turkey's first major arrival of non-European refugees occurred as a result of the Iran-Iraq war between 1980 and 1988. Despite having a larger refugee caseload, the UNHCR was able to resettle refugees within one to two years (Elite Interviewee AM).

This pattern changed in 1988, when Turkey received approximately 60,000 Iraqi Kurds following the use of chemical weapons by the Iraqi government (Ogata 2005). This was followed by a second arrival from Turkey's west, when approximately 300,000 refugees fled an attempt by the communist government in Bulgaria to assimilate ethnic Turks and Pomaks into a Bulgarian Slav identity (Kirisci 2003). Not long after in 1991, Turkey received approximately 450,000 refugees from northern Iraq after Saddam Hussein used force to suppress the country's Kurdish uprising (Ogata 2005).[2] As a result of the arrival of these three refugee groups, Turkey enacted the Asylum Regulation in November 1994, which was subsequently amended in 1999 and 2006. The regulation clarified who is eligible to receive temporary asylum protection in Turkey, effectively restating the parameters set forth in the 1951 Refugee Convention, but it was also criticized by civil society actors in Turkey for allowing significant administrative discretion in the processing of applications (Levitan et al. 2009). Ahmet İçduygu (2007) argues that while the 1994 regulation was "a positive attempt to regularize some rules and measures regarding asylum (and in part immigration as well), it did not reflect any liberalization of policy; rather, this move helped consolidate the authoritarian role of the state in immigration and asylum issues and increased power over these areas" (209).

Turkey received two more refugee migrations in the late 1990s: from Bosnia in 1996 and Kosovo in 1997 and 1998, although neither was prolonged. Up until that point, individual embassies were primarily responsible for determining an individual's refugee status and orchestrating resettlement. But after increased refugee arrivals in 1988, the UNHCR took on increased responsibility for this task, even though the organization still lacked an official country agreement with the Turkish government. A former external relations officer at the UNHCR in Ankara described how, "instead of going directly to the US embassy or the UK embassy, people were recommended to go to the UNHCR. Then the UNHCR became the filter for whether [asylum seekers] have good claims" (Elite Interviewee AM). As a result, a dual system of refugee recognition emerged.

In addition to registering with the UNHCR for international protection, asylum seekers were required to file a separate temporary asylum application with the Turkish Ministry of the Interior (MOI). The purpose of the government procedure was to determine whether the applicant had a legitimate need for temporary asylum in Turkey as specified by Turkey's national legislation (Levitan et al. 2009). Upon application, refugees were granted a six-month residence permit, which could be automatically renewed for another six months. At the end of this second period, extension of the residence permit fell under the discretion of the MOI prior to 2013 (Tokuzlu 2010) and subsequently falls under the Directorate General for Migration Management (DGMM), discussed below.

It is critical to point out that Turkey maintains geographic limitations to the 1951 Refugee Convention. Consequently, Turkey only grants full refugee status to individuals originating from countries that are members of the Council of Europe. In practice, this means only refugees coming from Russia or Caucasus states. All other refugees originating from countries outside Europe that arrive in Turkey and successfully undergo refugee status determination procedures are granted either conditional status or temporary protection by the Turkish government.[3] Another particularity of the Turkish asylum system is that the government established approximately sixty "satellite cities" used as temporary residences for refugees.[4] Once refugees register with Turkish authorities they are assigned to one of the cities, many of which are located in Turkey's internal provinces. As long as they remain living in the city, refugees have access to health care, schools and, depending upon the province, a modest stipend. Yet because the stipend is not usually enough to cover living costs and because there are few work opportunities in the fairly remote cities, many refugees decide to leave their assigned locale in search of work in Istanbul or one of Turkey's other metropolises, thereby forfeiting their legal status.

5.3 The 1980s–2008: Indifference

As Turkey received increased numbers of refugees and irregular migrants in the 1980s, 1990s, and 2000s, Turkish civil society and international organizations stepped in to fill the service-provision gap left by the national government.[5] The UNHCR took primary responsibility for refugees, but responsibility for irregular migrants and refugees residing outside their satellite city was left to international and domestic NGOs. The founder and director of a prominent legal and advocacy NGO based in Istanbul recalled the absence of government involvement during this period:

Very early on we identified that although Turkey was actually receiving refugees, there was no domestic law framework for Turkey to manage asylum and actually migration asylum, you could say. It was a field left to the national police, foreigners' department of the police, to manage from a very narrow security perspective with insufficient expertise and resources .... Basically, our assessment was that refugees were arriving in Turkey, [and] they had zero access to any kind of legal information, counseling, and assistance. And a lot of them actually didn't know where to go, how to apply. A lot of times they were having problems with the UNHCR procedure at the time. (Elite Interviewee AJ)

Between 2009 and 2010, the international and domestic NGOs providing information and services to migrants and refugees formed a network and began to cooperate via an online platform and monthly in-person meetings (Elite Interviewee AN). This included both secular and religious NGOs and INGOs such as Caritas, the Union Church of Istanbul, and Toplum ve Hukuk Araştirmalari Vakfi (Social and Legal Studies Foundation [TOHAV]), the Helsinki Citizens' Assembly, the Human Resource Development Foundation, and the UNHCR. This pool later expanded to include the Turkish NGO Human Rights and Freedoms (İHH), the Humanitarian Aid Foundation, and others.

Like Egypt and Morocco, there is a divide in Turkey between support and advocacy. Some NGOs provide only health, shelter, and legal services for migrants and refugees; other groups, such as Helsinki Citizens Assembly and the Migrant Solidarity Network partly or primarily focus on advocacy.[6] Remaining neutral allows service-providing organizations more access to government contacts and a less conflicted working relationship. The director of the Human Resource Development Foundation, which primarily provides material support to migrants and refugees, explained that his organization refrains from involvement with advocacy groups for fear of reprisal from Turkish authorities:

We have contacts with [advocacy groups], but we did not get into those networks. Because we are working or providing services to refugees. But those networks published reports or had press meetings or directly announced a crime or something like this. But for NGOs that are providing services, we have too much contact with Turkish authorities. So, we do not want to be in those networks because Turkish authorities or the individuals at the units, we experienced that they … behaved badly to refugees when we accompany them. When they hear that this NGO signed a press document, then they may be behaving badly to refugees. For this purpose, we do not enter into those networks, but we provide information to those networks. (Elite Interviewee AH)

In addition to NGOs and INGOs, there are numerous migrant CBOs operating throughout the country, particularly in large cities. Some are founded by migrants of Turkish descent, including associations established by Meskhetian Turks, Crimean Turks, Kazak Turks and Turks from Azerbaijan and East Turkistan (Toksöz et al. 2012). Because of the ease with which these groups can acquire citizenship, their activities tend to be culturally focused or related to maintaining ties with a home country (Toksöz et al. 2012). Other non-Turkish migrant groups from the Balkans, the Caucasus, Central Asia, and Iraq also developed migrant associations that tend to be more politically focused, aimed at raising awareness about migrant rights. Some of these organizations historically lobbied for migrants' rights in Turkey and developed social service programs – such as the Iraqi Turks Association of Culture and Solidarity and the Afghan Turkmen Social Assistance and Solidarity Association – although migrants without legal status generally refrained from engaging in protests or other forms of overt advocacy (Biehl 2013).

A notable protest did occur in 2008, when migrants being held at the Kumkapı Foreigners' Guest House[7] in Istanbul started an uprising in protest of the poor conditions in which they were being held. Treatment in detention centers was previously widely criticized by various human rights organizations. Migrants complained of being unable to apply for asylum, not understanding why they were detained or when they would be released, and of unhealthy detention conditions and physical abuse (Biehl 2013). The two-hour long protest at Kumkapı received national and international attention and was brought before the Turkish Human Rights Council of the Governor's Office and resulted in Turkey establishing the Commission on Migrants, Refugees, and Human Trafficking and some improvements to the conditions of the Istanbul Kumkapı facility. Nonetheless, Kristen Biehl (2013) notes that the Commission was handicapped in its ability to enact any major reforms in the absence of national legislation pertaining to migrants and refugees.

In terms of access to employment, refugees technically have access to the Turkish labor market, but in a de facto sense refugees face legal, administrative, and language barriers associated with receiving work permits (Levitan et al. 2009). For a company to hire a refugee, it must have at least five Turkish nationals already employed: a five-to-one ratio for every foreigner. Additionally, the company must be able to prove that no Turkish national is equally eligible for the job, and the refugee must possess certain skills or training that makes him or her more qualified than any Turkish national for that position (Norman 2014). Despite this, there is a shortage of labor inspectors in Turkey as a whole and especially in major cities like Istanbul, and neither employers nor migrants have an incentive to report violations of the requirements against hiring foreigners (Toksöz et al. 2012). Consequently, refugees as well as migrants have found employment in low-wage sectors including leather and textile manufacturing, restaurants, construction, agriculture, tourism, sex work, and domestic care (Elite Interviewee AI; Elite Interviewee Q; İçduygu and Aksel 2012), although the ability to access various types of informal work can vary greatly by geographic location, gender, legal status, and nationality. For example, in a survey of African migrants and refugees living in Istanbul, Kelly Brewer and Yükseker Deniz (2006) found a difference between West African irregular migrants and East African asylum seekers in terms of their economic survival strategies in Istanbul. West African migrants were more likely to be engaged in trade activities such as selling clothing, trinkets, electronics, or food. Asylum seekers were more likely to resort to marginal survival activities like begging, peddling, or sharing crowded apartments (Brewer and Deniz 2006).

While a system of policing through checkpoints does exist to monitor the legal status of migrants and refugees and their participation in the informal economy, a UNHCR spokesperson in Istanbul noted that this system is fairly lax. In his opinion,

[Turkey] is not a country that is really working on – it's not really hard on irregular migrants; it's not really hard on their access to services, or access to labor market. If they really want, [government] could develop a better supervision system, but it's not what's happening in Turkey. (Elite Interviewee K)

Even for refugees who leave their assigned satellite city and thereby forfeit their legal status or for rejected asylum seekers who are eligible for deportation, Turkey's willingness to police and remove these individuals is minimal (Brewer and Deniz 2006). According to a 2006 study of migrant and refugee populations living in Istanbul, the Foreigners' Police would notify an individual that their residence permit had expired and that he or she needed to leave the country within fifteen days, but police officials also admitted that they only provided a notification of the *intention* to deport. The police instead allowed these individuals to become "tolerated foreigners" in Turkey because "it is difficult to determine the whereabouts of such persons, and such a pursuit would be costly in terms of labor and time" (Brewer and Deniz 2006, 26).

5.4 Turkey's New Law on Foreigners and International Protection

Turkish-EU relations started to gain new pace in 1999. In order to be considered for candidacy, Turkey needed to make various changes to its domestic policies to meet the Copenhagen Criteria for membership eligibility, including in the area of migration. Specifically, Turkey would have to remove its geographic limitation to the 1951 Convention and transfer all asylum matters to a civilian authority (Kilberg 2014). Moving forward, Turkey and the EU agreed to an Accession Partnership on March 8, 2001, which detailed the various actions Turkey needed to take in order to harmonize its domestic legislation with EU laws. The partnership was later revised on March 26, 2003, after which Turkey declared its intentions to introduce changes to its immigration and asylum policies (İçduygu 2007). Three years later, the accession negotiations hit several roadblocks, including disagreements over the Cyprus issue, pushback from certain EU member states – notably Austria, Germany, and France – and slow progress from Turkey on the required reforms, leading the EU to freeze negotiations in December 2006 (Castle 2006).[8]

Despite the breakdown of the accession process, Turkish officials took steps the following year to consider specifically reforming domestic legislation in the area of migration. According to the former head of external communications for UNHCR Turkey and current director of an Ankara-based research group İltica ve Göç Araştırmaları Merkezi (Migration and Asylum Research Center [IGAM]), high-level meetings between Turkish government representatives and EU officials in charge of accession negotiations took place in 2007, during which EU officials emphasized the importance of reforming Turkey's migration policy (Elite Interviewee AM). While the issues of migration and asylum were not high priorities on Turkey's domestic political agenda at the time, the director of the Helsinki Citizens' Assembly in Istanbul argued that a select group of individual bureaucrats from the Asylum and Migration Bureau – under the Turkish Ministry of the Interior at the time – and a small group within the Turkish Ministry in charge of EU negotiations, became aware of the significance of migration and asylum in a regional sense:

The way in which it was such an important political issue in many EU member states, and the way in which migration, asylum, and borders was gradually turning into a very comprehensive, broad agenda of cooperation between Turkey and the EU that, you know, actually went beyond the confines of the accession. (Elite Interviewee AJ)

In other words, Turkish officials realized that the issue would be an increasingly important bargaining chip in its negotiations with the EU going forward, and Turkey was in a critical geographic position when it came to migration toward Europe.

Turkish government officials responded to EU requests by tasking two inspectors from the MOI with conducting a needs assessment of the migration field in 2008. The MOI inspectors reached out to civil society actors across Turkey and international organizations including the IOM and the UNHCR that had been providing services and filling the protection gap for years. Once they collected testimonials and information from civil society groups, the inspectors concluded that piecemeal reform would not be sufficient to address all the existing gaps.[9] According to an IOM representative in Ankara:

[The inspectors] took a quite open and participatory approach, and then they had the ability [and] capacity to understand that this is not something that you can really solve through adopting secondary legislation or doing some partial work, and somehow they developed a vision that it goes beyond periodic changes .... They decided to come up with a more comprehensive framework, after seeing such a huge gap. (Elite Interviewee M)

Consequently, the MOI inspectors received permission and support to organize the drafting of new comprehensive legislation on migration and asylum.

The role of international shaming and Turkey's concern over its image with respect to Europe was also key to the decision to reform the country's migration legislation. Kemal Kirişci (2012) argues that the understanding among Turkish officials of the importance of the migration issue was due at least in part to several cases brought before the European Court of Human Rights (ECtHR). In particular, Turkey was painted in a negative light by the 2009 case of *Abdolkhani and Karimnia v. Turkey*, in which the Turkish government deported two Iranian refugees to Iran and denied them access to contest the deportation decisions. With assistance from Turkish and international human rights lawyers and the Human Rights Association, a Turkish NGO, the two deportees successfully brought their case before the ECtHR (Aydin and Kirişçi 2013). The landmark decision in the *Abdolkhani and Karimnia v. Turkey* case was then followed by twelve additional cases that led to convictions against Turkey (Kirişçi 2012). Thus, while initial efforts toward EU accession spurred discussion of reshaping existing legislation related to migration, the impetus to continue reforming the policy area even after EU negotiations fell apart was informed by an understanding and acceptance of Turkey's geostrategic position among a specific and critical faction of the government, coupled with a response to international shaming at the European level. In support of this, Kemal Kirişci (2012) argues that the impact of the EU on Turkey's decision to enact migration reform is difficult to assess since the accession negotiations of the early and mid-2000s took place when a "paradigmatic shift" was already under way among Turkish officials (73).

In 2009, a core group of experts was assembled to begin the drafting process for the new law, including experienced bureaucrats from the Foreigners, Borders, and Asylum Department – part of the Ministry of the Interior – as well as policy and legal experts seconded from the UNHCR and the IOM. One IOM employee seconded to work on the drafting process attributed the new law's success to the leadership of one of the MOI inspectors, Atilla Toros. According to the IOM employee, Toros used his diplomatic nature to keep the issue of migration from becoming politicized domestically while he still attempted to convince various ministries, human rights organizations, and members of parliament that the new legislation was necessary and beneficial to Turkey (Elite Interviewee M). The IOM employee explained:

You know, if [we] went to an EU ministry, we were referring to the EU *acquis* [*communautaire*], or if we went to a human rights body, we were prompting human rights standards, or at the Ministry of Labor, we were showing examples of other developed countries who had given priorities to highly skilled migrants. He [Atilla Toros] knew the state of play, and so, accordingly, he had been convincing people. But at a substantive level, not only at a discourse level.

The issue of migration became controversial in Turkey with the arrival of Syrian refugees, but migration and asylum was not yet politicized at the time of drafting the new law, and Toros's team was able to focus on issues such as human rights, rather than "discrimination, access to the labor market, unemployment, these kinds of issues" (Elite Interviewee M). Toros's careful and comprehensive strategy was successful, and Law No. 6458 on Foreigners and International Protection was adopted in 2013, passed unanimously by the Turkish parliament. One of the most important changes embedded within the new law – which covers both regular and irregular migrants in Turkey as well as refugees and asylum seekers – was the creation of a new civil body, the Göç İdaresi Genel Müdürlüğü (Directorate General for Migration Management [DGMM]), which took over responsibility for all migration and asylum matters from the Turkish police. The DGMM began operating in mid-2015, and Atilla Toros was named the first director general.

The civil society organizations and INGOs that managed Turkey's migrant and refugee caseload over the previous decade had wide-ranging responses to the new law. The head of the Istanbul UNHCR office described the implementation of the new law as Turkey "shifting to a rights-based approach" to migration (Elite Interviewee J). The director of an NGO in Istanbul referred to both the new law and the government's investments in the DGMM as "ambitious" (Elite Interviewee AP). However, the new law also had critics. When the official transfer of responsibility from the police and the Ministry of the Interior to the newly created DGMM took place on May 18, 2015, the DGMM was not yet fully prepared in terms of capacity and staffing. A representative of the Association for Solidarity with Asylum Seekers and Migrants (ASAM), an NGO that assists with refugee status determination processes and service provision in Ankara, explained that in the provincial DGMM offices, "they just switched all the positions from Turkish national police positions into DGMM positions. I mean, one police officer just took off the uniform and now he's wearing this DGMM uniform" (Elite Interviewee AL). NGOs and international organizations in Ankara also spoke of the DGMM's lack of experience in conducting refugee status determination procedures, citing examples in which the DGMM seemed to be making decisions about who qualified for status or for resettlement based on unclear and nontransparent criteria, as well as collecting insufficient data (Elite Interviewee K; Elite Interviewee N). Coupled together and considering that Turkey still maintains a geographic limitation to the 1951 Convention, domestic NGOs and international organizations interviewed in 2015 were unsure whether the new law was instigated purely for political gain – both domestically and internationally – with

Figure 5.1 Aksaray neighborhood in Istanbul.
Photo credit: Kelsey P. Norman, 2015

little change on the ground, or whether the law reflected a genuine transformation in the way the Turkish government considered its role as a host state for migrants and refugees.

The lax approach to internal policing had also not drastically changed by the time of interviewing in 2015. This was abundantly clear from a trip to Aksaray, a neighborhood located just past Sultanahmet in Istanbul's tourist center and depicted in Figure 5.1. While Sultanahmet is packed with tourists of all nationalities that come to Istanbul to marvel at historic mosques and palaces, Aksaray is populated with migrants that come to Turkey looking to make a profit or to find a way to Europe.

The neighborhood operates at a bustling pace, with carpets, kilims, bedding, and clothes wheeled rapidly through the streets, and vendors selling fruit on street corners to customers of all nationalities. Men from various West African countries sell watches or shoes on the street, carefully laying out their products on a blanket on the ground, or – if they are slightly more established – on foldable wooden tables. Asian, African, and Eastern European women also pass through the neighborhood – some in pairs, some alone – but the number of men in this locale vastly outnumbers the women. Aksaray is also the best neighborhood in Istanbul to locate smugglers of all nationalities: Syrian, Cote D'Ivorian, and Russian, among others.

One man I met in Aksaray, Amir, who is originally from Senegal, explained that he had lived in the neighborhood for two years. He returned to Senegal one time during this sojourn in Turkey so that he could obtain a new visa but found that it was too expensive (€500 or €600 per trip) to do so more than once. In mid-2015 he was residing in Turkey on an expired visa, selling watches on the street. I asked Amir whether that led to problems with the authorities, but he told me, "No, I don't have trouble. There's this one type of car that you have to watch out for. But not the regular police." In general at the time of interviewing, migrants were able to exist in relative anonymity.

5.5 The Arrival of Syrians

Although the 2013 law moved Turkey closer to a liberal engagement policy, the arrival of nearly 4 million Syrian refugees in Turkey since 2011, coupled with the increasingly authoritarian policies of the ruling Adalet ve Kalkınma Partisi (Justice and Development Party [AKP]), worked to undermine any legislative progress made in the area of migrant and refugee rights. As an IOM employee in Ankara explained, in the wake of the Syrian refugee crisis the Turkish government has regressed toward viewing migration solely through a security lens (Elite Interviewee M).

The initial government response to Syrian refugees was welcoming and financially generous. Interviewees from civil society and international organizations in Turkey noted that the government responded with an uncharacteristically open hand to the arrival of Syrian refugees. As an NGO director in Istanbul who has worked on refugee issues in Turkey for more than 20 years stated,

Turkey has by and large responded positively, uncharacteristically positively, to the refugee influx from Syria. This looks nothing like what Turkey did in response to the Kurds from Syria in the aftermath of the first and second wars in Iraq. This looks nothing like how Turkey has been treating the mass influx of people from the Balkans throughout the '90s, this looks nothing like the way Turkey has been treating Iraqis, Iranians, and Afghanis who have been arriving. (Elite Interviewee AJ)

Interviewees also concurred that the Turkish government initially attempted to manage the Syrian crisis on its own terms. An individual at a UN agency in Ankara explained, "The government, at the beginning, was clear that they would provide all the services. So, there wasn't much space for international agencies at the beginning of the crisis" (Elite Interviewee N). A representative of ASAM explained that Turkey wanted to project the image that the country "is strong enough to tackle this problem, and the Syrians are our brothers, [so] please don't try to interfere [with] our relation[ship]. Turkey has the capacity to manage this" (Elite Interviewee AL). The government's initial reluctance to accept international aid and its pride in self-reliance was an attempt to exude an image of capacity both domestically and internationally.

The director of the Helsinki Citizens Assembly in Istanbul also described the AKP's Syrian refugee policy as "an extension of their Syrian policy at large" (Elite Interviewee AJ). Early on in the Syrian crisis, Turkish President (at the time, prime minister) Erdoğan condemned Syrian President Bashar Assad for his violent crackdown on protestors, and the Turkish government was accused of supplying arms and providing intelligence training for Syrian rebel groups (Manna 2012). Syrians were permitted to enter Turkey through an open door policy. To support the arrival of Syrian refugees, the Turkish government constructed refugee camps in Turkey's southeast, putting the Afet ve Acil Durum Yönetimi Başkanlığı (Disaster and Emergency Management Presidency of Turkey [AFAD]), in charge of supervising the camps. At the time of interviewing in 2015, the Syrian refugee population in the camps was approximately 250,000, or about 23 percent of the Syrian refugee population in Turkey. A representative from the UNHCR called the camps "outstanding," saying that "the conditions are remarkable, those are the best camps that ... not just UNHCR Turkey, [but that] UNHCR [as a whole] has ever seen. UNHCR would not be able to build 10 percent of these camps" (Elite Interviewee K). Turkey's leading role was also reflected through financial allocations. As of mid-2018, Turkey spent US$30.2 billion on hosting Syrian refugees (Farooq 2018), although this money was primarily directed toward the government-run refugee camps with international organizations and domestic NGOs continuing to provide most services in urban areas.

When Syrian refugees began entering Turkey in 2011, they were given "temporary protection" status – rather than conditional refugee status – which is a designation that can be assigned to any nationality of refugee entering Turkey en masse. Unlike other refugee groups, Syrians in Turkey were allowed greater freedom of movement and were not subject to the mobility restrictions imposed by the government's satellite city system. Syrians could still lose access to full health care and education by choosing to leave their city of registration, and officially the government required them to seek a travel permit before traveling or moving to another province. But some refugees chose to forego access to these services in search of employment. Ali, a young Syrian man from Aleppo, originally arrived in Adana – a city in Turkey's southeast – and registered with the local DGMM office but chose to leave his family and travel to Istanbul in search of better work opportunities. He explained, "My family is in Adana. There it is not so expensive, but for me it's not good. There I work like fourteen hours [a day]." Ali was able to locate a job working informally at a coffee shop in a touristy area of Istanbul, making a much better wage for fewer hours. A UNHCR representative explained the relatively lax system of monitoring the movements of Syrians:

There has not been a checking system yet for Syrians. Like there's no system to go and have signatures, fingerprints, whatsoever. So, with Syrians, the only problem they really have is that they can't benefit from services if they're registered in Mardin, and they come to Istanbul without the valid reason. They can't really have access to some of the services in Istanbul. But they can get basic education and emergency health. If they live in Mardin and there's a particular health problem that cannot be solved in Mardin, then they can come to Istanbul. Apart from the Syrians, there is a very strict rule for non-Syrians, they should stay in their satellite city. If they miss the signature duty for a period of three times, their file will be closed. (Elite Interviewee K)

The representative elaborated that while the government planned to fully implement a system confining Syrians to one city, it had not yet been fully put in place by mid-2015.

Government and NGO assistance dwindled following the initial years of more generous assistance and hospitality. Most Syrians I spoke with by mid-2015 in Istanbul and Gaziantep were subsisting by participating in the informal economy. For example, Noora, introduced in the beginning of this chapter, found informal work in a restaurant in central Gaziantep. She explained that when she first arrived in Turkey, she received some assistance from NGOs, but that by 2015 things had changed: "In the past, three years ago, there was some [assistance]. Now, there's none. And Ramadan is coming, so there needs to be help. There has to be help." Reem, a young Syrian woman living in Istanbul and working at a restaurant, had previously lived in Iraq before coming to Turkey. She found the access to aid in Iraq easier, stating, "No, the Turkish government doesn't have anything for Syrians. In Iraq it was better, from the government and also the people. Every week there was rice, food, but not here."

International organizations and NGOs clearly noted the participation of Syrians in the informal economy. A spokesperson for the UNHCR operation in Gaziantep explained:

Lots of people are working informally. You know, during my day here, I may go get my car washed and it's a Syrian working there, or I go to get my shirts cleaned and there's a Syrian working there. Or I go to eat and there's Syrians working in the restaurant. They're working everywhere, but they're all working without benefits and without insurance. (Elite Interviewee Q)

While the presence of Syrians and their participation in the informal economy did not initially provoke political backlash and nativist objections from Turkish nationals and politicians, this changed in 2014. Syrian refugees were accused of stealing Turkish jobs, increasing local rents, and unfairly accessing universities without having to sit for the same examinations as Turkish students (Cetingulec 2014). Syrian refugees were also a major point of contention in the lead up to the June 2015 parliamentary election. The main opposition, the Cumhuriyet Halk Partisi (Republican People's Party [CHP]), went so far as to propose sending refugees back to Syria if the party successfully came to power (Daily *Sabah* 2015).

As a result of this type of criticism, the AKP government took measures in 2015 to limit the gathering of data related to Syrian refugees by UN bodies, humanitarian NGOs, and academics affiliated with universities and research centers. A deidentified UN official opposed this policy, arguing that it was difficult to provide services and assistance when very little is known about the demographic in need (Elite Interviewee N). It also made the process of recommending refugees for resettlement extremely challenging. Another UN employee stated,

We would recommend having more information, to get more detailed information from Syrian refugees, because otherwise they will need to do the whole process again. They do fingerprint scans; they take biodata. It's not very advanced registration; it's very basic. They took like, the size of the shoe, the size of the person, in case of assistance. So, you can see it's [very] concentrated on the aspect of assistance. However, it should be more concentrated on the aspect of protection and, in case of resettlement, the authorities will be the ones providing for resettlement. They will be the ones coordinating with the UNHCR to identify the most vulnerable. So, their vulnerability assessment should have been stronger. (Elite Interviewee K)

At the end of 2015, Turkey capitalized on the increased arrival of asylum seekers from Turkey to Europe by negotiating an aid package worth up to €6 billion. The European funds were to be allocated in part to fund services and access to formal employment for Syrian refugees in Turkey and in part to help fortify borders and to further prevent irregular migration from Turkey to Europe by supporting the DGMM to "manage, receive and host" migrants (European Commission 2017a). This agreement, known as the "EU–Turkey deal" (officially, the EU–Turkey Joint Action Plan), was agreed to in March 2016 amid objections from international organizations and human rights groups. The main premise of the agreement was that for every Syrian national returned to Turkey from Europe, one Syrian would be resettled from a Turkish refugee camp to one of the EU member states. The Europeans hoped that the possibility of being returned to Turkey would deter asylum seekers – Syrians, but also other nationalities – from attempting to travel to Europe irregularly. In addition to the aid package, Turkey was also promised that it could reopen the defunct accession negotiation process and that Turkish citizens would be eligible for visa-free travel to the EU.

As a result of this deal, some of the bureaucratic barriers to entering the formal labor market were eased for Syrians in 2016. But because the new measures required Turkish employers to pay Syrian employees the minimum wage and provide them with health benefits, most were reluctant to do so. In a saturated labor market with so many Syrians willing to work informally without these additional requirements, the new policy only saw 5,500 more Syrians obtain work permits six months after implementation (Kaymaz and Kadkoy 2016). The deal also had the effect of disincentivizing the registration of Syrians in Turkey. After the promulgation of Turkey's new law in April 2014 and the issuing of a Temporary Protection Regulation in October 2014, a new foreigner identification document, or *yabancı tanıtma belgesi*, was introduced for Syrian nationals specifically (UNHCR Turkey 2016). Beginning in 2015, Syrians were only allowed to remain in Turkey for a maximum of ninety days before they needed to either obtain a temporary residence permit or register for temporary protection status (Norman 2016a).[10] However, many Syrians were reluctant to apply for the identification document if they still hoped to travel irregularly to Europe. After the EU–Turkey deal, the fear of being returned to Turkey if they had previously registered with the Turkish government increased. As such, many Syrians remained unregistered and without access to services or official residency.

Beyond the EU–Turkey deal's minimal – and in some cases deleterious – effects for Syrians in Turkey, progress on other aspects has been slow. The failed military coup of July 2016 and Prime Minister Erodğan's increasingly authoritarian response to those he claims were involved threatened to dismantle any progress toward EU visa liberalization, accession talks, or the creation of a customs union. Turkey's interference in domestic European politics in 2017 also adversely affected negotiations. In the most brazen example, Erdoğan called on ethnic Turks in Germany not to vote for political parties that he deemed to be "enemies" of Turkey in the summer 2017 legislative election, namely, the Christian Democratic Union, Christian Social Union, and the Green Party (Pierini 2018). German Foreign Minister Sigmar Gabriel called Erdoğan's proclamation an "unprecedented act of interference" in German sovereignty (*Deutsche Welle* 2017).

As long as the EU views migration from Turkey as a threat, cooperation between the two entities will likely continue on some level, despite the increasingly unsettling domestic situation for Turkish citizens and non-nationals alike. Assaults on freedoms of expression and of the press picked up pace following the foiled July 2016 coup attempt that aimed to remove Erdoğan from power. As of July 2018, more than 151,000 state officials, teachers, bureaucrats, and academics were dismissed from their posts and 150,000 were detained (Turkey Purge 2018) for alleged links to the "Fethullah Terrorist Organization" (referring to the movement based on the teachings of Fethullah Gülen), which the government claims orchestrated the coup attempt. A state of emergency, first declared in July 2016, has since been renewed seven times, allowing Erdoğan to issue more than thirty executive decrees that bypass parliamentary and judicial scrutiny and allowing him to carry out his crackdown (Amnesty International 2018). With fears of a weakening economy, Erdoğan called for early presidential and parliamentary elections on June 24, 2018, in an attempt to further consolidate his power, winning 52.5 percent of the presidential vote and granting him a new role as both head of state and head of government (Kirişci 2018). As a result of the increasing authoritarian situation and the crippling of civil society, Amnesty International (2018) argued that "sections of society most at risk of human rights abuses – such as women and girl survivors of sexual and gender based violence, LGBTI people, refugees and migrants – are [being] denied crucial support and solidarity as they struggle to defend their rights."

In 2019, the Turkish government implemented a campaign to arrest Syrians living outside their cities of registration, using raids of workplaces and checkpoints and arresting both those with valid registration documents and those without. Instead of sending Syrians back to their initial city of registration, however, Turkey began deporting Syrians to northern Syria in violation of international law and *refoulement*. In an attempt to avoid criticism, Turkish officials have convinced or coerced many of these individuals into signing "voluntary" deportation agreements (Gall 2019). These developments seem to coincide with increasing domestic criticism from both opposition parties and voters, although such objections have existed since at least 2015, as detailed earlier in this chapter. What was most likely a decisive factor in Erdoğan's decision to implement a repressive policy toward Syrians was the AKP's electoral defeat in the Istanbul rerun election in June 2019, coupled with a struggling Turkish economy. Once Erdoğan's hold on power was genuinely threatened, he decided to use Syrian refugees as a scapegoat to mitigate domestic fallout. Furthermore, a better use of Syrian refugees from the viewpoint of the AKP became evident: in September 2019 Erdoğan announced his plan to establish a twenty-mile-wide "safe zone" in northern Syria populated by Syrian Arabs that would act as a demographic buffer against the Kurdish-controlled region (Gall 2019).

5.6 Conclusion

This chapter explored Turkey's policies toward migrants and refugees over the last three decades, as well as the 2013 migration policy reform. Like Egypt and Morocco, Turkey used indifference to manage its growing migrant and refugee population in the 1990s and 2000s, permitting and monitoring the work of international organizations and civil society actors who provided services in the absence of direct government engagement. Yet once government officials perceived that reforming its migration policy could yield diplomatic benefits, the state undertook a major policy change that was five years in the making. When the new law passed in 2013, Syrian refugees had already been arriving in Turkey for two years, but the approximately 400,000 Syrians in the country at that time pales in comparison to the almost 4 million Syrians Turkey hosts at the time of writing. The enormity of the Syrian population may account for why Turkey's move toward a more liberal policy in 2013 has not yet to fully taken shape on the ground, but more recent developments suggest retreat from any liberal policy. Migrants and refugees continue to participate primarily in the informal economy, and nongovernmental and international organizations continue to do much of the heavy lifting in terms of service provision. I argue that the primary reason for this gap between policy outputs (formal law and policy) and outcomes (policy implementation) in both Turkey and Morocco is best understood by the incentive structures that drove Morocco and Turkey to liberalize their policies in the first place.

When liberal democracies – primarily those in Europe – were reforming their domestic migration policies in the 1970s and 1980s, their decisions were largely based on demands from domestic actors, whether labor unions, judiciaries, human rights advocates, or migrants themselves, with only the partial influence of international legal norms (Hollifield 1992; Joppke 1999b; Soysal 1994). Instead, transit-turned-host states like Morocco and Turkey are embedded in geographic and geopolitical systems where they must consider the interests of and potential benefits from both domestic and international constituents in a two-level game (Putnam 1988). In both Morocco and Turkey, reform was driven by a combination of international shaming and perceived diplomatic and economic benefits, rather than domestic legal institutions being forced to bring migrants and refugees into the social and economic structures of the host state.

As I argued in Chapter 4, international shaming was an effective technique in Morocco because of the country's sensitivity to and reliance on foreign – and specifically European – aid. For Turkey, shaming at the international level, and specifically at the European Court of Human Rights, was effective during a decade when Turkey was still hoping to gain privileged access to European markets and visa-space for Turkish nationals. While both countries were rewarded diplomatically and economically for enacting liberal policy frameworks, they may not perceive the same sort of benefits from following through to ensure that implementation outcomes for migrants and refugees match the new laws and policies in place (Norman 2019). Consequently, we see resulting policies that are de jure liberal, but which continue to look much like indifference for migrants and refugees residing in Morocco and Turkey. Furthermore, such policies are subject to future, rapid backlashes should a state's geopolitical calculus change, as evidenced by events unfolding in Turkey as this book is being finalized (Norman 2020).

Thus far, I focused almost entirely on national policies, and have considered migrants and refugees as a blanket non-citizen group residing in a host state. As such, I have not directly addressed whether different nationalities of migrants and refugees have differing experiences or receive differential treatment from authorities in their respective host states. The next chapter switches perspectives to address this question head-on. It pays particular attention to whether a migrant or refugee's experience in a host state – and specifically the treatment incurred by host state authorities – varies according to perceived cultural proximity, rather than how long an individual spends in the host state and his or her legal status.

6 | *Differential Treatment by Nationality?*

Ethnicity, Religion, and Race

6.1 Introduction

One fall day in 2014, on my trip back from the neighborhood of Zamalek to the frenzied streets of downtown Cairo, my cab driver asked me about my research. Why was I living in Cairo, he wanted to know, and not back in the United States? I explained that I was a doctoral student conducting interviews about migrants and refugees living in Egypt. When I told him that there were many migrants and refugees residing in Cairo, as well as other parts of the country, he nodded in understanding. "Yes," he concurred, "lots of Syrians." This conversation occurred approximately one year after the ousting of former President Mohammed Morsi and the politicization of Syrian refugees living in Egypt.

In response I told him, "Syrians, yes, but there are many other nationalities of refugees and migrants in Egypt as well. From African countries, for example." He replied, gesticulating emphatically, "Of course, there's Sudanese. But they're not refugees, they've been here forever." Egypt and Britain ruled Sudan as a joint protectorate between 1899 and 1922, and even in the postcolonial era Sudanese nationals were able to live in Egypt with relative ease until 1995.

I continued, "Not just Sudanese though, other groups too. Eritreans, Somalis." He thought about this for a brief second, and then, in typical Egyptian fashion, responded with a joke. He used a twist on a well-known expression, saying, "Of course. Because Egypt is the cradle of civilization, and all her children want to come to her." In Egypt, as well as in other parts of the Arab world, Egypt is referred to as *umm al-dunyā*; literally, the "mother of the world," but is understood as the "cradle of civilization." Naturally, the taxi driver joked, all of her children (other nationalities) want to come to her. What interested me most about this conversation was not the taxi driver's play on a common expression, but his inclination to first think of Syrians, then Sudanese, and finally other nationalities residing in Egypt. What makes some nationalities of migrants and refugees more understood or accepted than others?

This chapter investigates whether varying nationalities of migrants and refugees experience differential treatment in their respective host states. I focus primarily on Egypt and Morocco for two reasons. First, I was able to conduct a comparable number of migrant and refugee interviews in these two states (thirty-three in Egypt and thirty-eight in Morocco). In the final section of the chapter I discuss differential treatment in Turkey, but the comparatively lower number of migrant and refugee interviews conducted in Turkey does not allow me to make the same quantitative comparisons as in Egypt and Morocco. Second, both Egypt and Morocco predominantly receive migrants and refugees from sub-Saharan Africa as well as other Middle Eastern countries, as was explored in Chapters 3 and 4, allowing me to compare these two groups. The demographics of Turkey's migration picture are more complex.

To examine whether differential treatment occurs in Egypt and Morocco and to address whether cultural factors are behind any such treatment, I call attention to the racial hierarchies established by the dividing line of the Sahara. Contemporary Western scholarship often draws a stark conceptual distinction between North and sub-Saharan Africa, pointing to the Sahara Desert as a natural divide that demarcates qualitatively different regions. In this thinking, North Africa belongs to the Arab world – an epistemology that is aptly captured in the popular MENA (Middle East North Africa) acronym – while sub-Saharan Africa, according to some, represents a race-based, geopolitical term that lumps together a vast range of states and cultural groups. This border is now an accepted political, economic, and cultural division in academia and beyond. As Ali Abdullatif Ahmida (2009) writes,

a case in point is the colonial division of the study of Africa into North and South of the Sahara, which was accepted in modern academic scholarship: North Africa is included in the Middle East Studies Association, while the so called "Sub-Sahara" Africa is within the Association of African Studies. This colonial category has been accepted uncritically by African nationalists and continues to be reproduced at the turn of the twenty-first century. (3)

Regardless of its origin, this divide has had meaningful consequences for economic growth, trade relationships, and cultural and social connections across the continent, and in this chapter, I explore its implications for the treatment of migrants and refugees originating from these disparate regions who reside in North African host states.

6.2 Race, Ethnicity, and the Sahara as a Dividing Line

The cultural embeddedness thesis purported by Rogers Brubaker (1992) is the idea that the cultural foundations of nation-states act to restrain and bind a community through nationhood. Brubaker argues that the historical path a country takes toward nationhood, embodied in distinctive ways of thinking about belonging, informs the ways that a country develops rules for citizenship and policies toward noncitizens (Brubaker 1992). While other scholars have since criticized Brubaker's cultural embeddedness thesis as too rigid (Joppke 1999b), the general assertion that states possess institutional and cultural legacies that affect how they conceive of and treat noncitizens remains intact. Furthermore, the perception of shared culture, from the perspective of host states as well as individual immigrants, is cited in the migration literature as a strong indicator of successful socioeconomic integration outcomes in Western countries (Kymlicka and Norman 2000; Adida et al. 2010; Dancygier and Laitin 2014).

Integration is a two-way street, however, meaning that both host state policies and individual migrants' decisions can affect whether or not an individual becomes economically or socially integrated into a host state society.[1] In the context of host states like those in Europe, North America, and Australia, much attention has been paid to the factors that determine an immigrant's willingness and ability to participate politically in his or her new society. The literature tells us that many of the demographic traits associated with political activity among native-born individuals are also associated with immigrants' political and social activity, including race, gender, education, occupation, language ability, marital status, and age (Hochschild and Mollenkopf 2009). But there are also characteristics that are distinctive of immigrants – such as nationality, duration of stay, date of entry, and perception of nativist threat – that are relevant for immigrant integration outcomes (Hochschild and Mollenkopf 2009). Tariq Modood (2009) also demonstrates that an immigrant's religious background may facilitate or hinder his or her involvement with host state political activities, such as participating in a protest movement, a moral crusade, or supporting a candidate for office.

Although culture, religion, and race have not been studied to the same extent, all have the potential to influence integration outcomes – and host state treatment – for migrants and refugees in host states in the Global South, as they do in the Global North, although these factors may operate differently. James Milner (2009) argues that in postcolonial states like Kenya and Tanzania undergoing political and economic liberalization, nationality and citizenship have come to be more critical for integration outcomes than ethnicity, thereby eroding affinity between the local population and refugees. Claire Adida (2014) finds that Nigerian migrants in Benin, Ghana, and Niger with co-ethnic ties to the host population are less likely to assimilate because migrants tend to organize around informal leaders who have a self-preserving incentive to resist assimilation on behalf of their constituents.

This chapter examines how the cultural embeddedness thesis operates in North Africa, and whether individuals considered to be co-ethnics due to religious, racial, or ethnic background are more likely to receive preferential treatment. For the primary countries considered in this chapter – Egypt and Morocco – co-religious migrants are most likely to be individuals who are Muslim. In both Egypt and Morocco, religion and the state overlap in various capacities (Brown 2002; Hirschl 2010), and both states declare Islam as the state religion as well as a principal source of the national legal framework (Lombardi and Brown 2006). Co-ethnic or co-racial migrants are most likely individuals considered to be Arab because of historic skin-color-based slavery. Both Egypt and Morocco have a history of slavery during the Islamic period that may have contributed to racial hierarchies still in existence today. According to Bernard Lewis (1992), "black slaves were brought into the Islamic world by a number of routes – from West Africa across the Sahara to Morocco and Tunisia, from Chad across the desert to Libya, from East Africa down the Nile to Egypt, and across the Red Sea and Indian Ocean to Arabia and the Persian Gulf" (12). The lasting implications of this period mean that African or Black individuals in Arab states may be subject to racism and discrimination (El Hamel 2012; Hassan 2011).

However, a body of academic work has attempted to examine how the desert dividing sub-Saharan and North Africa also acted as a bridge rather than a barrier. Pointing to the precolonial period, Ali Abdullatif Ahmida (2009) highlights two historic routes for communication, trade, and cultural exchange: the Hajj Routes from the north west of Africa to holy sites in Arabia, and the trade routes between central and West Africa and the Mediterranean. Hamdy Hassan (2011) argues that it was not until the onset of colonialism in the Sahara and Maghrib that Europeans attempted to cut the economic, cultural, and political links between civilizations in North and sub-Saharan Africa, redirecting Arab and African economies toward the colonizing states.

In the mid-twentieth century, the era of anticolonial struggles saw African and Arab leaders, as well as civil society movements, attempting to reforge these links through political means. Egypt's Gamal Abdul-Nasser is especially credited as a proponent of African-Arab relations, and Nasser is remembered for offering refuge to the family of assassinated Congolese Premier Patrice Lumumba and to the family of Kwame Nkrumah, Ghana's first postindependence leader, after he was toppled by a coup that Nasser claimed was backed by "imperialist forces" (Manna 2012). Kwame Nkrumah's son, Gamal Nkrumah, remembers Nasser's reign as the "golden era" of African-Arab relations (Manna 2012). Later, the first official Arab-African summit was convened in Cairo in 1977 under then President Anwar Sadat.

These movements lost momentum in the 1980s. According to Hassan (2011), an "environment of suspicion and mistrust" developed between North African and sub-Saharan African states. Hassan (2011) attributes this at least in part to the Egyptian–Israeli peace agreement, which led to "a state of confusion and chaos in Arab-African relations. The Arab state had abandoned the ideological and strategic foundation which supports the assumption that Afro-Arab ties are a necessity for the common interests and security considerations of both parties" (x). Simultaneously, however, there was a resurgence of pan-Africanism led by Libyan leader Muammar Gaddafi. Gaddafi's strategy was marked by his diplomatic and financial support of the African Union, his encouragement of migrant workers from sub-Saharan African countries to Libya, and his support of the African National Congress in the fight against apartheid in South Africa, among other policies.

The 1995 Barcelona Process led to a further deterioration. Fifteen European countries met with the leaders of twelve mostly Arab states bordering the Mediterranean, including all of North Africa (with Libya as an observer). The process had three goals: to create a common area of "peace and stability" through political dialogue, to construct a zone of "shared prosperity" by removing economic barriers and eventually creating a free trade zone, and to develop human resources and cultural exchange (Suzan 2002). Of course, this process further solidified the economic and political divide between North and sub-Saharan African states because the latter region was not invited to participate.

With this historical background in mind, the next two sections examine migration that crosses the divide between North and sub-Saharan Africa, comparing it to intraregional Middle Eastern migration, focusing first on Egypt as a host country and then turning to Morocco. Using both quantitative and qualitative data, these sections assess whether perceptions of ethnicity, race, or religious identification affect the treatment experienced by migrants and refugees in North African host states. Furthermore, this section examines how these factors interact with others that might influence treatment – such as how long an individual spends in a host state, or his or her legal status – as well as state interests, namely, diplomatic, economic, or security concerns.

The question of whether certain groups of migrants and refugees receive preferable treatment in Global South host states needs to be separated into its de jure and de facto aspects. Examples of de jure privileging include instances in which certain nationalities are given access to host state services or are not required to obtain work permits in order to participate in the host state economy. The following sections focus on de jure instances of privileging in each host state, with some references to de facto practices, as well as reactions from individual migrants and refugees to any perceived preferential treatment.

6.3 Differential Treatment in Egypt

Of the migrant and refugee groups present in Egypt, Sudanese and Syrians received de jure access to certain services that are not allotted to other nationalities at the time of interviewing for this research. Specifically, Sudanese and Syrian refugee children were permitted to attend Egyptian primary school at no cost. In the case of the Sudanese, this was due to the Four Freedoms Agreement signed in 2004,[2] and in the case of Syrians, the Egyptian Ministry of Education issued an exceptional decree in 2012 (Elite Interviewee A). This de jure privileging of Syrians and Sudanese by the Egyptian government in comparison to other national groups was most often attributed to cultural familiarity. Jemal, a refugee from Eritrea, noted, "Eritrea has a different language, different culture, so they have a harder time integrating. It's like, Sudanese, they're Arab. Like Egypt, like Syria. But Eritrea has its own culture. So, life here is hard for Eritreans." Yet the idea of shared culture between migrants or refugees and the Egyptian population is not easily demarcated.

Some South Sudanese and Sudanese migrants and refugees interviewed for this study expressed a sense of African solidarity in that they believe the Egyptian government privileges Syrians and other Arab nationalities over those from Africa. Kamal, who is from a contested region between North and South Sudan explained, "There's discrimination from the [Egyptian] government, because Syrians are also from an Arab state, and Egypt is an Arab state . . . . Africans are all treated the same. We're all on the same level, but there's no real solidarity." Ahmed, another Sudanese refugee, spoke of the racism and harassment that Sudanese individuals face in Egypt due to the color of their skin, particularly for those from South Sudan.

Any Sudanese is going to have problems with Egyptians. I mean it depends on whether your skin is black. And there's more problems for women. There's some very bad things from the Egyptians. Harassment is a very difficult problem. You hear words, talking. You hear harassment. You hear "Hey you Black" [*yā iswid*] at any time. You hear "Hey you slave [*yā ʿabd*]." I say, "What slave?" Or you hear "Hey you monster [*ya waḥsh*]."

Nonetheless, three of six Eritreans interviewed explained that in their view, Sudanese are considered by the Egyptian government and populace to be Arabs, as opposed to Africans. Kedija, an Eritrean asylum seeker, argued, "Yes, there's some discrimination. For example, if you're Eritrean and you don't have your residency visa, they'll throw you in jail. But it's not like that for Sudanese or Syrians." From the perspective of Eritreans, this Arab-ness comes with certain privileges. Sudanese migrants and refugees can therefore be simultaneously African and Arab, depending on the point of view in question.

The responses from Syrians in regard to preferential treatment were mixed. Some Syrians believed their national group to be the worst off in terms of treatment. Nizar, a Syrian man living in Alexandria, explained, "The treatment here [makes] us want to leave. Maybe from the sea, to another country. The treatment is very, very bad. Unlike the Sudanese, or the Libyans, and Somalis. No, the treatment is very bad for the Syrians." Others indicated that Syrians are treated more favorably, even in light of the events that targeted Syrians specifically following the removal of former President Mohammed Morsi from political office. Hady, a Syrian man living in Cairo, argued:

I think Africans have it worse than Syrians. Maybe it's because they always come here illegally. And right after Morsi was forced out, things were bad for Syrians, mostly from the Egyptian people. They didn't trust us, they thought we were all affiliated with the Muslim Brotherhood [al-ikhwān]. But in general, Egyptians trust the Syrians more. We're they're Syrian brothers, you know? For Africans, it's more difficult.

While de jure privileging of Sudanese and Syrians does occur in Egypt regarding access to education, and in some cases health care, the perception that this is based on culture requires more examination, especially as each national group is likely to perceive themselves as receiving the worst possible treatment from host state authorities.

To examine more closely whether the treatment incurred by migrants is based on nationality as opposed to other factors, I divided my interview respondents into two groups: those considered to be a privileged nationality in Egypt (Arabs, including Syrians and Sudanese) and those considered to be nonprivileged (Africans, including South Sudanese and other African nationalities), although the distinction between African and Arab ethnicity is malleable. As explained previously, Sudanese migrants and refugees can be simultaneously African and Arab, depending on the point of view in question. Nonetheless, this demarcation is employed in order to further examine the thesis that host state outcomes depend on whether a migrant or refugee is considered a co-cultural. I compare the results to three other factors that may affect outcomes according to the existing literature: an individual's self-identified gender, the length of time that a migrant or refugee spends in the host state,[3] and whether an individual has legal status in the host state.[4] I consider the following outcomes: whether a migrant or refugee believes the host government provides services; access to hospitals and whether financial assistance is provided; access to education for migrants or refugees with children and whether financial assistance is provided; treatment and policing by host state authorities; and two types of participation in the host state: political activism, and participation in migrant/refugee community groups.

Table 6.1 *Attitudinal measure of whether the host state government provides services, Egypt*

	Thinks the host state government provides services, % (*n*)	
	No	*Yes*
Total	75.8 (25)	24.2 (8)
Privileged group	85.0 (17)	15.0 (3)
Nonprivileged group	61.5 (8)	38.5 (5)
Male	71.4 (15)	28.6 (6)
Female	83.3 (10)	16.7 (2)
Less than 2 years	100.0 (9)	0.0 (0)
More than 2 years	66.7 (16)	33.3 (8)
Has legal status	68.0 (17)	32.0 (8)
No legal status	100.0 (8)	0.0 (0)

To ascertain perceptions, I asked interviewees about whether they believe that the Egyptian government provides any services for them. As Table 6.1 shows, 75.8 percent of respondents did not believe the government provides any services, while 24.2 percent believe that the government provides at least one service. In this case, individuals from the privileged group – those from Syria and Sudan – were less likely to believe that the host government provides services. However, the larger discrepancy was between those who had spent less than two years versus more than two years in the host state, as well as between those with legal status and those without.

Next, I asked interviewees about accessing two specific types of services: health care and education for their children, if applicable. In response, 42.4 percent of individuals said they had been to a hospital or clinic during their stay in Egypt. Of those individuals, only 9.1 percent had some form of financial assistance when doing so. Respondents from the nonprivileged group were slightly more likely to visit a hospital but were slightly *less* likely to have assistance to do so. Once again, the larger discrepancy was between individuals who spent less than two years versus more than two years in Egypt, as well as between those with legal status and those without. See Table 6.2.

Table 6.2 *Access to a hospital by migrant and refugee characteristics,*
Egypt

	Visited hospital, % (*n*)		Financial assistance for visiting hospital, % (*n*)	
	No	Yes	No	Yes
Total	51.5 (17)	42.4 (14)	36.4 (12)	9.1 (3)
Privileged group	57.9 (11)	42.1 (8)	77.8 (7)	22.2 (2)
Nonprivileged group	50.0 (6)	50.0 (6)	83.3 (5)	16.7 (1)
Male	63.2 (12)	36.8 (7)	71.4 (5)	28.6 (2)
Female	41.7 (5)	58.3 (7)	87.5 (7)	12.5 (1)
Less than 2 years	66.7 (6)	33.3 (3)	100.0 (3)	0.0 (0)
More than 2 years	50.0 (11)	50.0 (11)	75.0 (9)	25.0 (3)
Has legal status	62.5 (5)	37.5 (3)	75.0 (9)	25.0 (3)
No legal status	52.5 (12)	47.8 (11)	100.0 (3)	0.0 (0)

Only 39.4 percent of interviewees had school-aged children with them in Egypt. One hundred percent of those interviewees with children enrolled them in school (whether government-run, community organized, or private), and 90.0 percent of those with children in school received some form of financial assistance. Individuals from the nonprivileged group were slightly more likely than the privileged group to receive assistance for enrolling their children in school. See Table 6.3.

Next, I asked interviewees about two perception questions relating to the privileging of certain nationalities by Egyptian authorities. First, I asked whether treatment from Egyptian authorities varied by nationality; in other words, are certain nationalities privileged over others? In response, 24.2 percent stated that privileging does occur, while 57.6 percent claimed that they believe all migrant and refugee groups are treated the same. Of those who felt that privileging of certain groups does occur, the most common nationality mentioned was Syrians. It is important to contrast this to statements made earlier in this section, which anecdotally indicate that privileging occurs. However, my data indicate that it is the minority, not the majority, of migrants and refugees who perceive that certain nationalities are privileged, although members of the nonprivileged group were more likely to think that privileging occurs (50.0 percent) compared to members of the privileged group (17.3 percent). See Table 6.4.

Table 6.3 *Access to education by migrant and refugee characteristics, Egypt*

	If has children in host state, do they attend school? % (*n*)		Financial assistance for school, % (*n*)	
	No	Yes	No	Yes
Total	0.0 (0)	100.0 (12)	10.0 (1)	90.0 (9)
Privileged group	0.0 (0)	100.0 (9)	12.5 (1)	87.5 (7)
Nonprivileged group	0.0 (0)	100.0 (3)	0.0 (0)	100.0 (2)
Male	0.0 (0)	100.0 (6)	0.0 (0)	100.0 (5)
Female	0.0 (0)	100.0 (6)	0.0 (0)	80.0 (4)
Less than 2 years	0.0 (0)	100.0 (6)	0.0 (0)	100.0 (6)
More than 2 years	0.0 (0)	100.0 (6)	25.0 (1)	75.0 (3)
Has legal status	0.0 (0)	100.0 (9)	0.0 (0)	100.0 (7)
No legal status	0.0 (0)	100.0 (3)	33.3 (1)	66.7 (2)

Table 6.4 *Attitudinal measure of host state privileging of certain nationalities, Egypt*

	Believes some nationalities are privileged in host state, % (*n*)	
	No	Yes
Total	57.6 (19)	24.2 (8)
Privileged group	82.4 (14)	17.6 (3)
Nonprivileged group	50.0 (5)	50.0 (5)
Male	64.7 (11)	35.3 (6)
Female	80.0 (8)	20.0 (2)
Less than 2 years	66.7 (4)	33.3 (2)
More than 2 years	71.4 (15)	28.6 (6)
Has legal status	66.7 (14)	33.3 (7)
No legal status	83.3 (5)	16.7 (1)

Second, I asked migrants and refugees whether certain nationalities are targeted by police or other authorities in Egypt. In response, 72.7 percent stated they do not think migrants and refugees are targeted by host state authorities, while 24.2 percent felt that these groups

Table 6.5 *Attitudinal measure of host state targeting of certain nationalities, Egypt*

| | Believes certain nationalities are targeted by host state authorities, % (*n*) | |
	No	Yes
Total	72.7 (24)	24.2 (8)
Privileged group	68.4 (13)	31.6 (6)
Nonprivileged group	84.6 (11)	15.4 (2)
Male	65.0 (13)	35.0 (7)
Female	91.7 (11)	8.3 (1)
Less than 2 years	77.8 (7)	22.2 (2)
More than 2 years	73.9 (17)	26.1 (6)
Has legal status	66.7 (16)	33.3 (8)
No legal status	100.0 (8)	0.0 (0)

are targeted. Individuals from the nonprivileged group were less likely, on average, to say that certain groups are targeted by the police. See Table 6.5.

In addition to asking about the perception of policing of certain groups, I also asked interviewees whether they ever personally had trouble with Egyptian authorities. Some examples include being subject to a neighborhood raid, experiencing difficulty at a checkpoint, or having trouble while trying to renew a residency permit. Most, 81.8 percent, of interviewees responded negatively to having trouble with an Egyptian authority, while only 18.2 percent reported having trouble with an authority during their residency in Egypt. Individuals from the privileged group were slightly more likely to have had trouble with an Egyptian authority, although the larger discrepancy was between men and women, those who spent more than two years in Egypt versus those who spent less than two years, and those who had legal status versus those without. See Table 6.6.

Third, I asked interviewees questions about their community and political participation in Egypt in order to gauge their connectedness to other migrants and refugees. In response, 51.5 percent of interviewees participated in community organizations run by migrants and refugees themselves, whether only with members of their same nationality or in

Table 6.6 *Trouble with host state authorities by migrant and refugee characteristics, Egypt*

	Has had trouble with host state authorities, % (*n*)	
	No	Yes
Total	81.8 (27)	18.2 (6)
Privileged group	80.0 (16)	20.0 (4)
Nonprivileged group	84.6 (11)	15.4 (2)
Male	85.7 (18)	14.3 (3)
Female	75.0 (9)	25.0 (3)
Less than 2 years	88.9 (8)	11.1 (1)
More than 2 years	79.2 (19)	20.8 (5)
Has legal status	80.0 (20)	20.0 (5)
No legal status	87.5 (7)	12.5 (1)

a community group open to various nationalities, while 48.5 percent stated that they did not belong to any community group. Interviewees from the nonprivileged group were more likely to participate in a community organization, though the larger discrepancy was between those who spent less than two years in Egypt versus those who spent two years or more. See Table 6.7.

Only 12.1 percent of interviewees participated in some kind of political activity in Egypt, while 87.9 percent had not. Interviewees from the nonprivileged group were only slightly more likely than interviewees from the privileged group to participate in a political activity, although most refugees and migrants of all backgrounds refrained from political participation. See Table 6.8.

To summarize, being part of the privileged group (individuals considered to be Arab and thus culturally similar in Egypt) did not lead to better reported treatment or outcomes for migrants. Members of the nonprivileged group were more likely to perceive that some nationalities are treated better than others in the host state, but the actual outcomes – access to education, hospitals, being arrested or detained by host state authorities – do not correspond to this perception. For most outcomes, cultural factors do not appear to matter as strongly as whether an individual has legal status or the amount of time that an individual has spent in Egypt.

Table 6.7 *Participation in a community organization by migrant and refugee characteristics, Egypt*

	Participates in a community organization, % (*n*)	
	No	Yes
Total	48.5 (16)	51.5 (17)
Privileged group	55.0 (11)	45.0 (9)
Nonprivileged group	38.5 (5)	61.5 (8)
Male	47.6 (10)	52.4 (11)
Female	50.0 (6)	50.0 (6)
Less than 2 years	100.0 (9)	0.0 (0)
More than 2 years	29.2 (7)	70.8 (17)
Has legal status	48.0 (12)	52.0 (13)
No legal status	50.0 (4)	50.0 (4)

Table 6.8 *Participation in political advocacy by migrant and refugee characteristics, Egypt*

	Participates in political advocacy, % (*n*)	
	No	Yes
Total	87.9 (29)	12.1 (4)
Privileged group	90.0 (18)	10.0 (2)
Nonprivileged group	84.6 (11)	15.4 (2)
Male	81.0 (17)	19.0 (4)
Female	100.0 (12)	0.0 (0)
Less than 2 years	88.9 (8)	11.1 (1)
More than 2 years	87.5 (21)	12.5 (3)
Has legal status	84.0 (21)	16.0 (4)
No legal status	100.0 (8)	0.0 (0)

Furthermore, when preferential treatment of a particular nationality by a host-country government does occur, it is more likely driven by political strategy rather than perceived cultural affinity with the host population. The case of Syrian nationals in Egypt discussed in Chapter

3 illustrates this well. In 2012, Egyptian President Mohamed Morsi allowed all Syrian children residing in Egypt to enroll in public schools regardless of their status with the UNHCR, and Syrian families could access Egyptian public hospitals for free. It was assumed by many at the time that a preference for cultural similarity accounted for this preferential treatment of Syrian refugees, which was not extended to nationalities of refugees from sub-Saharan Africa. This move was seen as particularly generous given the comparatively large number of Syrians who arrived in Egypt in 2012 and 2013 compared to other refugee groups. If a supposed lack of capacity had been preventing Egypt from extending state services to other groups previously, then one would expect this to have been an even more difficult challenge with Syrians.

History reveals that this decision was not motivated by cultural affinity for Egypt's so-called Syrian brothers but was instead politically motivated by Morsi's desire to demonstrate solidarity with Syrian opposition forces (Norman 2016c). Because of this link to Morsi's presidency, Syrians were later subject to a government-organized defamation campaign following his removal from power in July 2013 that targeted Morsi's political proponents and any other group presumed to support him (Elite Interviewee A). The military government that followed technically upheld the special treatment – de jure access to health care and primary education – extended to Syrians under Morsi, but the de facto treatment of Syrians changed dramatically, causing many Syrians to flee to other countries if they had the financial means to do so.

By the end of 2014, the situation was less dire for Syrians, but other national groups also experienced difficult periods when the relations between the Egyptian government and their home country became fraught. For example, Ethiopians in Egypt were impacted by a disagreement between the Egyptian and Ethiopian governments in June 2013 over the construction of the Grand Renaissance Dam in Ethiopia (Witte 2013). Both countries consider the Nile River to be a vital source of water and electricity, and Egyptian news reports at the time condemned Ethiopia and predicted nationwide water and electricity shortages in Egypt. Egyptian state-owned media helped to make this foreign-policy issue highly personal for Egyptian citizens, and as a result of public outrage, Ethiopian migrants and refugees were evicted by Egyptian landlords and harassed by Egyptian nationals in the street (Elite Interviewee C).

In 2015, the Sudanese migrant and refugee community in Cairo also experienced a difficult period marked by the increased arrest of Sudanese nationals and stories of abuse in police custody (Center for Refugee Solidarity 2016). According to the Center for Refugee Solidarity, which was monitoring the situation, this uptick was due to rising tensions between Egypt and Sudan in the leadup to Egypt's parliamentary elections at the end of 2015. There were accusations from Sudan that Egypt planned to hold elections in the Halayeb Triangle, a disputed territory on the border of Sudan and Egypt (Center for Refugee Solidarity 2016). While Sudanese migrants in Egypt have previously benefited from historic ties between the two countries, as well as from the 1976 Wadi al-Nil Agreement and increased cooperation between the Sudanese and Egyptian governments in recent years, the period of tension in 2015 indicates that Sudanese migrants are as susceptible as other nationalities should diplomatic relations with a nationality's home country become strained.

Contrasting the case of Syrians with Ethiopian and Sudanese nationals illustrates that negative host state relations with a sending country can impact culturally similar and dissimilar migrants and refugees alike. While culturally similar migrants and refugees (Syrians and, by some considerations, Sudanese) may receive de jure preferential treatment, all migrants and refugees are at risk of exclusionary treatment if they are perceived as a security risk or if the relations between their home state and Egypt become antagonistic.

6.4 Differential Treatment in Morocco

Like in Egypt, there are de jure policies in place in Morocco that privilege specific nationalities of migrants. One widely recognized de jure preferential policy is that certain nationalities of migrants are not required to complete the normally burdensome process for obtaining a work permit. As mentioned in Chapter 4, nationals of Tunisia, Algeria, and Senegal are exempt from having to go through the process run by the Agence Nationale de Promotion de l'Emploi et des Compétences (ANAPEC), which requires individuals to demonstrate that they are more qualified than Moroccans for a position (Escoffier et al. 2008). Normally, an employer seeking to hire a foreign national is required to post an advertisement in both French and Arabic to determine if there are any Moroccans that are qualified for a position, and then give preference to any Moroccan applicant. Consequently, among West African migrants in Morocco, Senegalese are seen as members of a privileged group who do not have to comply with this requirement. Regarding this perceived favoritism, Bertrand, a migrant from Cameroon, remarked, "Yes, Senegalese, they get some benefits because of the relationship between Senegal and Morocco. [It's] better than [Morocco's relationship with] Cameroon, for example." Issa, a migrant from Mali, attributed this privileging to political, cultural, and religious factors, saying, "The Senegalese community, they [have] a priority in everything ... because Senegal and Morocco have a good relationship. You know, diplomatic relations, race relations, religious relations. And the relation[ship] is very, very good."

Some Senegalese agreed with this depiction, asserting that religious and linguistic ties are the factors behind the privileging of Senegalese. Hachim, a Senegalese migrant, explained:

Well with Moroccan people, they like people from Senegal. They're gonna think, oh Senegal, good. Muslim. You have two things, you're Muslim and you speak French. But if you're from, like, Nigeria, you're not Muslim and you don't speak French. You know, it's not the same. You have more difficulties to speak with people, to make them understand who you are, what you want.

Still, many Senegalese, who are de jure privileged regarding the ability to access employment in Morocco, can face other barriers. For example, Senegalese must still obtain a residence permit, or *carte de séjour*, in order to remain legally in the country. As a representative of the Conseil National des Droits de l'Homme (CNDH) noted,

if in practice [the exception] makes it easier for Senegalese to get a job, and then through that job, being able to apply for a *carte de séjour*, is different.... It's a lot more hassle to hire someone who has to go through an ANAPEC process, but that doesn't necessarily mean that those who are exempt have it much easier. (Elite Interviewee AZ)

Like other West African migrants and refugees, Senegalese individuals reported that they face discrimination and racism in Morocco regarding access to employment and other necessities like housing. Hachim from Senegal argued that Moroccans

think that people from France or from America . . . when you have the same diploma, and you are applying for the same job, they're going to prefer these people to you. Yeah. For me, it's racism. Or if me and you are going to rent a flat, they're going to rent to you, but for me, they think, oh he's Black, he's going to make noise. You have clichés, and stereotypes.

Moussa, also from Senegal, commented,

Yes, sometimes it seems like Senegalese get treated better. Yes, we are their brothers. Yes, we are their friends. But then also, you know, I ask them: but how many Senegalese got killed last year? Three. There's still racism, there's still discrimination.

In addition to Senegalese, many migrants and refugees perceive Syrians as a favored group by the Moroccan government and among Moroccan nationals. Syrians themselves described preferential treatment and attributed this to cultural factors. Bassem, a Syrian man residing in Rabat, explained, "Maybe for the Moroccans, maybe they love the Syrians more than the Africans. Because there is a relationship, with language, with religion, with history."

It is critical to note, however, that most Syrians residing in Morocco arrived well before the 2011 crisis; some had been living in the country for decades. As a result, these individuals have had many years to establish business relations with Moroccan nationals and form their own community networks in the host state. This longevity may have also affected their de facto treatment in Morocco. Zain, a thirty-five-year-old Syrian man, came to Morocco when he was only two months old. He spent his entire life residing in Morocco, eventually establishing a Syrian restaurant with his father in 2010. Bassem, another Syrian man, had lived in Morocco for thirty-five years when we spoke in 2015 and was the head of the Syrian Community Association of Morocco (rābṭat al-jālīya al-sūrīya bi-l-maghrib). He explained, "Most Syrians leave [Syria] for business, to set up a business here. There's lots of ties with Morocco. For sixty years there's [*sic*] been Syrians here."

As in the analysis on Egypt, I examine these perceptions of privilege by dividing my interview respondents into two groups: those considered to be a privileged nationality in Morocco (including Syrians and

Senegalese), and those considered to be nonprivileged (all other African nationalities). As with Egypt, I compare the results to three other factors: an individual's self-identified gender, the length of time that a migrant or refugee has spent in Morocco, and whether an individual has legal status.

First, I asked interviewees whether they believe that the Moroccan government provides services for migrants and refugees. In response, 63.2 percent did not believe the government provides any services, while 36.8 percent believe that the government provides at least one service. Individuals from the privileged group were more likely to believe that the host government provides services, although the larger discrepancy was between those who had spent less than two years versus more than two years in the host state. See Table 6.9.

Next, I asked interviewees about accessing health care and education for their children, if applicable. In response, 28.9 percent of individuals said they had been to a hospital or clinic in Morocco. Of those individuals, only 13.2 percent had some form of financial assistance when doing so. Respondents from the privileged group were slightly more likely to visit a hospital and much more likely to have assistance to do so. However, this is equivalent to the discrepancy between males and

Table 6.9 *Attitudinal measure of whether the host state government provides services, Morocco*

	Thinks the host state government provides services, % (*n*)	
	No	*Yes*
Total	63.2 (24)	36.8 (14)
Privileged group	54.5 (6)	45.5 (5)
Nonprivileged group	65.4 (17)	24.6 (9)
Male	60.0 (15)	40.0 (10)
Female	69.2 (9)	30.8 (4)
Less than 2 years	100.0 (10)	0.0 (0)
More than 2 years	50.0 (14)	50.0 (14)
Has legal status	54.5 (12)	45.5 (10)
No legal status	75.0 (12)	25.0 (4)

Table 6.10 *Access to a hospital by migrant and refugee characteristics,*
Morocco

	Visited hospital, % (*n*)		Financial assistance for visiting hospital, % (*n*)	
	No	Yes	No	Yes
Total	57.9 (22)	28.9 (11)	18.4 (7)	13.2 (5)
Privileged group	55.6 (5)	44.4 (4)	25.0 (1)	75.0 (3)
Nonprivileged group	69.6 (16)	30.4 (7)	75.0 (6)	25.0 (2)
Male	68.2 (15)	31.8 (7)	75.0 (6)	25.0 (2)
Female	63.6 (7)	36.4 (4)	25.0 (1)	75.0 (3)
Less than 2 years	90.0 (9)	10.0 (1)	0.0 (0)	100.0 (1)
More than 2 years	56.5 (13)	43.5 (10)	63.6 (7)	36.4 (4)
Has legal status	55.6 (10)	44.4 (8)	62.5 (5)	37.5 (3)
No legal status	80.0 (12)	20.0 (3)	50.0 (2)	50.0 (2)

females and between those who spent less than two years in Morocco
and those who spent more than two years. See Table 6.10.

Only 21.1 percent of interviewees had school-aged children with
them in Morocco, and only 37 percent of those individuals enrolled
their children in school (whether government-run, community organized, or private). There were no members of the privileged group with
children in school in Morocco among my interviewees, so I am not able
to assess whether members of the nonprivileged group have
a comparatively difficult time enrolling their children in school or
accessing funding to do so. See Table 6.11.

Next, I asked interviewees about two perception questions relating to
Moroccan authorities privileging certain nationalities. First, I asked
whether treatment from Moroccan authorities varied by nationality. In
response, 37.9 percent stated that privileging does occur, while 62.1 percent claimed that all migrant and refugee groups are treated the same. Of
those who felt that privileging of certain groups does occur, the most
common nationality mentioned as privileged was Senegalese. Similar to
Egypt, my data indicate that a minority, not a majority, of migrants and
refugees perceive that certain nationalities are privileged. Interestingly,
and in contrast with data from Egypt, members of the privileged group
were more likely to think that privileging occurs (66.7 percent) compared
to members of the nonprivileged group (33.3 percent). See Table 6.12.

Table 6.11 *Access to education by migrant and refugee characteristics, Morocco*

	If has children in host state, do they attend school? % (*n*)		Financial assistance for school, % (*n*)	
	No	*Yes*	*No*	*Yes*
Total	62.5 (5)	37.5 (3)	75.0 (3)	25.0 (1)
Privileged group	0.0 (0)	0.0 (0)	0.0 (0)	0.0 (0)
Nonprivileged group	62.5 (5)	37.5 (3)	75.0 (3)	25.0 (1)
Male	66.7 (4)	33.3 (2)	100.0 (2)	0.0 (0)
Female	50.0 (1)	50.0 (1)	50.0 (1)	50.0 (1)
Less than 2 years	0.0 (0)	100.0 (1)	0.0 (0)	100.0 (1)
More than 2 years	71.4 (5)	28.6 (2)	100.0 (3)	0.0 (0)
Has legal status	66.7 (4)	33.3 (2)	100.0 (3)	0.0 (0)
No legal status	50.0 (1)	50.0 (1)	0.0 (0)	100.0 (1)

Table 6.12 *Attitudinal measure of host state privileging of certain nationalities, Morocco*

	Believes some nationalities are privileged in host state, % (*n*)	
	No	*Yes*
Total	62.1 (18)	37.9 (11)
Privileged group	50.0 (4)	50.0 (4)
Nonprivileged group	70.0 (14)	30.0 (6)
Male	57.1 (12)	42.9 (9)
Female	75.0 (6)	25.0 (2)
Less than 2 years	85.7 (6)	14.3 (1)
More than 2 years	54.5 (12)	45.5 (10)
Has legal status	70.6 (12)	29.4 (5)
No legal status	50.0 (6)	50.0 (6)

I then asked migrants and refugees whether certain nationalities are targeted by police or other authorities in Morocco. In response, 58.1 percent stated they did not think that certain groups of migrants or refugees are targeted by Moroccan authorities, while 41.9 percent

Table 6.13 *Attitudinal measure of host state targeting of certain nationalities, Morocco*

	Believes certain nationalities are targeted by host state authorities, % (*n*)	
	No	Yes
Total	58.1 (18)	41.9 (13)
Privileged group	33.3 (3)	66.7 (6)
Nonprivileged group	66.7 (14)	33.3 (7)
Male	57.1 (12)	42.9 (9)
Female	60.0 (6)	40.0 (4)
Less than 2 years	75.0 (6)	25.0 (2)
More than 2 years	52.2 (12)	47.8 (11)
Has legal status	53.8 (7)	46.2 (6)
No legal status	61.1 (11)	38.9 (7)

felt that certain groups are targeted. Individuals from the nonprivileged group were less likely, on average, to say that certain groups are targeted by the police. See Table 6.13.

In addition to asking about perceptions of policing of certain migrant and refugee groups, I also asked interviewees whether they ever personally had trouble with Moroccan authorities. In response, 68.8 percent of interviewees reported not having trouble with a host state authority, while 31.3 percent reported having trouble with an authority during their residency in Morocco. Individuals from the privileged group were much more likely to have trouble with a Moroccan authority compared with individuals from the nonprivileged group. See Table 6.14.

Third, I asked interviewees questions about their community and political participation in Morocco in order to gauge their connectedness to other migrants and refugees. In response, 73.7 percent of interviewees participated in community organizations run by migrants and refugees themselves, whether with members of their same nationality or in a community group open to various nationalities, while only 26.3 percent stated that they did not belong to any community group. Interviewees from the nonprivileged group were almost equally likely

Table 6.14 *Trouble with host state authorities by migrant and refugee characteristics, Morocco*

	Has had trouble with host state authorities, % (*n*)	
	No	Yes
Total	68.8 (22)	31.3 (10)
Privileged group	40.0 (4)	60.0 (6)
Nonprivileged group	81.0 (17)	19.0 (4)
Male	68.2 (15)	31.8 (7)
Female	70.0 (7)	30.0 (3)
Less than 2 years	62.5 (5)	37.5 (3)
More than 2 years	70.8 (17)	29.2 (7)
Has legal status	77.8 (14)	22.2 (4)
No legal status	57.1 (8)	42.9 (6)

Table 6.15 *Participation in a community organization by migrant and refugee characteristics, Morocco*

	Participates in a community organization, % (*n*)	
	No	Yes
Total	26.3 (10)	73.7 (28)
Privileged group	27.3 (3)	72.7 (8)
Nonprivileged group	26.9 (7)	73.1 (19)
Male	16.0 (4)	84.0 (21)
Female	46.2 (6)	53.8 (7)
Less than 2 years	80.0 (8)	20.0 (2)
More than 2 years	7.1 (2)	92.9 (26)
Has legal status	4.5 (1)	95.5 (21)
No legal status	56.3 (9)	43.8 (7)

to participate in a community organization. The largest discrepancy was between those who spent fewer than two years in Morocco versus those who spent two years or more. See Table 6.15.

At a rate slightly higher than in Egypt, 18.9 percent of interviewees participated in some kind of political activity in Morocco, while

Table 6.16 *Participation in political advocacy by migrant and refugee characteristics, Morocco*

	No	Yes
	Participates in political advocacy, % (*n*)	
Total	81.1 (30)	18.9 (7)
Privileged group	90.0 (10)	9.1 (1)
Nonprivileged group	76.0 (19)	24.0 (6)
Male	79.2 (19)	20.8 (5)
Female	84.6 (11)	15.4 (2)
Less than 2 years	100.0 (10)	0.0 (0)
More than 2 years	74.1 (20)	25.9 (7)
Has legal status	71.4 (15)	28.6 (6)
No legal status	93.8 (15)	6.3 (1)

81.1 percent did not. Interviewees from the nonprivileged group were slightly more likely than interviewees from the privileged group to participate in a political activity, though for the most part refugees and migrants of all backgrounds refrained from doing so. See Table 6.16.

On the whole, being part of a privileged group – comprising individuals who are considered to be culturally similar in Morocco – did not correspond with better treatment or outcomes. As in Egypt, cultural factors did not appear to matter as strongly as whether an individual had legal status or the amount of time that an individual spent in Morocco.

While this analysis looks at perceptions of treatment from the perspective of migrants and refugees themselves, these findings are in line with those of a recent study from Matt Buehler and Kyung Joon Han (2019). The authors conducted the first statistically representative public opinion poll of Moroccans' opposition toward migrants, surveying 1,500 citizens carried out in Morocco's Casablanca-Settat region. The survey asks whether Moroccan nationals have a preference for "Arab" versus "African" migrants, finding that if respondents expressed more opposition toward sub-Saharan African migrants, this was due to concerns over labor market absorption and economic competition, rather than concerns over cultural threats, including assumptions about the race, ethnicity, or religiosity of sub-Saharan African migrants.

Furthermore, like in Egypt, my discussions with both migrant and elite respondents in Morocco suggest that any privileging of certain migrant nationalities over others is more likely a result of the Moroccan state's domestic and foreign-policy interests rather than cultural factors. This relates specifically to Morocco's diplomatic and economic interests in West Africa, as well as the political issue of Western Sahara. In addition to the factors discussed in Chapter 4, a key diplomatic factor that may have incentivized the timing of Morocco's 2013 policy reform – which regularized thousands of irregular migrants from various West African countries – was Morocco's desire to play a leading role in Africa, both economically and geopolitically (Cherti and Collyer 2015). If Morocco wanted to take on a leadership position in West Africa, then it needed to act hospitably toward migrants originating from the region. As Myriam Cherti and Michael Collyer (2015) argue, Morocco's 2013 policy liberalization "suggests a change in the way that Morocco thinks of itself – less orientated toward the North and more receptive to its Southern neighbours than it has been over the decade that new patterns of immigration have become established" (602).

Connected to the foreign-policy goal of projecting influence in Africa, some interview subjects speculated that the 2013 reform was related to Morocco's foreign-policy goal of garnering support among African countries for Morocco's continued control of Western Sahara, an ongoing conflict that remains a taboo subject in Morocco (Norman 2016b). Morocco's ownership over Western Sahara has been a critical issue for the monarchy since Spain announced its decolonization of the territory in 1974 (Zunes and Mundy 2010). Spain handed Western Sahara over to Morocco in 1976, leading to a guerilla conflict fought between Moroccan forces and Sahrawi nationalists, led by the Polisario Front, between 1975 and 1991 (Zunes and Mundy 2010). From a Moroccan perspective, the claim to Western Sahara is not purely political or economic but also a matter of religion. The Moroccan king wields influence as a religious leader, officially "Commander of the Faithful" ('amīr al-mu'minīn), as the monarch claims direct descent from the Prophet Mohammed (Abdel-Samad 2014). James Sater (2010) argues that even under Spanish colonial rule, residents of Western Sahara looked to the Moroccan monarch as a religious authority, meaning that the present-day possibility of Sahrawi independence threatens the religious legitimacy of the Moroccan crown.

Since Hassan II's rule (1961–99), the monarchy has considered gaining diplomatic support for Morocco's claim to Western Sahara a critical foreign-policy issue. Sater (2010) argues that Morocco has compromised on trade issues with the EU to garner support for its Western Sahara policy and has been willing to take a soft stance on the Arab–Israeli issue in exchange for US support on Western Sahara. Indeed, the United States, France, and several other EU countries were willing to recognize Kosovo's independence but have refrained from advocating for the independence of Western Sahara, suggesting that their bilateral interests with Morocco have priority over efforts to seek a fair and long-term solution to the conflict (Theofilopoulou 2010).

Historically, nations on the African continent have not provided much support for Morocco on the issue of Western Sahara. This may be because African nations have generally accepted the principle of inherited colonial borders, leading to broad support of the Sahrawi's right to self-determination (Sater 2010). Minds might be changing however. Just prior to the announcement of the 2013 policy reform, King Mohammed VI embarked on a tour of West African countries, which yielded successful backing for his Western Sahara policy. In May 2013, Mohammed VI visited Senegal where he and Senegalese president Macky Sall signed six bilateral agreements, increasing cooperation between foreign ministries and strengthening investment. President Sall also praised Morocco's Western Sahara policy, stating, "Morocco's initiative for a broader autonomy of the Western Sahara region constitutes the ideal solution to the conflict" (MACP 2013). In July 2013 – just two months prior to the September migration policy reform – President Sall visited Morocco to discuss the treatment of Senegalese nationals residing in Morocco, some of whom had recently protested ill treatment from Moroccan authorities by occupying the Senegalese embassy in Rabat (*Jeune Afrique* 2013a, 2013b). In order to maintain economic and diplomatic support from Senegal, King Mohammed VI may have realized he needed to decisively address the migrant issue.

Moroccan diplomacy also won favor in Côte d'Ivoire. Just ahead of a visit from the Moroccan monarch in 2013, Côte d'Ivoire President Alassane Ouattara issued a statement proclaiming that the proposal to grant autonomy to Western Sahara under Moroccan sovereignty is "an appropriate solution to definitively settle the conflict" (MEO 2013). Two years later in 2015, the ambassador of Côte d'Ivoire to the United Nations was removed from office after stating that Western Sahara was the only territory not yet autonomous in Africa (*News Abidjan* 2015). Additionally, Morocco rejoined the African Union in January 2017 after an absence of thirty-three years, in a bid to exert further political and economic influence across sub-Saharan Africa and gain further legitimacy and support on the issue of Western Sahara (Woldemariam 2017). These diplomatic activities suggest that timing of the 2013 reform in Morocco was at least partly related to Morocco's diplomatic and economic interests in West Africa, as well as the country's claim of ownership over Western Sahara.

Furthermore, several migrants interviewed in Morocco believed that the Western Sahara issue factored into the everyday treatment of certain migrant nationalities. While some individuals suggested that cultural proximity and language skills were the primary factors affecting the differential treatment of certain nationalities, others attributed this disparity to whether or not one's home country supports Morocco's Western Sahara policy. Adjo, a migrant from Ghana, expressed a view supporting the latter:

If you're from West African countries, you're a friend of Morocco. But if you're from a country that's supporting the Polisario [the Sahrawi liberation movement] it's trouble. And the police know. But this, they won't tell you. No migrant would dare to say this, but everyone knows.

Government-affiliated officials interviewed for this research were unwilling to discuss the topic of Western Sahara directly, but an individual from an international organization in Rabat affirmed what some migrants observed:

Yes, that's definitely the case. I mean, there would be no indication from the government. But if they [the government] tell authorities that they should treat [migrant] nationalities differently, then obviously the Western Sahara topic comes up. (Elite Interviewee I)

These interviews suggest that Morocco's diplomatic and economic interests may factor into the everyday treatment of migrants or refugees residing in the host state, and that geopolitical factors, rather than perceptions of cultural differences, may be behind any differential treatment experienced by certain migrant nationalities.

6.5 Differential Treatment in Turkey

While I have not collected the same quantitative data to examine the differential treatment of migrants and refugees in Turkey, there is qualitative evidence to suggest that the privileging of certain nationalities occurs, as discussed briefly in Chapter 5. For example, the increased attention paid to Syrians in Turkey has in some cases provoked resentment from other refugee groups who have been residing in the country for longer. Syrians themselves acknowledged the de jure privileging of their nationality. Tareq, a young Syrian man living in Gaziantep, alluded to the privileging of Syrians over Iraqis and Iranians, saying, "For example, the Iraqis and Iranians, the difference for them in Turkey [is that] the Syrians are fortunate to receive a lot of help from the Turkish government." Tareq elaborated, saying that he did not see himself as a refugee in need of protection, explaining, "I think, other people, they need help. I mean, there's a number of people who need help. There [are] some people who are worse off than me. I have work, praise be to God. Another person, he doesn't have work, and he doesn't have a home and he doesn't have food. I have everything; it's good." But other Syrians disagreed, believing that the sheer number of Syrians in Turkey was leading to exclusionary treatment and pushback from Turkish nationals and political opposition parties. Reem, a Syrian woman in Istanbul, commented, "Yes, Syrians have a more difficult time because of the number. There's so many Syrians now."

Within the Syrian population there is also de facto differential treatment. Some Syrians are ethnically Turkmen, a Turkic ethnic group whose language is much closer to Turkish than Arabic and thus have an easier time integrating within the Turkish community. A UN employee focused on the issue of education for Syrians in Turkey explained, "Turkmen Syrians speak the language more or less .... Depending if they live in a community that's heavily Syrian or more mixed with Turkish, they may already speak some Turkish" (Elite Interviewee N). Conversely, Syrian Kurds face a difficult situation in Turkey due to the ongoing tensions between Kurdish minority areas and the central Turkish government. When the city of Kobani was under siege in northern Syria in 2014, the Turkish government initially refused to allow Kurdish Syrians to cross the border, although it eventually relented and established temporary camps for them inside Turkey (Elite Interviewee AM).

There are also historical precedents for the Turkish government providing specific nationalities with benefits if the state perceives political gains from doing so. Farhad, an Afghan migrant in Istanbul, explained that in his view, Afghans – like Syrians – received favorable treatment in Turkey because of ties as diverse as religion, economics, and a shared military past:

One [factor] is religion. [Afghans] share the same religion, most are Muslim Sunnis. And the other thing is history. Turkey and Afghanistan have a history. In World War I when they were fighting the Ottoman Empire, Afghans and Pakistan people, like Muslims from South Asia, they came here to help the Ottoman Empire. They're always talking about this. Turkish companies are doing lots of investments in Afghanistan. And they always say, "Yeah, you are our Muslim brothers, you helped us many years ago and now we're helping you." That's how they are doing business; it's a capitalist thing that they do.

Farhad arrived in Turkey from Afghanistan in the 2000s, but there were earlier groups of Turkmen Afghans who arrived in Turkey as refugees during the Cold War in the 1980s.[5] These groups formed organizations that were eventually able to lobby the Turkish government for citizenship in exchange for political support (İçduygu and Kirisci 2009).

Perhaps knowing this history, political opponents criticized the AKP's warm and financially generous reception of Syrian refugees since 2011 as a ploy to gain future voters. Proving these critics correct, Turkish President Erdoğan announced in July 2016 that "our [Syrian] brothers" would be granted citizenship (Hintz and Feehan 2017).[6] Voting rights thus granted provide "a mechanism for transforming refugees' gratitude into political support" (Hintz and Feehan 2017). Opponents fear that if Syrians are offered a pathway to citizenship, they could constitute a sizable bump in Erdoğan's political base. Turkish officials stated ahead of the June 2018 presidential and parliamentary elections that approximately 55,000 Syrians had been granted citizenship (Farooq 2018). While in a country of nearly 58 million registered voters this constituency is too small to make an impact in the AKP's favor (Farooq 2018), the issue has nonetheless been highly contentious among opposition parties and the general public (Atasü-Topçuoğlu 2018). Nonetheless, this favoritism toward Syrians can be easily reversed should a state's geopolitical calculus change, evidenced by the roundup and deportation of Syrian nationals beginning in mid-2019 discussed in Chapter 5.

6.6 Conclusion

This chapter primarily explored whether migrants and refugees residing in North African countries experience differential treatment according to their perceived cultural proximity to host state nationals. Using quantitative data derived from interviews with individual migrants and refugees of various backgrounds in Egypt and Morocco, I found that the perception of a migrant or refugee as a co-cultural can have a bearing on integration outcomes in some instances, but in general, other factors better explain the treatment incurred by various nationalities, namely, the length of time an individual spends in the host state, and whether he or she has legal status. Migrants and refugees from south of the Saharan border, considered to be African as opposed to Middle Eastern, are viewed as more culturally distant and may be subject to racialized treatment in either host state. Furthermore, migrants and refugees are likely to internalize this narrative as well; they may consider themselves to be more distant and consequently view local integration as less possible or desirable. This narrative is certainly present in the qualitative interview data presented in this chapter.

But, looking at the migrant and refugee data in their entirety, a different narrative emerges. As time passes and once they acquire legal status, migrants and refugees, regardless of their co-ethnic status, hold better opinions of the host state and are more involved in community activities. This change in perception complicates the racial hierarchy narrative, indicating that it is actually the minority rather than the majority of migrants and refugees, regardless of cultural background, that believe certain groups are treated in a privileged manner. In other words, the importance of the Sahara as a demarcating line diminishes in the aggregate picture, lending credence to the idea that shared culture is a malleable concept since both African-ness and Arab-ness are constructed identities.

Second, this chapter explored the importance of the cultural embeddedness thesis in comparison to other factors, including the diplomatic and security interests of the host states in question. An analysis of the political incentives underlying the de jure and de facto treatment of certain nationalities in Egypt and Morocco using qualitative interview data show that the privileging of co-cultural migrants or refugees may actually emanate primarily from the state's diplomatic and political interests rather than as a result of cultural factors. This is also true of Turkey, where specific migrant and refugee nationalities have received favorable treatment from the government when there are perceived benefits – such as creating a future loyal voting bloc – from privileging a specific group. However, the analysis also showed that any privileging of a particular nationality can be overridden should a culturally similar group be perceived as a security threat in the host state, and culturally similar and dissimilar nationalities can be equally vulnerable during times of domestic instability or periods of tension between a migrant sending state and host state.

This chapter narrowed in to examine engagement at the sub-national level and to explore whether different nationalities of migrants and refugees residing in each host state experience differential treatment. The next chapter zooms back out to focus on another possible influence on host state engagement decisions: the role of international actors within domestic policy space.

7 | The Domestic Influence of International Actors

UNHCR and IOM's Role in Host State Policy Outcomes

7.1 Introduction

In October 2014, I had the opportunity to attend an International Organization for Migration (IOM) workshop in Cairo titled "Training about State Migration Laws." It took place at the Semiramis Intercontinental, one of Cairo's most luxurious hotels, directly facing the Nile River and Tahrir Square. The attendees were a mix of IOM employees based at the Cairo office, two speakers from IOM's headquarters in Geneva who led the training, high-ranking public servants from the Ministry of Foreign Affairs and the Ministry of the Interior, members of the Egyptian judiciary, researchers from Egyptian national bodies who focus on children and youth, and a former ambassador representing the National Coordinating Committee for Combating and Preventing Illegal Migration (NCCPIM). Everyone in attendance wore a sleek suit or dress, and participants sat at polished, wooden tables facing a high-tech touch screen, while the lower-ranking IOM and Committee employees sat near the side of the room at a long table, note-taking and emailing.

The first two days of the three-day conference were led by a well-dressed and well-spoken Swiss IOM employee who tried her best to walk a fine line while addressing touchy issues. The third day was led by her counterpart, a Swedish IOM employee with the same smiling and pleasant demeanor. IOM's agenda for the training was fairly clear: host and transit countries like Egypt have responsibilities toward migrants or asylum seekers on their territory. There are established international legal guidelines that host states must follow when they detain or arrest a migrant, and human rights must be considered in addition to security. But this agenda was not fully in line with that of the Egyptian participants. The ambassador – head of the National Coordinating Committee for Combating and Preventing Illegal Migration – and the Egyptian public servants and researchers in attendance only wanted to discuss Egyptian emigrants, and specifically how to take measures to prevent Egyptian youth from traveling irregularly to Europe.

On the third day of the workshop these tensions came to a head. The IOM chief for the Egyptian office addressed the audience in Arabic about the results of a study on youth and involuntary migration that IOM had conducted in various countries. His report was met with criticism from members of the Egyptian national research bodies. This criticism prompted the IOM chief of the regional office – the highest-ranking IOM figure in the room – to stand up and give an impassioned speech, claiming that the participants had lost sight of the bigger picture: thousands of migrants are dying each year. He cited cases of Sudanese migrants who were seized from a camp in Sudan and trafficked through Egypt. This outburst was met with condemnation from the former ambassador. She sternly lectured the IOM chief, "I'm speaking about Egypt. And I know the problems of these Africans. On what basis are you mentioning this migration? Did you make a questionnaire? Did you interview them?" Ultimately, the source of tension between the ambassador and IOM chief, and underlying the workshop more generally, was that the ambassador and her colleagues only wanted to address the stakes of Egyptian *emigration*, not Egypt's role as a host state.

This chapter addresses the question of what role international migration organizations – primarily the UNHCR and the IOM – have in shaping the policy decisions of migrant and refugee host states. Are international organizations able (or willing) to act as advocates for migrants or refugees in demanding more inclusive policies, or are they only subject to the whims of the host countries in which they operate? Are there certain red lines that cannot be crossed, or are they able to use mechanisms – such as funding infrastructure projects that benefit the host state – to convince governments to enact certain policies?

The literature on global governance and international organizations is fairly divided on the influence that international institutions can have on domestic decisions and outcomes. Realists view international institutions as reflecting the interests of powerful nations and not capable of affecting state decisions; institutionalists argue that international institutions are able to independently influence state behavior; constructivists see international organizations as capable of affecting domestic policy through norm development and institutionalization. Since the late 1980s, much of the literature has responded to a challenge posed by realists to demonstrate that international institutions can significantly affect state behavior (Martin and Simmons 1998). In particular, John Mearsheimer (1994) raised critical objections to the institutionalist research agenda, arguing that studies provided very little empirical evidence documenting that international organizations changed state behavior in any meaningful way. Yet by focusing so much scholarship on responding to the agenda set by realists, "models of international institutions have rarely taken domestic politics seriously," and "insufficient attention has been given to the mechanisms through which we might expect institutional effects to work" (Martin and Simmons 1998, 742–43).

This chapter evaluates the incentives and capabilities of international actors in affecting domestic policy choices, paying particular attention to the mechanisms through which international organizations can influence decision-making. It demonstrates that while the rise of supranational migration actors like the UNHCR and IOM in recent years has had a tangible impact on migration engagement decisions across the three states examined in this book, international actors have been able to influence policy outcomes to varying degrees depending on (1) the leverage they can offer host state governments and populations; (2) the preexisting relationships that intergovernmental or international organizations have in the host state; and (3) the extent to which the topic of migration has been politicized or securitized in the host state.

7.2 The Role of IOs in "Managing Migration"

The global governance of migration has been characterized as "substance without architecture," insofar as norms around migration and refugees exist, but these norms lack a coherent institutional framework through which to apply them (Aleinikoff 2007). Yet increased use of the term *migration management* in policy and political language indicates the desire of states – particularly Global North receiving states – to further govern, control, and regulate international migration. There is much debate over the actual meaning of the term, and Martin Geiger and Antoine Pécoud (2010) note that migration management has come to constitute a wide range of practices, including countertrafficking measures, information campaigns, smart border controls, and capacity-building activities. Some

have even asserted that the purpose of the concept of migration management is to bring the wide range of IOM's activities under a single label
(Georgi 2010). The concept of migration management is also intended to
cover all types of migratory movements, including the migration of asylum
seekers and refugees (Georgi 2010)

While there are ongoing normative and political debates over the
ethicality and efficacy of managing migration, there is little doubt that
intergovernmental organizations have become the key partners of
states attempting to implement and influence migration practices globally (Wolff 2015). Chief among these actors are the UNHCR and the
IOM,[1] which have attempted to influence domestic decisions about
engagement with migrants and refugees in Global South host states
over the last several decades. Officially these organizations use pro-
migrant-rights discourse in their communications and press conferences, but these organizations are "trapped in the realities of their day-
to-day operations. Beyond their role of advocates, UNHCR and IOM
are also 'migration managers'" (Wolff 2015, 16). In the Mediterranean
context specifically, countries in the EU have used these institutions in
their attempts to co-opt policy in sending and transit countries to
further manage migration (Wolff 2015).

As discussed in Chapter 1, member states of the EU have managed
their external relations with neighboring countries via the Global
Approach to Migration and Mobility (GAMM) since 2005 and
through bilateral and regional frameworks such as the European
Neighborhood Policy that implement the GAMM (Wolff 2015). In
addition to the GAMM, the Rabat and Khartoum processes – enacted
in 2006 and 2013, respectively – are two regional processes that the EU
uses to negotiate and collaborate with external countries on specific
issues relating to migration. However, these processes have been confronted with several limitations. First, many of the neighboring EU
countries engaging in dialogue do not have domestic asylum, migration, or trafficking policies through which to conduct negotiations
(Wolff 2015). Second, as illustrated in the previous section, many
neighboring states are more concerned with the treatment of their
own nationals abroad rather than migrants or refugees residing on
their territory (Wolff 2015).

Within these frameworks and processes, international organizations like the UNHCR and IOM have been key actors and facilitators
between European states – which are some of the primary donors for

these organizations – and countries of origin or transit. Sandra Lavenex (2007) examines how international organizations can be both counterweights to, as well as agents of "EU-ization," referring to the repercussions of the European integration process on the external world. With financial contributions from the EU and individual member states constituting a large portion of the operational budgets of these organizations, they "become partners and in some cases one could even say subcontractors to the EU and its member states" (Lavenex 2007, 253).

Yet the extent to which intergovernmental organizations operating in the Mediterranean region are able to convince host state governments to carry out the agendas or preferences of European states is less clear. Regardless of whether these organizations are pushing for more inclusive or repressive policies, their ability to have any influence is limited by the fact that they can only operate in a host state with the explicit permission of the host-country government. While actors like the UNHCR and IOM are often seen by EU states as more competent and reliable than host state governments in achieving the EU's objectives regarding migration policy outcomes in neighboring countries (Geiger and Pécoud 2010), their very ability to have any kind of influence is severely curtailed by the nature of state sovereignty.

Michael Barnett (2001) captures the limitations of the UNHCR and intergovernmental organizations more generally, explaining that "when states [created] humanitarian international organizations they made sure that they were highly circumscribed in scope and mindful of state sovereignty" (245). Yet, since the 1980s, "the changing character of sovereignty has transformed the meaning and practice of humanitarianism, allowing once-shy UN agencies to strut into new domains" (Barnett 2001, 246). The UNHCR's mandate in particular was enlarged following the adoption of the 1967 Protocol that removed the geographic and temporal limitations to the 1951 Refugee Convention, universalizing its operations (Orchard 2014). As the global number of refugees grew in the 1980s, and especially after the end of the Cold War, the UNHCR increasingly took on a humanitarian role in addition to its protection mandate that has led the organization to make political compromises, not always willing or capable of fulfilling the watchdog role it was meant to carry out (Loescher 2003; Roxström and Gibney 2003; Hoffmann 2016).

This conflicting relationship – attempting to fulfill both protection and humanitarian roles – has led to a careful balancing act. The following excerpt from the speech of UNHCR Spokesperson Melissa Fleming at a press briefing at the Palais des Nations in Geneva on October 18, 2013, illustrates the fine line that the UNHCR must walk in order to operate in Egypt:

Growing numbers of Syrians are crossing the Mediterranean from Egypt to Italy, citing increasing anxiety over their security as well as incidents of physical assault, verbal threat, detention and deportation. The Egyptian Government estimates that 250,000 to 300,000 Syrians currently reside in Egypt, of whom 122,774 are registered with UNHCR. We fully recognize and commend Egypt's generous hosting of so many Syrian refugees. (UNHCR 2013)

Fleming's speech simultaneously condemns Egypt's actions and praises the country's "generous hosting." With the limitation of sovereignty facing international migration organizations, what kind of influence can these institutions have on domestic migration policies?

In thinking through this question, it is important to take into account the specific dynamics of the international migration and refugee regimes and the hierarchical global system in which these organizations operate (Lake 2011; Mattern and Zarakol 2016). The issue of irregular migrant and refugee reception as a whole constitutes a global collective action problem, yet states in the Global South are much more likely to receive refugees and migrants and serve as first countries of asylum (Betts 2008; Betts and Loescher 2011). Given that the burden of hosting refugees and irregular migrants falls primarily to Global South states, which in turn rely on financial and material support from states in the Global North in the so-called grand bargain (Cuéller 2006), what recourse do Global South states have in negotiating for a more balanced burden-sharing scheme?

One course of action at a state's disposal is to deport or *refoul* migrants or refugees either to the territory of another state or to a migrant or refugee's home country. In the case of refugees or asylum seekers whose claims have not yet been assessed, this action contravenes international law, as a refugee or asylum seeker by definition faces persecution and the threat of violence in their home country. However, host states in the Global South have used this recourse in instances where Global North states failed to provide adequate financial support or resettlement options for refugees. As Alexander Betts (2008) notes, "Hong Kong, Malaysia, Pakistan, and Tanzania, for example, represented prominent examples of where this threat has been carried out over the last quarter-century" (159). More recently, states in the Middle East and North Africa hosting Syrian refugees, including Jordan, Lebanon, Turkey, and Egypt, have been accused at varying points of either *refouling* Syrians to Syrian territory or of forcibly deporting them to a third country, as will be explored further in Chapter 8.

Another option host states have is to expel the international organizations working on their territory. As mentioned in the previous section, international institutions like the UNHCR and IOM are permitted to operate and carry out their mandates only with the permission of the host-country government. If a host state senses that an international institution or an individual employee has crossed a red line or overstepped a boundary, the state can choose to discontinue the organization's operations, expel the organization from the country, or revoke the visa of an organization's staff member.

Host states might also attempt to make life difficult for refugees or migrants in order to extract further resources or increased resettlement opportunities from countries in the Global North. In the existing literature, these policies can include the use of detention; the denial or limitation of welfare, economic rights, and health care; reducing access to the court system; and the provision of temporary protection or residence rather than permanent protection (Morris 1998; Hassan 2000; Minderhound 1999). A state may also choose to end registration for refugees altogether, as occurred in Lebanon in 2015 with regard to Syrian refugees.

Last, states can threaten to send refugees or migrants *onward*, allowing them to continue their journeys and arrive in Global North states. Various leaders in the Middle East and North African context have used this threat in negotiations with European states – perhaps most notably former Libyan Prime Minister Muammer Gaddafi in 2010 – although this action speaks to a broader global phenomenon. Kelly Greenhill (2010) calls this tactic "coercive engineered migration" and finds that it has been used at least fifty-six times since the advent of the 1951 Refugee Convention.

The subsequent sections examine the dynamic between international migration organizations and MENA host states, whose interests may differ from those of their northern neighbors. How do negotiations between these two types of actors take place, and under what conditions can international institutions convince a host state to enact a particular policy? If a host state turns to one of the tactics for recourse outlined above, how do international organizations react, and what kind of actions can they take?

7.3 Egypt

The UNHCR has had a MOU in place with the Egyptian government since 1954, whereby the UNHCR agreed to carry out all activities pertaining to the registration, documentation, and status determination of refugees in Egypt. One of UNHCR's long-term goals is to have the government of Egypt take on responsibility for refugee status determination (RSD) but doing so requires that the Egyptian government first adopt a national asylum framework. There is an article in the Egyptian constitution that addresses the issue of the right of asylum, and Egypt is a signatory to the 1951 Convention and the 1967 Protocol, but there is no specific domestic legislation in place relating to the rights of refugees. A representative from the UNHCR office in Cairo's 6th of October city addressed this gap: "On a yearly basis we put our agenda in coordination with the government of Egypt on who we want to train, what are the main subjects and issues, and also our interest in capacitating the government so that it would take on the responsibility of asylum issues, but that is a long, lengthy process." As of 2014, the UNHCR had not yet made much progress on this front.

Similarly, the IOM, operational in Egypt since 1991, has advanced capacity-building measures in order for the Egyptian government to take on more responsibility regarding migration and border management. In the immediate post-2011 space this was particularly challenging. A representative of the IOM regional office, located in central Cairo, explained,

I joined this office two years ago, and then there was the end of this first crisis, the January 25 uprising. The first election year, that November, no one wanted to have a discussion of border management, because it's a very sensitive issue here. And then in June with the election of Morsi, and as soon as [he] had to select heads of departments, it changed again and Sisi came to power. So, in June, this year, we started re-liaising again. (Elite Interviewee D)

The continual change in political leadership and ministry leads created a difficult environment for the IOM to engage in relationship and trust building and to accomplish any of its migration management prerogatives. The head of the IOM Egypt mission, also located in Cairo, commented on this lengthy process:

So, things are not moving because they're still trying to ... they understand the problem, but it's not clear that they understand the solution we're proposing. That's why we're going through all these dialogues, so they can see and learn how other governments are dealing with it. And then they will hopefully work with IOM on addressing these issues. But I'm hopeful that once they get it, things will move much faster. (Elite Interviewee C)

Despite these difficulties, representatives from both the UNHCR and the IOM spoke of examples in which they were able to successfully advocate for more inclusive policies toward migrants and refugees in Egypt regarding small-scale measures, such as education for refugees. After the military coup in July 2013, the protection environment changed for Syrians. As a representative for the UNHCR office in Cairo stated, Syrians "were perceived as interfering in the domestic political process" (Elite Interviewee A). Some individuals lost their jobs in the informal economy, Syrian-owned shops were attacked by neighbors, Syrian children were beaten in the street, and both men and women were harassed and physically threatened. Although Syrians were granted permission to enroll in Egyptian public education, "many began having difficulty in accessing schools. Practically, when they were approaching schools and trying to get registered, we were facing a lot of difficulties. We were getting reports that they were informally informed that there were no places, and that they are not welcome" (Elite Interviewee A). The UNHCR appealed to the Minister of Education, asking him to renew the decree allowing Syrians access to Egyptian public schools that was issued under former President Mohammed Morsi's leadership. This was a bold move on the UNHCR's part in a political environment where any policies associated with Morsi and the Muslim Brotherhood were under attack. According to the UNHCR representative, "the Minister was somehow not convinced, because in his opinion, [Syrians] will be welcomed anyway, there is no need for the decree. But we were emphasizing that maybe it's better for Syrians to have a paper, not to face confusion, and so on. And it was successful, yes" (Elite

Interviewee A). The UNHCR viewed this instance as a major achievement given the contentiousness of the political situation at the time.

The very presence of the Syrian caseload, and emergency caseloads in general, opened more doors for relationship building between the Egyptian government and the UNHCR and IOM. Defining the situation as an emergency attracted international attention, and thus international funding, in a way that Egypt's previous caseloads had not. With more international funding, the UNHCR and IOM were able to offer incentives to the national government, and thereby Egyptian nationals, that the organizations hoped would entice the government to consider more inclusive policies toward migrants and refugees. A representative from the UNHCR noted that while the organization had a good relationship with the Ministry of Foreign Affairs as well as his main national counterpart, the same could not be said of the Ministry of Education or the Ministry of Social Solidarity, explaining that "the interaction is weak with other ministry bodies" (Elite Interviewee A). At the time of interviewing in 2014, the UNHCR was particularly hoping to enhance its interaction with the Ministry of Social Solidarity. A UNHCR representative stated that the Ministry seemed open to developing a stronger relationship, "especially [since] we're coming with proposals to have a more holistic approach in interventions and to have a more co-existence [*sic*] approach in order to support the communities also" (Elite Interviewee A). The shift by international migration organizations to support host-country governments and national populations in addition to refugees was part of a larger UN plan developed in 2014 that is explored further in Section 7.6.

7.4 Morocco

The UNHCR has operated in Morocco since 1965, and – like in Egypt – has long advocated for more host state responsibility regarding refugees. Specifically, the UNHCR has been pushing Morocco to adopt a new domestic asylum framework since 2005. Morocco ratified the 1951 Convention, the 1967 Protocol, and also adopted basic national asylum legislation in 1957, but by 2005 this regulation was outdated. The head of external relations at the UNHCR office in Rabat lamented the lack of progress on this issue in mid-2013, explaining that "we are in a situation, of frustration, let's say, impatience, as a UN organization, because we've been promised progress on asylum, especially a new asylum framework, and as of today there is no progress. Of course, there are political commitments. Operationally, it's more difficult" (Elite Interviewee G). The representative spoke of areas of successful collaboration between the UNHCR and Moroccan government, such as trainings held for Moroccan judges and security officials around the issue of refugee rights. But progress on asylum was proving to be much slower, despite the fact that "there are lots more refugees coming from sub-Saharan countries, and also from Arab countries, so the situation is a bit different. So that's why we need a new framework: more comprehensive, more detailed. And we've been talking about the new framework since 2005."

The Moroccan government was resistant to the issue of local integration for refugees as well as for migrants more broadly. The UNHCR spent years attempting to gently push for integration measures for refugees, but any such suggestions were dismissed by the government. The same UNHCR official explained that local integration was not a message the Moroccan authorities "appreciated" (Elite Interviewee G). The representative was told by a Moroccan authority that "no country is willing to see refugees settled in their country for the long term." The UNHCR representative added, "And it was a human-rights professional that said that to me, but he's realistic. And there's no country that's giving a good example. It's the case for European countries, it's the case for Morocco, it's the case for African countries."

This conversation took place in August 2013, and after the September 2013 reform announcement I spoke again with the representative by email. When asked about the timing of the reform and the UNHCR's involvement, the representative wrote, "The reasons that have motivated the decision of the King to endorse [the] CNDH recommendations remain ... in the head of the King and his advisors. All what [sic] we can say is that it was particularly timely for UNHCR" (Elite Interviewee G). The factors explaining the timing of the reform were already discussed in Chapters 4 and 6, but the representative's comments speak to the lack of UNHCR's influence over the king's decision to adopt asylum legislation and take on responsibility for refugees. While the UNHCR was pleased by the government's sudden decision, it did not see the new policy as stemming from its years of lobbying efforts.

Another policy area that the UNHCR had difficulty addressing with the Moroccan government was the request to open an office in Oujda, a city in the country's East that is often the first stop in Morocco for migrants and refugees arriving from West Africa via Algeria. The UNHCR wanted to better address the topic of mixed migration, acknowledging that within a population arriving in Oujda there are likely to be refugees and irregular migrants, as well as victims of trafficking. With an office in Oujda, the UNHCR would be better positioned to put in place a more tailored approach to registering and providing immediate services for individuals crossing into Morocco from Algeria. But when the organization asked the Moroccan government to open a field office in the city, it received a negative answer (Elite Interviewee G). The government feared that an individual entering the country through Oujda – who ultimately might not qualify as a refugee – could register in Oujda to receive protection for several months as an asylum seeker before undergoing RSD, thereby constituting a pull factor for further migration to Morocco.

The UNHCR did not feel it could push back further on this issue. A UNHCR official in Rabat explained,

Practically, when we told the government that we would like to open an office in Oujda, we received a negative answer. Which means that we can go on regular mission, but we cannot open an office .... If we had a presence there, we would have the tools to be able to make this kind of distinction [between migrants and refugees] in this sensitive area. So right now, the only way a migrant has the ability to apply for asylum is to come to Rabat. (Elite Interviewee G)

The UNHCR and IOM have been criticized in Morocco for not taking a strong enough stance against some of the Moroccan state's more repressive policies toward migrants and refugees. Médecins Sans Frontières (MSF) famously shut down its operation in Morocco in 2013 in objection to systematic violence against migrants on the part of Moroccan authorities. While this left a major gap in terms of access to health services for migrants and refugees residing in Morocco, MSF argued that continuing to operate in the country would condone the state's use of violence (MSF 2013). However, this may represent a key difference between the mandates of intergovernmental organizations like UNHCR and IOM and international NGOs like MSF. A representative from the IOM believed that objecting publicly to repressive policies would stretch beyond the organization's mandate, explaining that IOM and UNHCR cannot engage in political advocacy like INGOs. As a director of programs at the IOM Rabat office explained, "we as IOM are an intergovernmental organization; we are a UN member. For advocacy, we usually do it together with other UN agencies. Of course, associations have a different way to do advocacy" (Elite Interviewee I).

7.5 Turkey

The UNHCR has operated in Turkey since the 1960s, but Turkey did not sign a MOU with the UNHCR to formalize the organization's role in refugee registration and resettlement until 2016. In 2015, a UNHCR program officer in Istanbul reflected on this long-term precarity: "Maybe you also know that we don't have a country agreement with Turkey? So, most of our organizational interventions with the authorities are depending on our trust building with the government; that we have been doing since 1967. So, [the Turkish government] could easily close UNHCR. If they dare, they could do it. There is no legally binding document" (Elite Interviewee K). Due to the lack of formal status, the UNHCR felt a need to be very transparent in its discussions with the Turkish government regarding the topic of resettlement, especially pertaining to Syrians. The UNHCR is the primary actor responsible for liaising with countries who might accept refugees for resettlement (e.g., Australia, Sweden), but the Turkish government makes the final decision about whether to grant an exit visa to any individual selected for resettlement. Maintaining a good relationship with the Turkish authorities is thus critical for carrying out any of the responsibilities related to the resettlement process. The same program officer explained this tense relationship as one of assuaging Turkish needs of maintaining authority in the process:

So, who is going to do the vulnerability assessment? It's the Turkish authorities. How are we going to reach the vulnerable persons? Through the registration done by Turkish authorities. So we sit together and we identify the vulnerable persons, and then we go with the resettlement procedure. And then of course they have the right to assess our assessment. If we choose those for resettlement, if they want to say … why? We say okay. We are quite liberal in what we're doing. If you want, here are our files, just to feel good. And then if you have any problems, please come back. (Elite Interviewee K)

Even after Turkey drafted and implemented its new legislation concerning migration and refugees in 2014, UNHCR's role in Turkey's refugee protection and resettlement system remained ambiguous. The new law did not clarify UNHCR's role in registering refugees or conducting RSD; it only affirmed that the Turkish Directorate General for Migration Management (DGMM) is responsible for asylum seekers.

The UNHCR's deference to the Turkish government applies to cross-border operations as well. The UN Office for the Coordination of Humanitarian Affairs (OCHA) operates out of Gaziantep in Turkey's Southeast to coordinate UN bodies, INGOs, and NGOs responding to the Syrian crisis. OCHA has periodically been concerned about Turkey's willingness to keep its border with Syria open, both to allow Syrian refugees into Turkey and to allow Syrians and Syrian NGOs to cross back and forth. In 2015, Turkey implemented new residency requirements for Syrians that effectively made it impossible to cross into Syria and then back into Turkey (Norman 2016a). The director of OCHA explained:

[The new policy caused] a significant amount of stress among the Syrian community, including the Syrian NGOs that are not residents. And need to go back and forth, don't want to go back and forth for logical reasons, don't want to get their passports stamped for logical reasons, because they're running out of pages. There are very basic sort of human reasons why the change in policy has been quite negative. (Elite Interviewee P)

But as an international organization operating out of Turkey at the country's behest, OCHA did not feel it could ask the government to amend its border policy. The director explained that he "didn't sort of dig behind that, because, as this UN entity, our presence in Turkey is purely for Syria, and we're not accredited to be in Turkey for Turkey. So, our capacity to kind of question what the government is doing is extremely limited, and we're here at their good graces. Will the border reopen? Presumably it will. But again, hard to say" (Elite Interviewee P).

Asking for permission for refugees to work in Turkey has proved equally difficult. Most countries – in both the Global North and the Global South – have laws in place that privilege the hiring of nationals over foreigners, and refugees are often subject to these restrictions. A program officer with the UNHCR in Istanbul explained that the organization had pushed for special access to the Turkish labor market for Syrians, arguing that this would benefit the Turkish community and economy in addition to refugees:

Obviously, we are there with them, providing them with advice on how it should be, and of course for asylum seekers and refugees we always support that refugees are given access to the labor market because that's the only way that they can support themselves; that's the only way that they can support the host community. If we don't give them the opportunity, they won't be supporting the community that they're living in, which would be quite unfair to them and quite unfair to the Turkish community. (Elite Interviewee K)

Further access to the labor market for Syrians did come to fruition in 2016 as a result of European funding attached to the EU–Turkey deal examined in Chapter 5. However, the misaligned incentive structures of the Syrian employment policy meant that, in practice, few Turkish employers were willing to hire Syrians (Kaymaz and Kadkoy 2016).

Prior to the 2013 reform, the UNHCR also pushed for a more liberal migration policy in general, particularly regarding asylum and international protection. According to a former spokesperson for the central UNHCR office in Ankara, the period between 2006 and 2007 saw a rapid deterioration in the situation for asylum as well as for conditions in detentions centers holding irregular migrants (Elite Interviewee AM). The UNHCR, in addition to nongovernmental organizations, lobbied the government for better policies for years, and groups like the Migrant Solidarity Network held protests in Istanbul and Ankara (Elite Interviewee AK).

At the time, the UNHCR found that its concerns were being ignored. A former UNHCR spokesperson described the state of Turkish detention systems and instances of *refoulement*: "People were sent back to Iran, Iraq, detention centers; Afghans were put in planes and sent to Afghanistan. It was terrible, UNHCR was pleading to meet, to discuss the issues, and we were just rejected" (Elite Interviewee AM). After much effort, the Ministry of Foreign Affairs agreed in 2008 to meet with representatives from the UNHCR, who arrived at the meeting with a list of twenty issues to discuss with the government. The last point on the list pertained to an upcoming World Refugee Day event that the UNHCR was planning in conjunction with the Turkish Radio and Television Corporation (TRT). The former UNHCR spokesperson described Ankara's position:

We went there, it was the most terrible meeting I have ever had. The representative, deputy representative, and myself, and my assistant; we were four and they were four or five. I read the first bullet point about the

Afghan situation, and the ambassador raised up his hand, [saying]: "You are French, aren't you? You cannot teach us human rights. Our young diplomats during the Second World War saved many Jewish people from Nazi Germany. Next point!" No discussion, just insulting. Really, just very bad. As a Turkish national, I was ashamed. (Elite Interviewee AM)

After raising the last point, the Ministry of Foreign Affairs representative dismissively replied, "What is World Refugee Day? Okay, go to our cultural department and they can consult" (Elite Interviewee AM). After that remark, the meeting ended.

Although disheartened, the former UNHCR spokesperson was unaware that concurrently, two inspectors had been appointed by the Ministry of the Interior to begin looking into Turkey's migration situation. A mere two days after the disastrous meeting with the Ministry of Foreign Affairs, the two MOI inspectors began reaching out to Turkey's migration and refugee protection community, including local NGOs and international migration bodies like the UNHCR and IOM. According to the former UNHCR spokesperson, "we suddenly got a call from these two Interior Ministry inspectors asking us for a consultation meeting. We wanted to roll a red carpet out for them" (Elite Interviewee AM). The director of the Helsinki Citizens' Assembly, an NGO based in Istanbul, recounted a similar story. Prior to 2008, the group's relations with the Ministry of the Interior and police had been strained due to a report the organization published on the state of Turkish migrant detention centers. The director and his colleagues were consequently shocked to suddenly receive a phone call from the MOI inspectors in 2008. "The switch in mentality was night and day," the director explained (Elite Interviewee AJ). While the sudden communication and interest from the MOI was regarded as a victory by international organizations and NGOs, it speaks to an internal reform process rather than a UNHCR- or IOM-influenced decision.

Nonetheless, the UNHCR and the IOM had a definitive role in shaping the principles and legal language of the new 2013 law once the drafting process was under way. As discussed in Chapter 5, individuals from the UNHCR and IOM operations in Turkey were seconded by the drafting committee to lend their expertise directly. As a former UNHCR spokesperson explained, in the new law, "the usage of terminology, the meaning of terms like international protection, they are all due to the efforts of the UNHCR" (Elite Interviewee AM). But even with this influence, the UNHCR and IOM were not given a defined role in Turkey's new migration and international protection system. When asked in 2014 what the role of UNHCR would be after the new law's implementation, the head of UNHCR Istanbul office replied, "We will keep doing our role here in Turkey in any capacity that the Turkish government wants" (Elite Interviewee J). This finally changed on September 1, 2016, when the UNHCR and the Republic of Turkey signed a Host Country Agreement, ending more than sixty years of the UNHCR operating in Turkey without a formally defined relationship (UNHCR 2016).

Relationships and trust also matter for whether international organizations are able to gain access to host-country decision makers. UNICEF operated in Turkey for sixty years prior to the start of the Syrian crisis, working on issues of early childhood and primary education. According to an emergency coordinator at UNICEF, this is why the organization was allowed access to Turkish government-run refugee camps while other UN bodies and INGOs were not:

UNICEF was one of the first UN agencies allowed to start working in the camps, I think, because of our previous relationships with the Turkish government. So, with UNDP and UNHCR, they didn't have the same long-standing relationship with their line ministries. Although UNHCR had been here dealing with the refugee caseload. (Elite Interviewee N)

UNICEF was also adept at framing the organization's issues of concern. One of UNICEF's main priorities regarding Syrian refugees in Turkey is to increase the number of Syrian refugee children attending school, and it wanted the Turkish government to view this topic as a central priority. UNICEF was able to bring the Turkish government on board only after reframing the issue as a security threat instead of as a policy strictly about educational access.

At the start of the Syrian crisis, UNICEF embarked on a global campaign labeled the "No Loss Generation" in conjunction with Save the Children and other international organizations. The campaign argued that education and personal safety are as critical for children as daily necessities like food and water. Knowing that the Syrian conflict risked becoming a protracted crisis, and that the future of Syria and the region depended on having educated children to one day return to Syria, UNICEF asked donors to support and promote education and protection. UNICEF also saw the need to have the Turkish government understand this message but chose to relay the gravity of the situation through a security lens. The coordinator explained, "That's not how UNICEF looks at the out-of-school Syrian kids, but ... the government looks at those children as potential security risks if [they are] left on the streets and uneducated. So that's good, I mean I think we're getting a lot of attention on the education issue recently" (Elite Interviewee N).

Lastly, intergovernmental migration organizations learned that during a contentious political period, it is particularly difficult to convey messages to the government or advocate for certain policies. A program coordinator at the IOM in Ankara explained that in mid-2015, the organization raised the issue of vocational training for Syrian refugees with the Turkish government. The IOM argued that refugees could utilize technical skills in the local job market in Turkey or upon returning to Syria once fighting subsided. But with parliamentary elections looming, the proposal was "put on hold somehow, so for the moment we're just continuing with our old program and not initiating anything new. We want just for this period to [pass], because we do not want to face any problems, knowing the political tension in the country" (Elite Interviewee L). The organization learned that making difficult requests during a period of potential political change or upheaval was unlikely to yield results.

7.6 The Regional Refugee and Resilience Plan

A larger refugee caseload in a host country can open doors for international organizations, which was certainly the case for countries hosting Syrian refugees. In 2014, the UN instigated the Regional Refugee and Resilience Plan (3RP) which brought together the plans developed individually with national authorities of the countries most affected by the Syrian crisis – namely, Egypt, Iraq, Jordan, Lebanon, and Turkey – with the overarching goal of ensuring protection and humanitarian assistance for Syrian refugees, while simultaneously "building the resilience" of individuals, families, communities, and institutions in the most affected countries (3RP 2014). According to the plan's website, "the 3RP represents a paradigm shift in the response to the crisis by combining humanitarian and development capacities, innovation and resources" (3RP 2014). The largest difference from previous approaches was the focus on resilience, thereby addressing the vulnerable host-country nationals of the impacted communities – in addition to refugees – in recognition of the fact that Syrian refugees were residing in some of the poorest areas of less developed countries. In 2015, the total funding requirements for the 3RP were approximately US$3.4 million dedicated to refugees and US$2.1 million for "resilience," which would benefit host-country nationals through infrastructure projects, food subsidies, education and training activities, and private sector development, among other areas (3RP 2015).

The increased focus on host-country resilience was amplified following the mid-2015 European refugee "crisis," which will be further explored in the next chapter. The so-called crisis further highlighted the need, in Europe's eyes, to focus on supporting both refugees and host-country governments, if only to prevent further migration of individuals to Europe. In early 2016 various EU member states – including the United Kingdom, Germany, and Norway – met in London with the UN and officials from Middle Eastern host states to raise funds to support MENA countries. The conference raised more than US$12 billion in grants, including US$6 billion for 2016 and US$6.1 billion more for 2017–20.

The Jordan Compact was announced at the end of the conference. The Compact included a plan to create 200,000 jobs for Syrian refugees in Jordan in exchange for Jordanian access to European markets. One month later, in March 2016, the EU negotiated its 1–1 readmission deal with Turkey discussed in Chapter 5. And later that year, in November, the EU and Lebanon adopted a compact that foresaw an EU allocation of at least €400 million in 2016–17, in addition to bilateral assistance of more than €80 million. The EU also committed to increase support to private sector development in Lebanon, to provide assistance to help Lebanese businesses take advantage of existing market access to the EU, and to seek to reduce existing nontariff barriers to goods and services (Danish Refugee Council et al. 2017). Rawan Arar (2017) argues that these events led to a "new grand compromise," whereby Middle Eastern host states capitalized on European fears raised during the 2015 refugee "crisis" to negotiate better refugee hosting deals and increased development aid. Similarly, Gerasimos Tsourapas (2019b) examines how the migration deals that proliferated in the post-2015 period have led host states like Turkey, Lebanon, and Jordan to engage in rent-seeking behavior, leading to the commodification of refugees. This dynamic will be explored further in Chapter 8.

While a larger refugee or migrant caseload – such as the increase in Syrian arrivals in neighboring countries after 2011 – and subsequent increased international attention can therefore make host states more receptive to the involvement and requests of international organizations, this does not happen on its own merit. Organizations are most likely to have success if they can offer funding for national projects, provide benefits for local host communities, and demonstrate to the host government that the international community is interested in supporting its prosperity, beyond just hosting refugees.

7.7 Conclusion

International organizations face certain limitations when attempting to push their agenda or advocate for alternative policies in refugee and migrant host states, but there are also strategies and factors that organizations can utilize to be more effective in their work. Regarding limitations, I identify four primary areas that are either viewed as red lines or situations in which organizations are unlikely to have much influence. The first fairly clear red line for many Global South host states is that international organizations cannot appear to be asking for or encouraging the local integration of migrants and refugees, although exceptions to this rule were made in the context of the Syrian refugee crisis. Using the incentive of international funding or trade advantages, donor states convinced Jordan and Turkey to allow further inclusion of Syrians into certain sectors of the formal economy (Arar 2017), although this has not necessarily translated into substantially higher rates of employment for Syrians (Kaymaz and Kadkoy 2016; Lenner and Turner 2018). Second, host states are generally unwilling to enact a measure or policy that has the potential to serve as a pull factor for further migration, whether this is offering better access to social services or allowing an international organization to open a new office in a contentious area, as was the case with the UNHCR's request to open an office in Oujda, Morocco. Third, international organizations are less likely to accomplish their aims during periods of domestic contention or instability. Unfortunately for certain countries such as Egypt, this describes much of the post-2011 period. Last, international organizations are unlikely to be successful in pushing for new legislation relating to migration or asylum unless the incentives to reform legislation are already in place as a result of exogenous factors unrelated to an organization's advocacy work. In other words, international organizations can do little to request changes to national policy on their own.

Yet there are also areas in which international organizations have been successful in either influencing domestic policy or having a host government adopt a certain agenda. The first is asking for host states to follow through on the implementation of existing policies. In the case of Egypt, the UNHCR was able to convince the Egyptian Ministry of Education to reinstate a decree allowing Syrian refugee children to attend public schools even in a very contentious political environment. Second, host states have been willing to allow for international organizations to lend their expertise and carry out capacity-building programs within domestic institutions. Third, organizations are more likely to be successful over time, once they have developed relationships with host state political actors or institutions and built trust. Fourth, organizations that are adept at framing or reframing an issue – such as encouraging the Turkish government to view education policy for refugee children through a security lens – may have more success. Last, a larger refugee or migrant caseload and international attention can make a host government more receptive to the advice or requests of international organizations. This is especially the case for organizations that can offer funding for national projects and benefits for local host communities, and that can demonstrate to the host government that the international community is interested in supporting it. In the Mediterranean context, international organizations became particularly receptive to this idea beginning in 2014 with the instigation of the 3RP in response to the Syrian crisis.

But financial incentives are not all that matter. One might expect that Western donor states and international organizations exert greater influence over domestic policy outcomes when they are able to provide large financial incentives and funding to host states. What I have instead demonstrated in this chapter is that scholars should consider the question of international organizations' influence from the viewpoint of host states themselves. Financial incentives are important, but so are the following criteria: (1) whether the issue of migration or refugees has gained domestic political salience leading to more red lines; (2) the preexisting relationships that international organizations developed in the host state; and (3) the security concerns around migration or refugees. All of these factors matter at least as much as the financial incentives that donor countries and international organizations can offer.

To conclude, this chapter argued that there are certain circumstances under which international organizations are more likely to be successful in influencing domestic decisions around migration and refugee policy, but ultimately host states are strategic actors that consider financial support and external influence in conjunction with other factors such as domestic politics and state security. This chapter also briefly addressed the period beginning in 2014 and increasingly after 2015 when the relations between MENA host states, international organizations, and EU countries underwent restructuring. The next chapter will elaborate on these changes and the migration situation in the Mediterranean after the 2015 European refugee "crisis" more generally.

8 | *The Post-2015 Migration Paradigm in the Mediterranean*

8.1 Introduction

To get to the border of Ceuta – one of the two Spanish enclaves on the northern coast of Morocco – from Tangier, you can catch a *grand taxi* – usually a rundown Mercedes – from Tangier's *al-madīna al-qadīma*, the old city, for approximately MAD 50, or US$13. The taxi will drive along the coastal road and into the hills before steeply descending toward the small Spanish enclave. On the April morning that I traveled this route in 2015, it was overcast and foggy, giving the winding mountain road an ominous feel. Before my fellow passengers and I began the descent, I started to see sub-Saharan African migrants – mostly men in their late teens or early twenties – along the side of the road. Some of them were trying to hail passing cars, but others were slowly ambling along the narrow shoulder. Many migrants that hope to successfully cross the border into Ceuta camp along this highway, waiting for an opportunity either to jump the multiple layers of barbed wire fences and walls separating Ceuta and Morocco, or hide in the trunk of a vehicle. We passed through three police checkpoints on the short drive from Tangier to Ceuta. Our taxi was waved on at each checkpoint, but other cars and trucks were stopped and searched.

Once we began the steep descent, the Spanish enclave suddenly emerged from beneath the clouds. I could see rough hills and steep cliffs with a sprinkling of houses, and then a city appeared, albeit behind a heavily barricaded wall depicted in Figure 8.1. Upon reaching sea level, I got out of the taxi and into line with the many Moroccan nationals intending to cross the border, waiting for about half an hour before I could hand in my immigration sheet and receive an exit stamp to leave Morocco. After receiving the stamp, I was ushered through a cage-like structure with several sets of aisles, similar to the maze-like enclosures used in slaughterhouses. Once I passed through, I found

Figure 8.1 The border crossing between Morocco and Ceuta. Photo taken from the Spanish side of the Ceuta–Moroccan border.
Photo credit: Kelsey P. Norman, 2015

myself in another queue, this time with Spanish Guarda Civil authorities checking documents. There was a line of Moroccan men on my left, and, as I made to enter behind them, I was told by the Spanish guards to move forward. The men in the queue to my left seemed to be waiting indefinitely with no forward movement, stuck in limbo between Moroccan *emigration* and Spanish *immigration* control. One Spanish guard took my passport, and when I mistakenly told him "*shukrān*" after he handed it back, he scolded me in Spanish: "*shukrān*? What's that? You say *gracias* here." I continued on through the narrow, caged passage, having to pass down long alleyways before finally emerging to find myself facing a long corniche and a large blue sign reading "España." Of this border and others erected and fortified in the mid-2000s in countries close to Spain, Ruben Andersson (2014) writes, "Ironically, to close off, Spain first had to reach out. It had to create a zone of contact – that is, a frontier .... It had knocked on all the right doors in order to close its own" (83).

This chapter shifts to examine migration in the Mediterranean space in the wake of the 2015 European refugee "crisis," after which the stakes and power (im)balances between unwilling receiving counties in Europe and host countries of the Middle East were renegotiated and reconstituted (Arar 2017). So far, this book has captured the process of EU border externalization and its ramifications for Middle East and North African host states, as well as individual migrants and refugees, up until the middle of 2015. While refugees and migrants had been arriving in Europe in growing numbers since the beginning of the Arab Spring in 2011, there was a pronounced and sustained increase in arrivals – as well as deaths in the Mediterranean – beginning in 2015, leading to a period of increased panic among European officials and heightened international media attention surrounding the issue.

This chapter uses a lens of "migration diplomacy" – defined by Gerasimos Tsourapas (2017) as the use of "diplomatic tools, processes and procedures to manage cross-border population mobility" (2370) – to examine and understand the new migration paradigm in the Mediterranean region as a whole that resulted from the 2015 crisis. It provides insight into what this paradigm means for power politics and relations between Middle East host states and the EU, the continued and amplified use of mechanisms for preventing migration to Europe, as well as the consequences for individual migrants and refugees at the heart of an intensified migration management regime.

8.2 Migration Diplomacy

While migration has been considered a low-stakes issue in the field of foreign diplomacy (Oyen 2015), the use of migration diplomacy has a long history as means of persuasion and coercion in the Middle East context. Helene Thiolett (2011) argues that regional integration in the Middle East has been mainly fueled by formally or informally regulated labor-force transfers between countries, and as such migration decisions in the region "should be analyzed as an indirect form of foreign policy that uses the selection of migrants and quasi-asylum policies as diplomacy" (110). Of course, this is not only true of the Middle East. As discussed in previous chapters, individual European countries and the EU as a whole have used migration diplomacy to externalize their borders and export the role of managing migration to neighboring states – in exchange for visa access, trade deals, and development aid – over the last several decades (Geddes 2005; Lavenex and Schimmelfennig 2009). There has been notable pushback from Middle Eastern host states against the asymmetrical power relationships built into the use of migration diplomacy by European states. Most notable among examples is perhaps Colonel Muammar al-Gaddafi's 2010 threat to "turn Europe black" unless his government was paid several billion euros to keep its borders closed and prevent transit migration from and through Libya.[1]

This type of migration diplomacy is classified by Kelly Greenhill (2010) as "coercive engineered migration," referring to cross-border population movements that are deliberately created or manipulated in order to induce political, military, and/or economic concessions from a target state or states (in the case of Gaddafi's threat, Italy specifically and the EU generally). Greenhill finds that coercive engineered migration has been attempted fifty-six discrete times since the advent of the 1951 Refugee Convention (Greenhill 2010). In these cases, coercive engineered migration was instigated by three classes of actors: generators, who directly created or threatened to create cross-border population movements unless targets conceded to their demands; *agents provocateurs*, who did not create crises directly but who nonetheless deliberately acted in ways designed to incite others to generate outflows of migrants or refugees; and opportunists, who played no direct role in the creation of migration crises but who carefully exploited crises for their own gain (Greenhill 2010).

While Gaddafi and, arguably, Erodğan, fall under the category of generator in the context of the Middle East, other actors in the Mediterranean are opportunists, benefiting from the crises produced by others. The leaders of countries such as Lebanon, Jordan, and Egypt tangentially benefited from post-2015 European existential fear and became astute negotiators of migration diplomacy, despite unequal power hierarchies. They did not need to generate or threaten Europe with further refugee arrivals; European countries were already traumatized in 2015. As Greenhill (2010) states, "a crisis can help level the playing field, enhance the credibility of weak actors, increase the potency of their threats, and thereby improve their coercive capabilities" (23). I argue that all states hosting migrant and refugee populations in the Mediterranean region – and also farther afield in sub-Saharan Africa – benefited from Europe's post-2015 political crisis because they used migration diplomacy to extract more concessions than they were able to previously. Of course, those who benefited least from this new diplomacy paradigm were migrants and refugees themselves.

8.3 The 2015 European Crisis

In 2015, migration patterns in the Mediterranean region shifted dramatically. Before 2015, Italy received more migrants via the Central Mediterranean route than Greece did via the Eastern Mediterranean route. Suddenly, Greece received more migrants in the first six months of 2015 (68,000) than Italy had during all of 2014 (67,500) (UNHCR 2015). By early August 2015, the UNHCR announced that 250,000 migrants had arrived in Europe by sea so far that year: 124,000 in Greece and 98,000 in Italy. By the end of the year, approximately 1 million individuals arrived in Europe by sea – three to four times more than in 2014 – the majority (about 800,000) of whom arrived in Greece, rather than Italy (Holland 2015).

The shift from the Central Mediterranean route to the Eastern Mediterranean route can be traced to a domestic policy change in Macedonia. In early 2015, the Macedonian government lifted restrictive policing measures that had previously made transiting through the country highly difficult and dangerous (Sly 2015). With Macedonia more accessible, the route from Turkey to Greece and through the Balkans to Northern European countries opened up. In addition to this route being less dangerous than the Central Mediterranean route, it also dropped the price of a journey from the US\$5,000 to US\$6,000 needed to travel via Italy to approximately US\$2,000 to US\$3,000 (Sly 2015). According to Elizabeth Collett and Camille Le Coz (2018), European policy makers were not initially worried by the route change:

The short journey from Turkey to the Aegean islands was seen as less perilous than the long one from Libya to Italy, so the fact that this was becoming the more-used route was not questioned. Officials underestimated the attractiveness of a safer, more direct route for those seeking passage to Europe, and thus failed to grasp the levels to which these arrivals might climb. (13)

The increase in arrivals during 2015 is partly explained by the route change, lower price, and the spread of this information to other asylum seekers and migrants. Collett and Le Coz (2018) also point to an increase in the proportion of individuals arriving from war-affected countries during this period. While the EU has consistently received mixed flows of migrants and asylum seekers, approximately 90 percent of arrivals in 2015 were from Syria, Afghanistan, or Iraq (Collett and Le Coz 2018).

A final factor that incentivized an increase in arrivals was German Chancellor Angela Merkel's announcement in August 2015 that Germany would suspend the Dublin Protocol, allowing asylum seekers to remain in Germany rather than returning them back to their first EU country of arrival and registration (in most cases, Greece or Italy). Combined with a more affordable and less dangerous journey via the Eastern Mediterranean route, Merkel's decision served as a pull factor for individuals residing at the time in countries such as Turkey or Lebanon, or even those still in Syria, to attempt a voyage to Europe.

Only a few days after Merkel's August announcement, the tiny deceased body of three-year-old Aylan Kurdi – a Syrian national whose family had attempted the voyage from Turkey to Greece – was found on a Turkish beach and photographed by Turkish journalist Nilüfer Demir. The images quickly spread internationally, heightening Europe's shame over what was quickly being called a "crisis."[2] European Commission President Jean-Claude Juncker's speech on September 9, 2015, focused on a proposal to expand the EU's emergency internal relocation program from 40,000 to 160,000 asylum seekers (Collett and Le Coz 2018), and Merkel spearheaded a coalition of states willing to support the scheme (Weber 2016). Initially approved in September by a weighted majority of member states due to a lack of consensus, the plan saw dissent from Slovakia's Prime Minister Robert Rico, which then provoked a further backlash from other Central European countries (Weber 2016). With Slovakia unwilling to implement the scheme, other countries – France, Sweden, and Austria – also reneged from the proposal.

According to interviews collected by Collett and Le Coz (2018) of European officials and policy makers, the shift to a mandatory – as opposed to voluntary – relocation and distribution scheme for asylum seekers constituted "a turning point in the political discussion about managing the crisis, deepening divisions between Member States over how to share responsibility for asylum claims" (14). As Bobo Weber (2016) summarizes, "the failure of the EU's established crisis management revealed the core problem behind the refugee crisis: the EU's own unresolved internal problems which turned a manageable migration emergency into an existential issue for the EU." Unable to agree on an internal political solution, the EU quickly turned to an old playbook: developing mechanisms for reducing the number of migrants and refugees able to reach European shores in the first place. On November 29, 2015, the European Commission adopted the "Joint Action Plan on the Implementation of the EU–Turkey Statement," representing a consensus among various actors that arrivals from Turkey to Greece had to be stemmed (European Commission 2016c). Within six months, the EU negotiated the EU–Turkey deal discussed in Chapter 5.

8.4 Amplification of the EU–Turkey Model

The EU–Turkey deal has run into numerous problems since its implementation. First, very little progress has been made on a visa liberalization scheme for Turkish nationals, EU accession talks, or negotiations over a customs union (Vammen and Lucht 2017). Second, the deal has been contested in various legal venues, including the Greek domestic court system and the European Court of Human Rights, leading to the containment of asylum seekers in overcrowded and unhygienic facilities on Greek islands while waiting for court decisions about whether it was legal to return them. The deal was ultimately upheld in both venues, although since March 2018, only 2,177 Syrian refugees were returned from Greece to Turkey, either returning "voluntarily" or through coercion, but not through the parameters of the deal itself (Alpes et al. 2017). Furthermore, out of the nearly 4 million Syrian refugees in Turkey, only 12,778 Syrians were resettled from Turkey to the EU two years after the deal was implemented. Despite these failings, the model for the deal has largely been hailed as a success thanks to the diminished number of refugees arriving in Europe via the Eastern Mediterranean migration route. Consequently, European leaders sought to replicate the premise of the deal – which is similar in principle to prior agreements the EU established with neighboring countries – across the Southern Mediterranean in order to decrease arrivals along the Central Mediterranean migration route.

On the heels of alleged success with the EU–Turkey deal, the EU endorsed an agreement between Italian Prime Minister Gentiloni and Fayez al-Serraj, head of the UN-backed Libyan Government of National Accord. Al-Serraj's government is one of three rival governments in Libya, together with the House of Representatives in Tobruk – which did not support the EU agreement – and the unrecognized and Islamist-leaning National Salvation Government in Tripoli (Toaldo 2017). Libya agreed to prevent irregular migration to Europe, establish temporary refuge within its borders to screen asylum seekers, and repatriate individuals willing to return to their countries of origin. In exchange, the EU agreed to financially support Libya's coastguard in apprehending and returning boats carrying migrants, and to fund the improvement of Libya's "local reception centers" where migrants are housed (Palm 2017). The EU's support of Italy's agreement with Libya ignored human rights violations toward migrants in the country that were documented by numerous human rights groups and international organizations (UNICEF 2017), as well as violent and deadly actions taken by the Libyan coastguard in violation of international law (BBC 2016). Additionally, Libya has not ratified the 1951 Refugee Convention or the 1967 protocol and lacks domestic asylum legislation (Amnesty International 2012). Furthermore, Libyan law criminalizes unauthorized migration and does not distinguish between migrants, refugees, victims of trafficking, or others in need of international protection (Amnesty International 2012).

The deal with Libya received significant public criticism from UN officials and human rights organizations (OHCHR 2017), especially after it was reported that EU funding was used to support a Libyan militia commander to combat irregular migration in exchange for cars, boats, and the recognition of his force as a legitimate security body (Trew et al. 2017). Shocking images and video clips also surfaced of migrants in Libya being traded at slave auctions (Elbagir et al. 2017). Yet despite these grave human rights violations, the agreement has been touted by European leaders as a success for preventing migration to Europe and a model to be emulated elsewhere.

Egypt also attempted to capitalize on the increasing number of boat departures leaving from its shores in 2016 by enhancing its cooperation with the EU. Compared to 2015, the number of arrivals in Europe from Egypt doubled to approximately 7,000 in the first half of 2016, with most individuals coming from the Horn of Africa and Sudan, in addition to about 1,800 Egyptian nationals (Nielsen 2016). The boat journey from Egypt to Italy is particularly long and dangerous, taking up to ten days, and in exchange for further curtailing this route, Egyptian authorities began calling for financial support and development funding

(Naceur and Rollins 2017). While Egypt was previously less involved with the EU's migration externalization efforts in comparison to neighbors like Libya or Tunisia, in the post-2015 environment, Egypt did not want to miss out on taking advantage of the increased funding allotted for EU migration partnerships (Nielsen 2016). After nearly a year of negotiation from both sides, an EU–Egypt Migration Dialogue was launched on December 16, 2017 (Al-Kashef and Martin 2019).

While Morocco was already deeply involved with various types of EU migration agreements prior to 2015, it used the 2017 EU agreement with Libya to its advantage. As the arrivals of migrants and asylum seekers from Morocco to Spain grew in the fall of 2018, representatives from the Moroccan government claimed that the Italian government's decision to prevent the arrival of migrants from Libya to Europe was pushing smuggling networks to utilize the Moroccan-Spanish route instead (Bozonnet 2018). Morocco and Spain intensified their cooperation around the issue of migration in October 2018, with Spain's secretary of state for migration declaring that Spain would be Morocco's "voice" in Europe (Teevan 2018). Ultimately the EU approved the distribution of €140 million to Morocco to increase border controls, which the Moroccan minister for foreign affairs claimed was only a starting point for further negotiation on the issue, noting that Morocco had asked for much less than other countries (Bozonnet 2018).

Since 2015 and the European refugee "crisis," the EU has also directed hundreds of millions of euros in the form of development aid across the African continent. While these types of agreements and projects are not new – as has been detailed in previous chapters – Europe's desperation and fear has led it to engage in riskier and more brazen deals than it was willing to previously, and to provide enhanced funding. One example is the Emergency Trust Fund for Africa, established at the Valletta Summit on Migration in November 2015 and worth over €2.9 billion (Hopper 2017). The resources from the fund are allocated for "the creation of jobs and economic development, basic services for local populations, stability and governance, and migration management" (European Commission 2017b), with migration management referring to preventing irregular migration and fighting human trafficking. The agreement with Libya mentioned above was also partly financed by the Trust Fund, whereby Libya received €116 million (Hopper 2017). The logic behind the Trust Fund is that migrants will not choose to leave their home countries and embark on migratory journeys if economic circumstances and opportunities improve via development funding offered by Europe. Aside from the fact that a large portion of the Trust Fund's resources have gone toward border security rather than development projects (ICG 2017), this logic also contravenes empirical evidence strongly suggesting that economic and human development *increases* people's capabilities and aspirations and therefore tends to coincide with an increase, rather than a decrease, in migration in the short to medium term (de Haas 2007).

8.5 Renegotiating North–South Power Relations

Europe's dismissal of its responsibility toward asylum seekers who successfully arrived on its territory in 2015 had global ramifications for the way in which Global South countries considered their own responsibilities. This was immediately evident in Kenya, which hosts several highly populated refugee camps including Dadaab, the largest refugee camp in the world with approximately 333,000 mostly Somali residents. The Kenyan government announced in March 2016 that it would close Dadaab, citing security concerns and domestic threats after a series of terror attacks claimed by al-Shabaab (Mutiga and Graham-Harrison 2016). While Kenya had previously threatened to close Dadaab, the decision in 2016 was followed by immediate planning and action: the government set a timeline and budget and disbanded its Department of Refugee Affairs (Mutiga and Graham-Harrison 2016). The Kenyan announcement came a week before Turkey agreed to its deal with the EU after months of negotiations, and aid groups operating in Kenya suspected that the government might reverse its decision if further international assistance was provided (Mutiga and Graham-Harrison 2016).

In 2017, the government was forced to back away from the decision after a domestic court case in response to a petition filed by two Kenyan human rights organizations – the Kenya National Commission on Human Rights and Kituo Cha Sheria – found the closure unconstitutional (Kituo Cha Sheria: Legal Advice Centre 2017). Nonetheless, Kenya's 2016 announcement reflected a growing sentiment of the time. The EU was investigating new ways to return asylum seekers who had actually managed to reach its territory, and then presidential candidate Donald Trump announced his plan to block the resettlement of Syrian refugees to the United States. Global South countries were no longer willing to abide by the power structures implicit within the "grand bargain" described in Chapter 2. In Kenya, a statement released by the Ministry of Interior in May 2016 announcing the intended closure of Dadaab explained, "Governments across Europe and the Middle East have taken unprecedented efforts to limit refugee inflows into their countries on the grounds of national security. Kenya cannot look aside and allow this threat to escalate any further" (quoted in Hargrave et al. 2016, 15).

A 2016 report by the Humanitarian Policy Group investing the implications of European and Australian policies for Kenya, Jordan, and Indonesia explained that if Global North countries

with stronger economies and institutions, are reluctant to uphold their obligations under the Refugee Convention, then there is little incentive for poorer countries, in much more difficult circumstances, to persevere in doing so. Instead, restrictions in developed countries send a clear message that at best it is one rule for them and another for the rest of the world, or at worst that international obligations towards refugees simply do not hold any more – either way tilting the balance towards restriction. (Hargrave et al. 2016, 3)

Since 2015, Global South countries have become better negotiators. They are adept at demanding more resources in exchange for hosting migrants and refugees indefinitely and for preventing the onward migration of these individuals toward Europe or other Western regions. They also want more say over who enters their borders and how long migrants or refugees remain. The issue of the return of Syrian refugees from neighboring host states provides an illustrative example of this dynamic.

According to the UNHCR, between 2015 and September 2018 at least 107,927 Syrian refugees returned from Lebanon, Jordan, Turkey, Iraq, and Egypt (11.11.11 2018). These numbers can be deceiving, however, because during the same period, refugees were also leaving Syria. In 2017, nearly half a million Syrians were newly displaced to neighboring countries, and 37,000 of those Syrians who returned to their home in 2017 had to flee again after their return. In theory, the repatriation of a refugee should be safe and dignified and should not contravene the international norm of *non-refoulement*. Yet host states have been known to pressure refugees into returning to their home countries by making the host state situation so dire that refugees feel they have no other choice but to leave (Crisp and Long 2016). Understandably, host states and host communities suffer from hosting fatigue, especially as international funds to support protracted refugee situations dry up.

In the case of Syria, the narrative of a victory over ISIS began dominating headlines in late 2017, even as the war between opposition and regime forces lingered on. In early 2018, major government assaults on the opposition strongholds of Idlib and Eastern Ghouta intensified, and in January 2018 Turkish forces crossed into northern Syria to invade the Kurdish enclave of Afrin. Regardless of any evidence to the contrary, the Lebanese government considered the war in Syria to be over. After years of disagreement on how to handle the situation of refugees in Lebanon and the Syrian war more generally, a consensus formed among government officials and political parties. Lebanese President Michel Aoun – a supporter of the Assad regime – gave a speech before the UN General Assembly in September 2017, stating that with "85 percent of Syrian territories" recovered by the Assad government, the time had come to talk about the return of displaced Syrians to their homeland, and that the topic had become "urgent" (UN General Assembly 2017) But the president also spent part of his speech focusing on semantics, stating, "There are those who talk about *voluntary* return, while we speak about a *safe* return" (emphasis added).

It is unclear what a safe return of Syrians would look like in practical terms, especially for those who refuse to return to Syria while Bashar al-Assad remains in power or for those who escaped conscription into the Syrian military. Staying in a host state like Lebanon – where Syrians face extremely limited working opportunities and a complex bureau-cratic environment that leaves many without options for legal status – and eking out an existence versus risking whatever danger one might face upon return to Syria is a nearly impossible choice for many individuals and families.

Tensions over the issue of return came to a head between the Lebanese government and international organizations operating in Lebanon in June 2018 when the UNHCR and the Lebanese Ministry of Foreign Affairs engaged in a dispute over further returns of Syrians from Arsal in northeast Lebanon. Lebanese Foreign Affairs Minister Gebran Bassil accused the UNHCR of discouraging refugees from returning to Syria and of "spreading fear by asking questions about military conscription, security conditions, accommodations and living situations in Syria, along with possible halts to aid and the prospect of returning home without UN assistance" (Hamdan 2018). In response, the Ministry of Foreign Affairs ordered the Directorate of Protocol to stop processing residency applications for UNHCR staff in Lebanon, refusing to reverse the decision unless the UNHCR produced a plan for returning displaced Syrians from Lebanon to Syria (Hamdan 2018). This coercive strategy effectively amounted to the Lebanese government telling the UNHCR: comply with our policies or end your operation in Lebanon.

Jordan, which hosts between 650,000 and 1.3 million Syrian refugees, also deported Syrians in 2017. This stands in contrast to the fanfare around Jordan's progressive stance toward Syrians in 2016 after the announcement of the Jordan Compact. As discussed in Chapter 7, the deal between Jordan and EU donor countries envisioned the issuing of 200,000 work permits for Syrians in Jordan, in exchange for the establishment of special economic zones and preferential access to European markets for goods produced in Jordan by companies employing Syrians. Rawan Arar (2017) quotes a Jordanian official describing 2016 as "Jordan's golden year," or the year that Jordan was finally able to advocate for Jordanian interests in exchange for its hosting of refugees (308).

In implementing the terms of the compact, the Jordanian government only allowed permits to be issued in specific sectors – namely, manufacturing – ignoring the existent migrant workforce of Egyptians and South Asians who have long dominated the industry, albeit informally (Lenner and Turner 2018). As with Turkey, this left employers reluctant to take the required steps to formally employ Syrians when there was already a large and exploitable labor force willing to work for less. The 2016 promise of 200,000 formally employed Syrians had not come to fruition as of 2018. Just over 80,000 work permits were issued to or renewed by Syrians, and the number of work permits valid at any one point in time was considerably lower, estimated to be between 35,000 and 45,000 (Lenner and Turner 2018). With the program failing to live up to what was assured in 2016, Jordanian implementing agencies focused increasingly on unscrupulous ways to increase the number of work permits issued in order to obtain more funding from the World Bank and EU donor governments, rather than addressing the underlying problems of the agreement and its inability to drastically improve employment opportunities for Syrians (Lenner and Turner 2018).

With the Jordan Compact failing to deliver on promises for both the economic integration of Syrian refugees as well as Jordanian development goals (Arar 2017), and with increasing security concerns on the border between Syria and Jordan, the return of Syrian refugees became an increasingly pressing issue. Human Rights Watch reported that Jordanian authorities deported approximately 400 registered Syrian refugees per month in the first five months of 2017, in addition to about 300 unorganized returns of registered refugees per month that appeared to be voluntary (Human Rights Watch 2017). Another 500 refugees per month were estimated as returning to Syria with little known about the circumstances under which they left (Human Rights Watch 2017).

Turkish President Erdoğan also raised in the issue of returning Syrians, promising that his 2018 military incursions into northeast Turkey near Afrin would allow Syrian refugees residing in Turkey to return home. He alleged, "We will solve the Afrin issue, the Idlib issue and we want that our refugee brothers and sisters return to their country. [Syrian refugees in Turkey] also want this" (*Daily Sabah* 2018). In reality though, the military advances led to the further displacement of Syrians (Al Jazeera 2018b).

In July 2018, the issue of refugees returning to Syria gained momentum. Russia presented an assessment following the Helsinki Summit stating that 890,000 refugees could return to Syria from Lebanon in the near future, in addition to 300,000 from Turkey and 200,000 from EU countries (Perry 2018). Hoping to further encourage returns, the Syrian government issued a decree in October offering amnesty to civilian men who avoided military conscription, although the decree did not include those who fought against the government or joined opposition groups (Loveluck 2018). Then, in November 2018, Lebanese Caretaker Minister for Refugee Affairs Mouin Merehbi announced that twenty refugees who returned to Syria from Lebanon had been killed by the regime and their allied forces (*New Arab* 2018). For those fearful that the Assad government was not genuine in its guarantees of protection, this was devastating evidence that it was still too soon to promote large-scale returns.

Nonetheless, at the time of writing, all three major Syrian hosting countries are eager to return refugees – and some, like Turkey, have already taken concrete steps to do so – partly as a response to the lack of international assistance that has transpired. Despite the US$6 billion pledged for Syrian refugee-hosting countries at the London Conference in February 2016, the UN reported that appeals for the refugee response were only 60 percent funded at the end of 2016 (Danish Refugee Council et al. 2017). On April 5, 2017, the international community and the governments of refugee-hosting countries came together again in Brussels to build on the so-called success of the 2016 conference in London and confirmed the multiyear pledges made earlier. At the end of 2017, the UN reported that the appeal for the refugee response was 53 percent funded (UNOCHA 2018).

Aside from a lack of follow-through on financial commitments, changing dynamics between Global North and Global South host states can also be attributed to the new power hierarchies that were renegotiated after 2015. Major Syrian hosting countries discovered that they can return refugees with few negative consequences from the international community. They have been emboldened by Europe's fear and willingness to throw money at the situation instead of resolving its own internal political problems over the issue of asylum. If European countries are not going to fully deliver on the money that was promised in exchange for continuing to host Syrian refugees, then these countries see little to lose in repatriating them. At the end of the day, it is migrants and refugees themselves who benefit least from the race to the bottom scenario instigated by the EU's shirking of its commitments.

8.6 Implications for Refugees and Migrants

As mentioned in Section 8.4, as of November 2017, Greece had not yet deported a Syrian asylum seeker to Turkey on the grounds of the safe-third-country principle implicit in the EU–Turkey deal. Syrians successfully returned to Turkey had either "accepted to return, had received a negative asylum decision on grounds of merit or had, for various reasons, not been able or willing to complete their asylum procedure in Greece" (Alpes et al. 2017, 2). Those individuals returned to Turkey were temporarily held in detention where they underwent identification and security checks. They were then given the option of staying in government-run camps or leaving to live in an assigned satellite city where they were required to register with the local DGMM office. Yet two readmitted Syrians interviewed by Maybritt Jill Alpes et al. (2017) stated that they had not been able to register with DGMM authorities despite repeated attempts. One of the two Syrians interviewed decided to go back to Syria, explaining, "There was nothing for me in Turkey, I cannot get my *kimlik* [identity card]; I cannot get a work permit" (quoted in Alpes et al. 2017, 7). The other readmitted Syrian was planning to pay a smuggler to reenter the EU for the same reasons (Alpes et al. 2017).

Non-Syrians deported from Greece to Turkey were immediately detained upon arrival with the stated purpose of secondary deportation to respective countries of origin. Despite legal guarantees about access to information, non-Syrians and Turkish lawyers interviewed by Alpes et al. (2017) revealed that readmitted asylum seekers had not been informed about asylum procedures in Turkish detention centers. An interviewed Pakistani asylum seeker who was deported to Turkey in January 2017 was told by an officer at the Kayseri detention center in Istanbul, "Those people who got their asylum rejected in Greece, they are not allowed to apply for asylum in Turkey" and "You came here for deportation, you will all go back to your countries" (quoted in Alpes et al. 2017, 5). In terms of the treatment of migrants and asylum seekers in detention centers, Turkey appears to have reverted to the securitized, pre-2013 approach described in Chapter 5.

Asylum seekers and migrants who remained in Greece were effectively trapped at the threshold of Europe, unable to move onward yet reluctant to return to Turkey, having made risky and costly investments in their original journey. For example, thousands of migrants and asylum seekers were housed in Moira camp on the island of Lesbos, which is managed by the Greek government but financed by the EU. In March 2018, the camp had 5,300 residents in a space meant to accommodate approximately 2,000 people (Strickland 2018). According to a *New York Times* reporter who visited the camp, the conditions in Moira were deplorable:

Rain soaks through the tents, and there is a lack of electricity and hot waters in the showers, even in winter. The public toilets and showers are soiled with feces. As bad as the food is, it often runs out. The lines – for everything – are endless. Fights break out constantly. Violence, theft and rape are constant threats. (Strickland 2018)

Other camps aside from Moira – as well as makeshift centers run by volunteers in cities – were plagued by poor living conditions, unsanitary facilities, and tensions with local Greek communities, prompting human rights groups like Human Rights Watch to call for an end to Greece's containment policy (Strickland 2018). Though the number of arrivals in Greece in 2018 was far fewer than its peak in 2015 and 2016, individuals continued to make the voyage (Magra 2018).

Yet perhaps the most harrowing situation in the post-2015 space is the torture and enslavement faced by migrants and asylum seekers stuck inside Libya. Alarming interviews shared by rights groups and journalists told of human trafficking, smugglers who sell migrants and asylum seekers as slaves, torture, and rape. One eighteen-year-old man from Eritrea told Fatima Naib (2018) of being held captive in a large container-like shed in the city of Bani Waled, southeast of Tripoli. The young man recounted, "They (smugglers) kept us in a large, container-like shed. It was really a cramped area with around 320 of us and had one toilet to share. I stayed there for three months. There were women and children in the same container as the men, children as young as two years, and there were infants born as a result of rape by the Libyan captors" (quoted in Naib 2018).

The conditions in EU-funded detention centers in Libya were not much better. Most official detention centers are under the control of militias and armed groups who see them as moneymaking ventures (Reidy 2017). On an unannounced visit to a Department for Combatting Irregular Migration (DCIM)-affiliated facility, Hanan Salah – Libyan researcher for Human Rights Watch – found approximately 1,300 people in a room built to fit no more than 150 (Reidy 2017). According to Salah, people were sleeping in shifts and had limited access to toilets, and "the hygienic conditions were absolutely inhumane and absolutely disgusting. I spoke with people who hadn't been able to change their clothes in … six months" (quoted in Reidy 2017). The line between EU-funded DCIM detention centers and the criminal enterprises surrounding irregular migration was also unclear, and there were established links between those running official detention facilities and smugglers (Reidy 2017). Individuals who found themselves stuck in this system effectively had two unappealing choices: remain in detention in Libya indefinitely, or ask to be voluntarily repatriated, which for many was not a viable or safe option.

8.7 Conclusion

EU heads of state convened at a European Union leaders' summit in Brussels in June 2018, with migration as one of the key issues on the agenda. Leaders continued to disagree about any prospect for internal burden-sharing and resettlement schemes among EU member states, though they were in consensus about the need for further burden-shifting beyond EU borders. Specifically, leaders called for the establishment of migrant processing centers – described as disembarkation platforms – in North and sub-Saharan African countries such as Morocco, Algeria, Tunisia, Egypt, Libya, Morocco, Niger, and Tunisia. Instead of being permitted to remain in the EU, asylum seekers would be returned to these countries where their asylum claims could be assessed. Following the summit, the leaders of several of the countries mentioned in the proposal stated that they would be unwilling to host any such centers (Rankin 2018). Regardless of whether the processing centers eventually come to fruition, the conclusions of the summit represent a continued trajectory of the EU shirking its responsibility toward human rights commitments in favor of state security.

A parallel tactic to offshoring migrant and refugee hosting increasingly used by various European governments is the targeting of civil society and humanitarian organizations that attempt to assist migrants and refugees. The Italian government refused to allow humanitarian rescue boats to dock in its ports in June 2018 (Sunderland 2018), and Malta followed suit with a hardline approach, disallowing a rescue boat carrying 233 migrants to dock for five days (Masters and Schmidt 2018). On May 29, 2018, Hungary introduced draft legislation that restricted the ability of NGOs and aid workers to offer services to asylum seekers, enhancing limitations first introduced by the Hungarian Parliament in February (UNHCR 2018). All of these measures will have a negative, and potentially fatal, impact on migrants and refugees either at Europe's shores or already within its borders.

At the end of the day, migrants and refugees benefit least from Europe's continued border externalization efforts. In exchange for increased international assistance and development funds offered since 2015, Middle East host countries were meant to improve formal access to education, employment, and social services for refugees. In other words, financial assistance was meant to incentivize the adoption of a more liberal engagement policy. Yet with not all promised funding delivered, and with a lack of accountability mechanisms, the policies on the ground – at least for individuals residing in urban situations – continue to most closely resemble indifference. Migrants and refugees are employed in informal sectors, access to health care and education – when available – is primarily provided by INGOs and NGOs, and migrants and refugees are integrated into host state economies and societies in a de facto sense.

Europe's approach to migration externalization since the creation of the Schengen space has not changed course, though there was a momentary hesitation followed by a hastened return to business-as-usual policies in 2015. The previous chapters in this book explored the ramifications of this process. Transit-turned-host states in the Middle East and North Africa developed policies of indifference to mitigate the buildup of migrants and refugees effectively stuck within their borders. If the EU continues along the path of doing everything in its power to prevent migrants and refugees from arriving within its territory, we should expect to see other patterns repeated elsewhere as well. Host states in the Middle East may implement de jure liberal policies if there are diplomatic and economic gains to be had from doing so, or they may utilize repressive policies when migrants or refugees are deemed a security threat or their presence becomes highly politicized. Yet the day-to-day lives of migrants and refugees themselves will primarily continue to be characterized by informality and an uncertainty about whether to remain, to carry onward, or to return home.

9 | *Conclusion and Avenues Forward*

9.1 Scope Conditions and Generalizability

This book explored the phenomenon of migrant and refugee settlement in three Middle East and North Africa countries from the perspective of migrant and refugee groups as well as each host state. It asked: Why do host states permit migrants and refugees to remain indefinitely, and what determines whether host states treat them inclusively, exclusively, or with indifference? It argued that we can better understand the migrant and refugee engagement strategies of host states if we account for indifference as a policy option, in addition to liberal or repressive policies. Identifying indifference – and considering the possibility that it is a strategic option utilized by host states, rather than the absence of state capacity – helps to elucidate approaches that might otherwise be considered neglect or an absence of engagement. Incorporating the option of strategic indifference also allows us to grasp the extent of cross-national variation in migration and refugee policy outcomes in Middle East host states and capture changes in policy over time.

This book was primarily concerned with theory-building: constructing the concept of strategic indifference and examining its use for understanding the engagement strategies present in key transit-turned-host countries. Yet indifference may also be applicable to liberal democratic host states in the Global North where there is little done to prevent or control informal work by undocumented migrants (countries such as Italy, Spain, or the United States), or for democratic host countries in the Global South that have only recently become immigration-receivers. For example, although South Korea has sanctions in place for undocumented workers and their employers,

in practice the [South] Korean government mostly ignores the illegal hiring of foreign workers and usually does nothing to find or deport them. The law imposes a hefty fine (up to 10 million won) on employers of undocumented workers, but few employers pay any fine at all. (Seol and Skrentny 2004, 502)

While indifference may look qualitatively similar in these different contexts, the use of indifference as a policy through which to attract funding from international sources and the benefits that host states receive from such a policy are likely to be specific to Global South states due to their geopolitical positioning.

Regime type is also key. As demonstrated in Chapters 3, 4, and 5, indifference is a tenable strategy until the diplomatic, economic, or security incentives surrounding migration in a host state change. The incentives for switching from a policy of indifference to a more repressive or more liberal policy are likely to differ for nondemocratic states. While liberal democracies historically reformed their migration policies due to domestic legal institutions being forced to bring migrants and refugees into the social and economic structures of host states, the insights of this study demonstrate that nondemocratic states are likely to respond to different incentives.

The official government narrative of policy change in Morocco was that reform in 2013 emanated from civil society, but a closer examination in Chapter 4 revealed that a primary motivation behind the king's announcement of reform was international shaming. While it was local civil society actors who brought the topic to international attention, the Moroccan government acted in order to prevent the tarnishing of its image as a moderate, human rights–abiding state. The reform also allowed the government to co-opt civil society critics, including international and domestic NGOs and migrant community groups. By inviting these actors to the table regarding the implementation of the reform process and by undertaking periodic consultations with them, the government – in particular the newly expanded Ministry for Migration Affairs – reduced the risk of future criticism. The case of Morocco also demonstrated that the use of migration policy as an instrument of influence can be directed toward sending states. One explanation for the timing of the Moroccan policy reform discussed in Chapter 6 is the country's desire to play a leading role in West Africa, both economically and geopolitically. Because Morocco wanted to take on a leadership position, it had to put on a welcoming face toward migrants originating from West African countries. Tied to the foreign-policy goal of gaining clout among its southern neighbors, the migration reform was likely also at least partially a bid for the support of African countries in Morocco's control of Western Sahara.

For Turkey, the EU accession process of the early and mid-2000s provided the initial impetus for reform, leading Turkey to begin the process of examining and conforming its domestic legislation in several policy areas, including migration, in order to meet EU standards. Yet even after negotiations with Europe collapsed, reform in Turkey continued due to an understanding among a faction of the country's political elite that grasped the importance of Turkey's geostrategic position in regard to migration. The decision was also driven in part by several cases brought before the European Court of Human Rights (Kirişçi 2012), as well as perceived diplomatic benefits from Turkey's European neighbors.

As such, in both the Moroccan and Turkish cases, migration policy reform was used to minimize international shaming and gain diplomatic benefits from neighboring states. The cases of Morocco and Turkey suggest that these two factors are individually necessary and jointly sufficient for a transit-turned-host state to enact a more liberal policy. Yet this pathway to reform also suggests that while a resulting policy will be de jure liberal, in practice, state engagement will continue to look much like indifference. James Hollifield, Philip Martin, and Pia Orrenius (2014) pose the question: why do failed immigration control policies persist in today's labor-importing countries, often long past the point when it becomes apparent that they are not working? In translating and applying this question to countries of the Global South, we might similarly ask: why are new immigration policies introduced when they appear to be mostly for show? The answer lies in Morocco and Turkey's semi-authoritarian contexts.

Semi-authoritarian regimes are adept at imposing rules, and yet the outward appearance of democracy and human rights still matters (Brown 2011). Both Morocco and Turkey viewed the issue of migration, as well as migration reform, as a critical bargaining instrument to achieve other diplomatic and economic goals. This is in support of Katharina Natter's (2018) "illiberal paradox," whereby semi-authoritarian states are incentivized to enact more liberal migration policies, not because of prevailing human rights norms but because of economic or foreign-policy interests. It also helps explain why the liberal strategies adopted by Turkey and Morocco have not fully taken shape on the ground. While these states were rewarded for enacting more liberal policies, they may not see the same benefit from ensuring that the policies are fully implemented (Norman 2019). In both Turkey and Morocco, migrants and refugees continue to participate primarily in the informal economy, and international and nongovernmental organizations continue to be the leading providers of services and assistance. Furthermore, liberal policies developed primarily in response to economic and foreign-policy interests may be subject to rapid reversals, as evidenced by Turkey's changing policy toward Syrians in mid-2019.

The relative autonomy that the monarchy had in enacting policy reform due to Morocco's semi-authoritarian context is also notable. Turkey's reform process is perhaps more illustrative and generalizable for liberal democratic countries in that the legislative drafting committee – led by individuals from Turkey's Ministry of the Interior – had to successfully sell the legislation to members of parliament. It is also key that the issue of migration was not highly politicized at the time of reform in either Turkey or Morocco, making the new legislation less contentious and more palatable for a domestic audience. While semi-authoritarian governments have fewer veto points and are adept at stifling opposition and suppressing electoral competition (Olcot and Ottaway 1999), leaders may still worry about public discontent on issue-specific topics leading to a loss of regime legitimacy. In thinking about how and whether this explanation for shifting from an indifferent to a more liberal approach transfers to other regions, the top-down and semi-authoritarian governance context, as well as Morocco and Turkey's geographic and geostrategic location between powerful countries in the Global North and sending countries in the Global South, are both critical considerations.

Tunisia could be an interesting comparative case in this regard in that it is a transit-turned-host country in North Africa for migrants and refugees attempting to reach Europe, but Tunisia transitioned to – and has thus far maintained – democratic governance after its 2011 revolution. Since the early 2000s, Tunisia cooperated with the EU on issues of migration, agreeing to prevent irregular migration in exchange for development aid, increased trade, and visa liberalization for Tunisian citizens (Boubakri 2013). In the period after the revolution, Tunisia and the EU signed a mobility partnership which provides a framework for future cooperation on issues including readmission, border controls, and visa facilitation (Natter 2018). The new democratically elected government will thus have to decide whether to accept European development aid and enact securitized migration policies to the same extent as its authoritarian predecessor, or to take a more nuanced, less security-oriented approach (Natter 2015).

Unlike the cases of Morocco and Turkey, Egypt illustrates how political economy factors can incentivize a continued indifference toward migrant and refugee groups, although the unstable post-2013 political climate led to a more securitized approach whereby the state was willing to expend additional resources for the purposes of policing, detaining, and deporting migrants and refugees, moving Egypt closer to a repressive strategy. While African migrants and refugees were sometimes detained and deported prior to 2013, this increasing securitization began in earnest with the case of Syrian refugees following the Egyptian military coup that ousted former President Mohamed Morsi. Syrians became the subject of a government-organized media campaign that referred to them as terrorists allied with the Muslim Brotherhood and former President Mohamed Morsi's supporters. In 2014, concerns over terrorism and its alleged links with migrants in Egypt spread to all migrant and refugee nationalities, reflecting the increasingly authoritarian turn of the post-2013 military leadership and President el-Sisi's government more broadly. By 2015, the government was taking steps to further solidify and legalize its authoritarianism, drafting and implementing laws to curtail any form of opposition or contention (Hamzawy 2017). After the regime consolidated its hold on power, the issue of migration was no longer as politicized, and the government instead began looking toward Europe to capitalize on its ability to host migrants and refugees following in the footsteps of Morocco and Turkey.

In 2016, Egypt successfully passed a domestic anti-smuggling law, which was the culmination of the work of the National Coordinating Committee on Combatting and Preventing Illegal Immigration mentioned in Chapter 3. It also decreased the number of boats leaving its shores in the summer of 2017, leading the EU to shower Egypt with praise. In 2018, Austrian Chancellor Sebastian Kurz called Egypt "efficient" and commended Egyptian President Abdel Fattah el-Sisi for providing "an example when it comes to illegal migration and people smuggling" (Al Jazeera 2018a). In January 2019, the High Commissioner for Refugees, Filippo Grandi, met directly with President el-Sisi to applaud Egypt's refugee hosting and discuss el-Sisi's upcoming role as chair of the African Union (UNHCR 2019). And in February 2019, leaders from the EU and the Arab League met in Sharm el-Sheikh for an inaugural summit to discuss migration, security, and business opportunities. In exchange for European recognition and funding, the EU asked for Egypt's assistance in intercepting and returning migrant boats leaving from Libya (Cook 2019). Catherine Woolard, secretary general of the European Council of Refugees and Exile, summarized Egypt's new approach to the EU, stating, "It is quite clear that el-Sisi is playing the migration game. He understands how desperate Europe is to try and prevent people from arriving in Europe and he is willing to exploit that" (quoted in Segura 2018).

Of course, preventing migrants and refugees from traveling onward to Europe means that more individuals will end up residing semi-permanently in Egypt. As the cases of Morocco and Turkey demonstrate, increased interest and funding from Europe does not necessarily translate into better policies on the ground for individual migrants and refugees. This is because European funding has done little to incentivize Middle East and North African host states to invest enough resources to make long-term integration for migrants and refugees feasible or desirable. Instead, European money will probably continue to inoculate the el-Sisi regime from international criticism for its human rights abuses, all in the name of migration prevention.

The generalizability of this study is limited to other migrant and refugee-receiving host states that can be classified as semi-authoritarian and that are influenced by powerful neighboring states with strong migration control preferences. Yet even with these scope conditions, these findings have implications for understanding migration policy decisions in other parts of the world. In other words, the theory of strategic indifference – as well as the reasons host states switch from indifference to other policies – is not unique to the Mediterranean or the Middle East and North Africa. This theory and its methodology can travel to other regions such as South America or elsewhere in Asia where states are undergoing a similar transformation from countries of conduit to countries of settlement.

Australia has used safe-third-country agreements, the offshoring of asylum seekers, and capacity-building funding measures to convince Papua New Guinea and Indonesia to prevent and contain migrants hoping to reach Australia (FitzGerald 2019). Similarly, the United States has attempted to enact safe-third-country agreements with

Mexico, Guatemala, Honduras, and El Salvador, has made foreign aid to these countries conditional on effectively curtailing irregular migration, and in the late 2000s the US government financed the upgrading of Mexico's migration control databases in return for access to the information (FitzGerald 2019). Comparing the use of external migration controls in Australia, the United States, and the EU, David FitzGerald (2019) asserts that only certain aspects of Europe's policies are unique:

The individual pieces of the remote control strategies themselves are common, with the exception of Frontex, which does not have parallels in the North American or Australian cases. Restrictive visa policies, carrier sanctions, liaison officers posted abroad, readmission agreements, publicity campaigns trying to convince potential migrants to stay in place, safe third-country and origin-country agreements, and agreements on which country is responsible for hearing asylum claims can all be found in some form in the other contexts. What is unusual are the supranational factors that promote or restrain these policies and the many pathways that they develop. (190)

Given these similarities, we may also expect that the transformation of countries like Indonesia, Papa New Guinea, Mexico, or Guatemala into buffer zones – and thus countries of settlement – on behalf of Australia and the United States, respectively, will result in similar outcomes in the new host states as well. When differences occur, scholars should question whether they are due to domestic politics around migration, regime type and governance, the nature of the relationship with regional hegemons, or other factors not yet assessed. I propose that we are likely to see indifference at play elsewhere as new transit-turned-host countries contend with – and attempt to strategically manage – inward migration.

9.2 Accidental Ethnography

In conducting the research for this book I do not claim to have engaged in formal ethnography, but I did adopt an ethnographic sensibility as described by Lisa Wedeen (2010) and Lee Ann Fujii (2015). By recording informal interactions, seemingly mundane moments, and small geographic or aesthetic details in more than 300 pages of field notes, I was able to reflect – both in the field and later in the process of writing – on the broader political and social world in which such moments and details are embedded (Fujii 2015). For example, by both formally interviewing individual migrants and refugees while also paying attention to power hierarchies and the importance of networks, I came to understand the complexity of the system that migrants and refugees face in attempting to access services and assistance in host states.

In Egypt, I formally interviewed Amina – a twenty-six-year-old woman from Khartoum, Sudan – who is an employee of Tadamon, a migration-focused NGO with several locations in Cairo. I took an hour microbus ride in addition to a ten-minute tuk-tuk ride from central Cairo to meet Amina on the 6th of October at Tadamon office, located in a large villa in a residential part of the Cairo suburb. The villa was likely built to house a well-off Egyptian family, but without buyers it was being leased out to Tadamon with financial backing from the UNHCR. Inside her spacious office lit by afternoon sun, Amina and I spoke about Tadamon, her home in Sudan, and her life in Cairo. Her temperament during our interview was tranquil and friendly, but when an older couple – two Sudanese clients of Amina's – entered her office, she became serious and authoritative, meticulously walking the line between expressing concern and conveying efficiency in investigating their case. The couple came to Tadamon because they were having health problems as well as difficulty paying their monthly rent. Amina took down all their information – as well as that of their children – and assured them that Caritas, an international NGO, would be able to help them. Once the couple left, I asked Amina what she planned to do with the forms she had filled out and she explained, "Oh, that's just an average case. They're having the same problems as everyone else." She would give the information to another Tadamon employee up on the third floor, who would then get in touch with Caritas and the UNHCR to inform them of the case.

As Amina explained this process, I thought back to another interaction from several weeks earlier while speaking with a representative at the UNHCR office, also located in the city. I asked the representative about the refugees lining up outside the UNHCR office, whom I had noticed on my way inside. She smiled at me conspiratorially, informing me that "there'll always be people who wait out there, no matter how well or not well the system works. They think that if they're there physically, then we'll move through their case faster. Sometimes they even sleep out there." After my meeting I stood outside the UNHCR office checking my phone and was approached by a man who wanted to show me his yellow UNHCR card, designating his status as an asylum seeker. He started explaining his situation – how long he had been in Egypt and how he hoped to move onward – and asked for help. As he was speaking, more men and women gathered around me in a circle. As one person finished relaying their story – the difficulties they faced in Egypt and how badly they needed to be resettled – another individual would come and begin telling me his or hers. Most began by showing me their blue or yellow UNHCR cards or sometimes even health documents and medical receipts. Reading the dates on the UNHCR cards was heartbreaking. A blue or yellow card lists each time a person has met with someone at the UNHCR, and one woman's card read: 2009, 2011, 2014. She told me that her next appointment with the UNHCR was not scheduled until 2019.

I tried offering the names and phone numbers of the organizations I had learned about during the course of my research in Egypt: Caritas, PISTIC, All-Saints, Tadamon, the Egyptian Foundation for Refugee Rights, but those gathered around me responded despondently, saying they had tried the various organizations and no longer trusted them. Those with health problems had already visited Caritas. When I suggested Tadamon, one man told me the organization had a policy of only helping each client on one occasion. Presumably when these individuals saw me – a white American woman – standing outside the UNHCR office, they thought that I may be able to offer some better option than turning to the organizations that had thus far failed them.

Returning to my conversation with Amina, I wondered whether she was exaggerating the services and assistance offered by Tadamon. Were the individuals waiting outside the UNHCR not being forthcoming about having sought out the organization's services? What is more likely is that the migration and refugee assistance network in Egypt is confusing and overwhelming. It is informal, bureaucratic, and based on personal connections, reflecting in some ways the broader governmental environment in which it operates. Without knowledge of how the UNHCR-INGO-NGO system functions, and without friends or family directly connected to an organization, it is difficult to find one's way to any of the services on offers or to obtain correct information on policies and practices. Without the ability to triangulate my formal interview with Amina, my conversation with the UNHCR administrator, and my accidental ethnographic moment that occurred outside the UNHCR office, I may not have gained this further insight into the convoluted service-provision system that migrants and refugees must contend with.

While these anecdotes from Egypt highlight the downside of indifference for migrants and refugees – leaving them in a precarious and informal position, subject to rapidly changing security environments and absent important legal protections – my interviews with migrants and refugees and other moments of accidental ethnography also pointed to an upside. Thanks to this multifaceted approach, I understood how a policy of indifference sometimes benefits migrants and refugees, allowing them social and economic flexibility and the opportunity to exist in relative anonymity. For example, in Gaziantep, Turkey I met Tareq, a twenty-five-year-old Syrian man with shoulder length hair and an easy, nonchalant manner. Tareq originally left Syria for Egypt prior to the 2011 revolution to work in tourism with friends he knew there. He stayed just over two years until the end of 2012, but throughout that time he did not renew his residency. He returned briefly to Syria and then planned to travel again to Egypt but was denied entry for having overstayed his previous visa. Instead, he came to Turkey in 2013 and had not left the country by the time we spoke in mid-2015. He had friends in Gaziantep – mostly other Syrians originally from Aleppo – and through them he was able to find a position as a barista in a Syrian-run coffee shop.

One day as we were talking, Tareq's carefree manner of speaking turned heavyhearted as he discussed his family and friends still in Aleppo. He tried to gauge my opinions on the conflict in Syria, but mostly ended up telling me about his own frustrations. "I just want the war to end," he lamented. "The fighting has to end." He simultaneously wanted to return to Syria and to study in Europe or America, asking me, "Which is better, do you think? Europe or America? For studying international law?" In response to some of my questions about his life in Turkey and his interactions with government-run services, Tareq told me he never received any help from the government or any nongovernmental organization during his stay. "There are other people who need help more than me," he explained. "I have a job, the people without jobs need help. For me, life is good." He added, "They don't have a problem with Syrians working in Turkey, so that's something." For Tareq, a policy of indifference was something of a service in and of itself.

Perhaps the most critical observation I made through an ethnogra-
phically sensitive approach was a corrective to my own thinking about
the possibilities available to migrants and refugees living in Global
South states. All too often – in the interest of highlighting the securitized borders and violent policing practices that keep migrants and
refugees from accessing Western states (Jones 2016) – individuals who
do not make it past such borders and instead live in transit countries are
dismissed by researchers and the media. Because they reside in states
where their rights may not be recognized in law and formal policy, they
are perceived not to have agency and unable to contribute in important
ways to their temporary host state. This may be a result of the over-
stated focus on the lives and well-being of refugees residing in camps, as
addressed in Chapter 1. For example, Arthur Helton (2007) refers to
refugees in Dadaab camp in Kenya as "being condemned to wasted and
fearful lives" (154) in the absence of more effective humanitarian
action. Yet this assumption discounts the experiences of the vast majority of migrants and refugees who do not arrive in Western host countries and instead reside semipermanently in countries such as Egypt,
Morocco, and Turkey.

While individuals like Deng, Amadu, Youssef, Noora, Amina, and
Tareq – and all the other individuals who contributed their stories to
the research in this book – may live in precarity, their lives are not
forever put on hold while they await a chance to move on, to be
resettled, or to return home. This book demonstrates that migrants
and refugees residing in countries like Egypt, Morocco, and Turkey can
find access to livelihoods – albeit usually informally – and find ways of
sending their children to school, searching for access to health care,
forming communities, and engaging in social and sometimes political
activities. Their lives, struggles, and accomplishments – as well as the
policies they live under – are as worth understanding as the lives of
individuals who successfully make it across Western borders into states
in the EU and elsewhere.

9.3 Where from Here?

More than a decade ago Helton (2007) argued that Western containment policies toward refugee crises of the time were not a lasting
solution, and that a greater degree of international cooperation was
necessary to render refugee responses more workable and enduring.

Following the 2015 European refugee "crisis," most countries of the world seemed to agree with Helton's decade-old assessment that the containment of migrants and refugees was still not working, and that human migration should be managed with greater global cooperation and, allegedly, with a human-centered approach. In September 2016, 193 countries adopted the New York Declaration for Refugees and Migrants, laying out a process for the development of two global compacts; one on global migration and one on refugees.

These processes culminated in the adoption of the Global Compact for Safe, Orderly, and Regular Migration in December 2018 by 164 nations of the world – the United States and Australia being notable exceptions – and the adoption of its companion agreement, the Global Compact on Refugees, by 181 countries. The Global Compact for Safe, Orderly, and Regular Migration is historic, representing the first time that UN member states have formally agreed to govern migration in a comprehensive, multilateral manner. But what bearing will this non-binding agreement have on the current pattern of states outsourcing migration management to transit countries and making access to territory increasingly restrictive for both migrants and refugees? As the Assistant High Commissioner for Protection told the Executive Committee of the UNHCR in 2018, "we are facing a watershed moment where two sets of values have emerged in two distinct modes of discourse. It is difficult to reconcile how the positive developments of the past year have occurred alongside the seemingly endless volley of assaults on refugees" (quoted in McAdam 2019).

When United Nations member states convened in New York in July 2017 to finalize the text for the Global Compact for Safe, Orderly, and Regular Migration, General Assembly President Miroslav Lajčák stated that the compact "can provide a new platform for cooperation. And it can be a resource, in finding the right balance between the rights of people and the sovereignty of States" (UN General Assembly 2018). Europe's actions since 2015, and the subsequent actions of host states in the Middle East and sub-Saharan Africa, make it clear that the balance is currently weighted heavily in favor of state sovereignty, at the expense of the rights of migrants and refugees. Rather than greater responsibility and burden sharing in the wake of the 2015 refugee "crisis", European states have instead turned to increasingly far-fetched solutions in order to prevent the arrival of migrants and refugees within their borders. This will likely lead to further migrant deaths in the Mediterranean and will certainly lead to the further buildup of migrants and refugees residing semipermanently in transit-turned-host countries such as Egypt, Morocco, and Turkey.

For the compact to have a meaningful impact on the lives of migrants and refugees in the MENA region, European leaders must follow through with implementing the principles set out in the compact. Most notable among these is the idea of safe migration, which will only be ensured if EU countries provide significantly more pathways for legal immigration rather than pushing refugees, asylum seekers, and other vulnerable migrants toward dangerous voyages. The patterns of migrant and refugee settlement and the resulting implications for MENA host states analyzed in this book can be directly traced back to the EU's changing external security regime as a result of creating the Schengen space in 1985, closing off many of the previously accessible opportunities for obtaining visas or claiming asylum. In principle, objective (5) of the compact aims to reverse this, calling for the "enhanced availability and flexibility" of pathways for regular migration (Global Compact for Migration 2018). This includes facilitating regional and cross-regional labor mobility through international and bilateral cooperation arrangements, as well as providing humanitarian visas, private sponsorships, access to education for children, and temporary work permits for those forced to leave their countries due to "precarious situations" (Global Compact for Migration 2018, 11–12). It remains to be seen whether states are actually prepared to drastically increase the number of visas – for which an individual does not need to be highly wealthy or educated to obtain – and the number of resettlement spots it would take to ensure avenues for safe migration.

In the absence of a systemic change that allows for increased pathways for regular migration, the topic of host state policies in the MENA region – and the treatment of migrants and refugees therein – becomes more critical than ever. The research presented in this book makes it clear that engagement policies in MENA host states cannot be improved merely by throwing money at the situation and subsequently turning a blind eye, as has been the EU's modus operandi for several decades but especially following the 2015 refugee "crisis."

Chapter 7 examined the role of international migration organizations in Egypt, Morocco, and Turkey, finding that financial incentives will only go so far in allowing for influence over host state policies. Furthermore, the extent to which international organizations operating in the MENA region are able to convince host state governments to carry out the agendas or preferences of Western donor states depends on (1) the extent to which the topic of migration has been politicized or securitized in the host state; (2) the ability of international organizations to frame or reframe policy areas; and (3) the preexisting relationships that international organizations have developed in the host state. Chapter 8 looked at the relationships between international organizations, Global North states, and MENA host states – in addition to diplomacy and security in the Mediterranean region more broadly – after 2015, arguing that host states in the Mediterranean region, and sending states further afield in sub-Saharan Africa, benefited from Europe's post-2015 political crisis by using migration diplomacy to extract more concessions than they were able to previously. Those benefiting least from this arrangement are individual migrants and refugees who have even fewer options than they did previously for onward travel, most vividly evidenced by the torture and enslavement of migrants and asylum seekers either stuck inside or pushed back to Libya with the assistance of European funding.

The findings from both chapters demonstrate that host states in the Middle East and North Africa are not merely the recipients of the policy choices of more powerful states or international actors as they are often framed. They make strategic decisions about how best to allocate resources and pursue engagement policies, which may or may not be in line with the preferences of international organizations and donor countries in the Global North. In other words, these states are not merely migrant and refugee hosting vessels; they have their own stakes in the global migration and refugee system. Taking the incentives of MENA states more seriously and finding ways to give them a meaningful and equitable seat at the table while still ensuring that they are abiding by international standards and upholding migrant and refugee rights is undoubtedly a challenging task. Yet only in doing so can we develop a more just and effective migrant and refugee protection system that addresses the well-being of migrants, refugees, and host-country nationals at present and in the future.

Appendix A Elite Interview Table

ID	Organization	Location	Month of interview	Saturation	Format	Length	Recording	Language
Category: International migration bodies				High				
Elite Interviewee A	UNHCR	Cairo, Egypt	9/2014		Semistructured	56 min	Audio recording	English
Elite Interviewee B	UNHCR	Cairo, Egypt	10/2014		Semistructured	30 min	Audio recording	English
Elite Interviewee C	IOM Egypt Office	Cairo, Egypt	9/2014		Semistructured	1 h 15 min	Audio recording	English
Elite Interviewee D	IOM Regional Office	Cairo, Egypt	9/2014		Semistructured	25 min	Audio recording	English
Elite Interviewee E	IOM Egypt Office	Cairo, Egypt	10/2014		Semistructured	45 min	Concurrent notes & supplementary notes w/i 1 h	English
Elite Interviewee F	UNHCR	Alexandria, Egypt	10/2014		Semistructured	49 min	Audio recording	English
Elite Interviewee G	UNHCR	Rabat, Morocco	8/2013		Semistructured	35 min	Audio recording	English
Elite Interviewee H	UNHCR	Rabat, Morocco	1/2015		Semistructured	1 h 1 min	Audio recording	English
Elite Interviewee I	IOM	Rabat, Morocco	2/2015		Semistructured	1 h 4 min	Audio recording	English
Elite Interviewee J	UNHCR	Istanbul, Turkey	8/2014		Semistructured	45 min	Concurrent notes & supplementary notes w/i 1 h	English
Elite Interviewee K	UNHCR	Istanbul, Turkey	5/2015		Semistructured	54 min	Audio recording	English
Elite Interviewee L	IOM	Ankara, Turkey	5/2015		Semistructured	22 min	Audio recording	English

(cont.)

ID	Organization	Location	Month of interview	Saturation	Format	Length	Recording	Language
Elite Interviewee M	IOM	Ankara, Turkey	5/2015		Semistructured	1 h 4 min	Audio recording	English
Elite Interviewee N	UNICEF	Ankara, Turkey	5/2015		Semistructured	35 min	Audio recording	English
Elite Interviewee O	United Nations Population Fund	Gaziantep, Turkey	6/2015		Semistructured	30 min	Concurrent notes & supplementary notes w/i 1 h	English
Elite Interviewee P	Office for the Coordination of Humanitarian Affairs (OCHA)	Gaziantep, Turkey	6/2015		Semistructured	44 min	Audio recording	English
Elite Interviewee Q	UNHCR	Gaziantep, Turkey	6/2015		Semistructured	45 min	Concurrent notes & supplementary notes w/i 1 h	English

High

Category: Local NGOs/universities

ID	Organization	Location	Month of interview	Saturation	Format	Length	Recording	Language
Elite Interviewee R	Tadamon	Cairo, Egypt	9/2014		Semistructured	1 h 1 min	Audio recording	English
Elite Interviewee S	St. Andrews Refugee Services (StARS)	Cairo, Egypt	9/2014		Semistructured	1 h	Concurrent notes & supplementary notes w/i 1 h	English
Elite Interviewee T	African Hope Learning Center	Cairo, Egypt	10/2014		Semistructured	38 min	Audio recording	English
Elite Interviewee U	Egyptian Foundation for Refugee Rights (EFRR)	Cairo, Egypt	10/2014		Semistructured	1 h 33 min	Audio recording	English & Arabic

Interviewee	Organisation	Location	Date	Type	Duration	Recording	Language
Elite Interviewee V	Egyptian Foundation for Refugee Rights (EFRR)	Cairo, Egypt	10/2014	Semistructured	1 h 33 min	Audio recording	English & Arabic
Elite Interviewee W	Egyptian Initiative for Personal Rights (EIPR)	Alexandria, Egypt	11/2014	Semistructured	1 h 7 min	Audio recording	English
Elite Interviewee X	Egyptian Initiative for Personal Rights (EIPR)	Alexandria, Egypt	11/2014	Semistructured	1 h 7 min	Audio recording	English
Elite Interviewee Y	Refugees Solidarity Movement	Alexandria, Egypt	11/2014	Semistructured	1 h 6 min	Audio recording	English
Elite Interviewee Z	Association Marocaine des Droits Humains (AMDH)	Rabat, Morocco	1/2015	Semistructured	57 min	Audio recording	Arabic
Elite Interviewee AA	Organisation Démocratique du Travail (ODT)	Rabat, Morocco	2/2015	Semistructured	36 min	Audio recording	French & Arabic with interpretation assistance
Elite Interviewee AB	Groupe Antiraciste D'Accompagnement et De Defense Des Etrangers et Migrants (GADEM)	Rabat, Morocco	3/2015	Semistructured	40 min	Audio recording	English
Elite Interviewee AC	Fondation Orient-Occident (FOO)	Rabat, Morocco	3/2015	Semistructured	15 min	Audio recording	English & Arabic

(cont.)

ID	Organization	Location	Month of interview	Saturation	Format	Length	Recording	Language
Elite Interviewee AD	ABCDS	Oujda, Morocco	4/2015		Semistructured	30 min	Concurrent notes & supplementary notes w/i 1 h	English & Arabic
Elite Interviewee AE	Rascine	Casablanca, Morocco	4/2015		Semistructured	45 min	Concurrent notes & supplementary notes w/i 1 h	English
Elite Interviewee AF	Migrant Solidarity Network Istanbul	Istanbul, Turkey	8/2014		Semistructured	39 min	Audio recording	English
Elite Interviewee AG	Istanbul Bilgi University	Istanbul, Turkey	5/2015		Semistructured	40 min	Concurrent notes & supplementary notes w/i 1 h	English
Elite Interviewee AH	Human Resources Development Foundation (HRDF)	Istanbul, Turkey	5/2015		Semistructured	45 min	Audio recording	English
Elite Interviewee AI	Human Resources Development Foundation (HRDF)	Istanbul, Turkey	5/2015		Semistructured	52 min	Audio recording	English
Elite Interviewee AJ	Helsinki Citizens Assembly	Istanbul, Turkey	5/2015		Semistructured	1 h 30 min	Audio recording	English
Elite Interviewee AK	Migrant Solidarity Network	Ankara, Turkey	5/2015		Semistructured	44 min	Audio recording	English
Elite Interviewee AL	Association for Solidarity with Asylum-Seekers and Migrants (ASAM)	Ankara, Turkey	5/2015		Semistructured	1 h 6 min	Audio recording	English

| Elite Interviewee AM | Asylum and Migration Research Center (IGAM) | Ankara, Turkey | 5/2015 | | Semistructured | 1 h 54 min | Audio recording | English |

Category: International NGOs

Medium

Elite Interviewee AN	Catholic Relief Services (CRS)	Cairo, Egypt	10/2014	Semistructured	39 min	Audio recording	English
Elite Interviewee AO	Médecins Sans Frontières (MSF)	Alexandria, Egypt	11/2014	Semistructured	33 min	Audio recording	English
Elite Interviewee AP	Africa and Middle East Refugee Assistance (AMERA)	Cairo, Egypt	11/2014	Semistructured	56 min	Audio recording	English
Elite Interviewee AQ	Caritas	Cairo, Egypt	11/2014	Semistructured	29 min	Concurrent notes & supplementary notes w/i 1 h	English
Elite Interviewee AR	Caritas	Cairo, Egypt	11/2014	Semistructured	20 min	Concurrent notes & supplementary notes w/i 1 h	English
Elite Interviewee AS	Africa and Middle East Refugee Assistance (AMERA)	Cairo, Egypt	11/2014	Semistructured	30 min	Concurrent notes & supplementary notes w/i 1 h	English
Elite Interviewee AT	Caritas	Rabat, Morocco	3/2015	Semistructured	25 min	Audio recording	English
Elite Interviewee AU	Syrian-American Medical Society (SAMS)	Gaziantep, Turkey	6/2015	Semistructured	15 min	Audio recording	English

(*cont.*)

ID	Organization	Location	Month of interview	Saturation	Format	Length	Recording	Language
Category: Government officials				Low				
Elite Interviewee AV	Ministry of Interior	Cairo, Egypt	10/2014		Semistructured	20 min	Concurrent notes & supplementary notes w/i 1 h	English
Elite Interviewee AW	National Coordinating Committee for Combating and Preventing Illegal Migration	Cairo, Egypt	10/2014		Semistructured	31 min	Audio recording	English
Elite Interviewee AX	Palestinian Consulate	Alexandria, Egypt	11/2014		Semistructured	43 min	Audio recording	English & Arabic
Elite Interviewee AY	Ministry of Foreign Affairs	Cairo, Egypt	11/2014		Semistructured	1 h	Audio recording	English
Elite Interviewee AZ	Conseil National des Droits de l'Homme (CNDH)	Rabat, Morocco	3/2015		Semistructured	58 min	Audio recording	English
Elite Interviewee BA	Ministry of Foreign Moroccans and Migrant Affairs	Rabat, Morocco	4/2015		Semistructured	1 h 9 min	Audio recording	French & Arabic with interpretation assistance

Appendix B Migrant and Refugee Interview Table

Pseudonym	Gender	Age	City	Month of interview	Language	Nationality
Egypt						
Kareem	Male	30	Cairo	9/2014	English	Central African Republic
Hady	Male	36	Cairo	9/2014	English & Arabic	Syria
Mohammed	Male	29	Cairo	9/2014	Arabic	Syria
Ahmed	Male	42	Cairo	9/2014	Arabic	Sudan
Deng	Male	28	Cairo	9/2014	English	Sudan
Kamal	Male	44	Cairo	9/2014	Arabic	Sudan
Abdul Wahood	Male	38	Cairo	10/2014	Arabic	Sudan
Rayan	Female	41	Cairo	10/2014	Arabic	Sudan
Nadia	Female	42	Cairo	10/2014	Arabic	Sudan
Hiba	Female	27	Cairo	10/2014	Arabic	Sudan
Amina	Female	26	Cairo	10/2014	Arabic	Sudan
Ahmed	Male	35	Cairo	10/2014	Arabic	Sudan
Amirah	Female	38	Cairo	10/2014	English & Arabic	Sudan
Raoul	Male	42	Cairo	10/2014	English	Congo
Yonas	Male	25	Cairo	10/2014	Arabic	Eritrea
Jemal	Male	43	Cairo	10/2014	Arabic	Eritrea
Fatima	Female	34	Cairo	10/2014	Arabic	Sudan
Abdelrahman	Male	37	Cairo	10/2014	Arabic	Sudan
Kedija	Female	32	Cairo	10/2014	Arabic	Eritrea

Abdelaziz	Male	37	Cairo	10/2014	Arabic	Sudan
Mustafa	Male	43	Cairo	10/2014	English	Sudan
Winta	Female	18	Cairo	10/2014	English	Eritrea
Asmarina	Female	26	Cairo	10/2014	English	Eritrea
Malik	Male	27	Alexandria	11/2014	Arabic	Sudan
Ala'a	Male	29	Alexandria	11/2014	Arabic	Sudan
Nizar	Male	45	Alexandria	11/2014	Arabic	Syria
Sama	Female	42	Alexandria	11/2014	Arabic	Syria
Fathi	Male	40	Cairo	11/2014	Arabic	Syria
Hassan	Male	36	Cairo	11/2014	Arabic	Sudan
Usama	Male	34	Cairo	11/2014	Arabic	Syria
Munira	Female	42	Cairo	11/2014	Arabic	Sudan
Bashir	Female	25	Cairo	11/2014	Arabic	Sudan
Fikru	Male	36	Cairo	11/2014	Arabic	Eritrea
Morocco						
Amadu	Male	28	Rabat	1/2015	Arabic	Senegal
Adjo	Male	34	Casablanca	1/2015	English	Ghana
Hachim	Male	33	Mohammedia	1/2015	English	Senegal
Cheikhou	Male	28	Rabat	1/2015	English	Senegal
Boubacar	Male	30	Rabat	1/2015	French, with interpretation assistance	Guinea

(*cont.*)

Pseudonym	Gender	Age	City	Month of interview	Language	Nationality
Armand	Male	46	Rabat	2/2015	French & English	Democratic Republic of the Congo
Moussa	Male	40	Rabat	2/2015	French & English	Senegal
Francis	Male	40	Rabat	2/2015	French, with interpretation assistance	Cameroon
Basirou	Male	24	Marrakesh	2/2015	English	Gambia
Issa	Male	26	Rabat	2/2015	English	Mali
Yande	Female	30	Rabat	2/2015	French, with interpretation assistance	Senegal
Fatoumata	Female	22	Rabat	2/2015	French, with interpretation assistance	Côte D'Ivoire
Binta	Female	30	Rabat	2/2015	French, with interpretation assistance	Senegal
Camara	Female	29	Rabat	2/2015	French, with interpretation assistance	Senegal
Patrice	Male	44	Rabat	2/2015	French, with interpretation assistance	Democratic Republic of the Congo

Djeneba	Female	18	Rabat	3/2015	French, with interpretation assistance	Côte D'Ivoire
Adama	Male	28	Rabat	3/2015	French, with interpretation assistance	Senegal
Daniel	Male	35	Rabat	3/2015	English	Cameroon
Arafa	Female	53	Rabat	3/2015	French, with interpretation assistance	Chad
Claude	Male	36	Rabat	3/2015	English	Cameroon
Salomon	Female	45	Rabat	3/2015	French, with interpretation assistance	Democratic Republic of the Congo
Emmanuel	Female	50	Rabat	3/2015	French, with interpretation assistance	Congo
Affoue	Female	28	Rabat	3/2015	French, with interpretation assistance	Côte D'Ivoire

(*cont.*)

Pseudonym	Gender	Age	City	Month of interview	Language	Nationality
Koffi	Male	35	Rabat	3/2015	French, with interpretation assistance	Côte D'Ivoire
Reyna	Female	36	Rabat	3/2015	English	Philippines
Bertrand	Male	35	Rabat	3/2015	English	Cameroon
William	Male	30	Rabat	3/2015	English	Cameroon
Souleymane	Male	34	Oujda	4/2015	French	Mali
Rachid	Male	37	Oujda	4/2015	French	Burkina Faso
Kojo	Male	32	Oujda	4/2015	English	Ghana
Faycal	Male	24	Oujda	4/2015	French	Niger
Isaac	Male	22	Oujda	4/2015	French	Guinea-Conakry
Mariama	Female	38	Oujda	4/2015	French	Senegal
Abdou	Male	36	Tangier	4/2015	French	Cameroon
Kwaku	Male	38	Tangier	4/2015	English	Ghana
Adama	Male	28	Rabat	4/2015	French	Mali
Bassem	Male	60	Rabat	4/2015	Arabic	Syria
Zain	Male	35	Rabat	4/2015	Arabic	Syria
Turkey						
Ibrahim	Male	26	Istanbul	8/2014	English	Congo

Name	Gender	Age	City	Date	Language	Country
Ali	Male	25	Istanbul	5/2015	Arabic	Syria
Reem	Female	23	Istanbul	5/2015	Arabic	Syria
Amir	Male	32	Istanbul	5/2015	French	Senegal
Farhad	Male	30	Istanbul	5/2015	English	Afghanistan
Noora	Female	45	Gaziantep	6/2015	Arabic	Syria
Youssef	Male	26	Gaziantep	6/2015	Arabic	Syria
Tareq	Male	25	Gaziantep	6/2015	English & Arabic	Syria
Khalil	Male	30	Gaziantep	6/2015	Arabic	Syria

Notes

1 Introduction: Migration in the Global North and South

1. The names of all migrants or refugees used in this book have been changed to protect the identity of interview subjects.
2. While acknowledging the heterogeneity of countries in the Global South, throughout this book the designation Global South emphasizes geopolitical relations of power and is preferable to the phrase "developing countries," which emphasizes stages of development.
3. Specifically, David FitzGerald (2019) argues, "an underappreciated explanation for the increase in remote control of asylum seekers is that it grew out of the 1967 Protocol that stripped away the 1951 Convention's geographic and temporal limitations on who is considered a refugee .... The Protocol's opening of asylum to the persecuted throughout the world, including non-Europeans who had been excluded from mostly white countries of destination by racist immigration policies stripped refugee policies in the Global North of much of their value as tools for realpolitik and racial selection. Thus, destination countries subverted the spirit of the Refugee Convention with remote controls" (44).
4. Although Turkey maintains geographic limitations to the Convention, as explained in Chapter 5.
5. The data collection for this study is covered by two IRB approvals: HS# 2012-9054 (obtained October 3, 2012) and HS# 2014-1407 (obtained September 12, 2014).
6. While interviewees were asked a predetermined list of questions, interviews were semistructured, allowing interview subjects to elaborate on questions or to go off on tangents. I also asked follow-up questions when appropriate. Often nonscripted questions revealed important factors I had not considered when designing my interview questionnaire, thus leading to potential new factors or themes for understanding migration policy decisions.
7. Often this snowball sampling would entail asking to meet a friend or family member of someone I had already spoken with. Other times I frequented coffee shops or restaurants in neighborhoods with large populations of migrants and established a rapport with a particular

migrant or refugee employee, eventually asking that person whether they would agree to be interviewed. I used a set list of questions to guide my interviews but also let migrants and refugees tell their stories, elaborating about additional topics that were not directly related to my research question, such as the journey from their home country to the host state. While elite interviews generally lasted between forty-five minutes and one hour, migrant/refugee interviews were as short as twenty minutes and as long as four hours.

8. It is difficult to estimate the number of irregular migrants residing in a host state because these individuals are unlikely to be registered with the government or an international migration body. Furthermore, it is difficult to approximate a migrant population when this number is likely in flux due to new arrivals and frequent departures from the host state. See Kamal Sadiq (2009) for a discussion on the problems associated with accepting data on irregular migration at face value.

2 Host State Engagement in the Middle East and North Africa

1. This pattern has started to change with recent publications that focus exclusively on state policy (including Mourad 2017b; Dionigi 2017; Arar 2017).

2. Noora Lori's (2019) work on citizenship in the United Arab Emirates (UAE) also focuses exclusively on state policy, though the subject of her investigation is national minorities rather than immigrants or refugees. Nonetheless, she examines how national minorities who lack citizenship – *bidūn* – are treated as temporary residents by the Emirati state until their citizenship is ultimately "offshored" to the Union of the Comoros. Lori argues that both the UAE's strategy of making people wait for status and the decision to outsource the citizenship of the *bidūn* to the Comoros were policies designed to transform domestic minorities into documented "foreign" residents. In other words, the *bidūn* were neither entirely excluded nor entirely included within Emirati state structures through intentional policy, with similarities to a policy of strategic indifference employed by Egypt, Morocco, and Turkey toward migrants and refugees.

3. Scholars also examine power relations between Global North and Global South states in the field of global migration governance, which is a less developed and less cohesive area of international cooperation in comparison to the refugee regime (Betts 2011). For a discussion of South–South cooperation (or lack thereof) within the field of global migration governance, see Randall Hansen et al. (2011).

4. Using this type of approach to examine state inaction, Lama Mourad (2017) argues that a "nonpolicy" on behalf of the Lebanese government in response to the Syrian crisis necessitated that other actors – both at the local and international levels – adopt certain actions. While Mourad is unable to say with certainty that this "inaction" was a strategy rather than a lack of capacity, she demonstrates that this nonpolicy subsequently "structur[ed] the responses that did emerge, both 'below' and 'above' the state, that is namely by local authorities and international agencies" (49).

5. Egypt, Morocco, and Turkey are all classified by Polity as "closed anocracies" (Marshall 2017), a term that is synonymous with semi-authoritarianism. Monty Marshall and Gabrielle Elzinga-Marshall (2017) describe anocracy as a "middling category rather than a distinct form of governance. They are societies whose governments are neither fully democratic nor fully autocratic but, rather, combine an often-incoherent mix of democratic and autocratic traits and practices" (30). While Steven Levitsky and Lucan Way (2010) classified Egypt as "fully authoritarian" in their 2010 study, Egypt underwent significant liberalization in 2011 and has also seen authoritarian retrenchment post-2013; see Chapter 3 for details. Turkey has also moved further toward full authoritarianism since 2013 and particularly following the 2016 attempted coup; see Chapter 5.

3 Egypt: From Strategic Indifference to Postrevolutionary Repression

1. For an extensive analysis of the presence of Palestinians in Egypt as well as their treatment under the government of Gamal Abdel Nasser and subsequent Egyptian presidents, see Oroub El Abed (2009).

2. Specifically, Egypt claimed reservations to Article 12.1, thereby waiving the responsibility of determining the personal status of refugees, as well as Articles 20, 23, and 24, which claim that refugees should be afforded equal status to nationals in regard to rationing, public relief, assistance, and labor laws/social security, respectively (Zohry and Harrell-Bond 2003).

3. Primarily these services are available to refugees who have officially registered with the UNHCR in Egypt, though the UNHCR and IOM also fund some services for migrants who do not have proof of status.

4. Prior to 1995, the 1976 Wadi al-Nil agreement between Sudan and Egypt gave Sudanese access to education, health services, property ownership,

and employment, but this ended in 1995 after an assassination attempt on former President Mubarak, allegedly committed by individuals linked to the Sudanese government (Karasapan 2016). The Four Freedoms agreement signed in 2004 reenacted some of these rights for Sudanese citizens residing in Egypt, but it is not necessarily enforced in practice (CARIM 2004).

5. The NCCPIM was eventually merged with the National Committee on Countering Trafficking in Persons (NCCTIP) to form the National Coordinating Committee for Combatting and Preventing Illegal Migration, Trafficking in Persons (NCCPIM, TIP) in 2016.

6. An exception was a rise in the deportation of Eritreans in 2008 (Elite Interviewee AP).

7. A law came into effect in November 2013 that required three days' notification before protesting. The Egyptian Ministry of the Interior also has the right to cancel, postpone, or move any protest.

4 Morocco: From Raids and Roundups to a New Politics of Migration

1. Unlike other countries in the Middle East and North Africa, Morocco has received relatively few refugees from other MENA states over the last ten years, and the majority of migrants from sub-Saharan Africa do not qualify for official refugee status.

2. MSF closed its operation in Morocco in 2013 because it objected to violence used by Moroccan and Spanish border authorities against migrants.

3. The CNDH is accredited by the UN according to the Paris Principles as a transparent, independent human rights organization, but it nonetheless receives its funding from the Moroccan government. One of the main activities of the Council is to write an annual report that summarizes the state of human rights in the country and to issue advisory opinions on thematic issues.

4. This number later increased to more than 25,000 after the conclusion of the appeals process (Schuettler 2017).

5. Specifically, the Islamist association Unification and Reform (*ḥarakat al-tawḥīd wa-l-iṣlāḥ*) was permitted to join the Popular Democratic and Constitutional Movement (MPDC). Following the election in 1998, the group changed its name to the Justice and Development Party (PJD) or *ḥizb al-ʿadāla wa-l-tanmīa* (Willis 1999).

6. The CNDH was established in 2011 by Royal Decree with a broader mandate than the CCDH. Its remit is to "protect and promote human

rights, but also to enrich thoughts and debate on human rights and democracy issues" (CNDH 2014).

5 Turkey: From Strategic Indifference to Institutionalized Control

1. "Guestworker" or labor export agreements were signed between Turkey and Germany, the Netherlands, Belgium, Austria, France, and Sweden during the 1960s.
2. Ultimately refugees fleeing Iraq were housed in camps along the Iraqi–Turkish border until they were returned to the Kurdish autonomous zone (Sassoon 2009). In both 1988 and 1991 Turkey was reluctant to accept Kurdish refugees, fearing this could affect Turkey's demographic balance or incite tensions with Turkey's Kurdish minority (Sassoon 2009; Ogata 2005).
3. In Turkish popular media and political speeches, the word *misafir* is used to describe refugees, which translates to "guest" or "visitor."
4. Unlike other refugee nationalities, Syrian refugees are not subject to the satellite city system.
5. Kristen Biehl (2013) gives an analysis of the ways in which the local government in Istanbul responded to migration.
6. Festus Okey, a migrant from Nigeria, died on August 20, 2007, from gunshot wounds while in detention at the Beyoğlu Police Station. His mysterious death was perhaps one of the most important turning points in the public becoming aware of police treatment of undocumented migrants in Istanbul, which led to the creation of the Migrant Solidarity Network (Biehl 2013).
7. Effectively, Foreigners' Guest Houses are migrant detention centers where apprehended foreigners are held until deportation arrangements can be made (Biehl 2013).
8. Despite the EU's freezing of accession talks in 2006, Lisel Hintz (2019) argues that Erdoğan's Adalet ve Kalkınma Partisi (AKP) was able to use the changes required to domestic institutions as part of the EU's Copenhagen Criteria to its own benefit. Specifically, the nine harmonization packages undertaken by the AKP government between 2002 and 2004 helped to reduce the role of the military in politics, change the powers and makeup of the judicial system, and reduce the traditional influence of opposition parties (Hintz 2019).
9. Despite the reform process, Turkey maintains its geographic limitation in regard to the United Nations 1951 Refugee Convention. According to a key informant who was involved with the drafting process, lifting the

geographic limitation was never up for debate (Elite Interviewee K). The drafting committee was fearful that addressing this controversial issue would jeopardize the success of the entire law. Ahmet İçduygu (2007) claims, "The issue of lifting the geographical reservation of the 1951 Geneva Convention, which is very central to the asylum regimes in Turkey, is also often regarded as an element of change which may subsequently harm the notion of homogenous national identity" (203).

10. Prior to the outbreak of the Syrian conflict, Syrian nationals were able to enter Turkey without obtaining a visa.

6 Differential Treatment by Nationality? Ethnicity, Religion, and Race

1. Nonstate actors such as employers can also affect an immigrant's socioeconomic integration outcomes and have been shown to display preferences for certain types of immigrants. For example, employers in Western Europe have been shown to favor immigrants who are co-ethnics or from the same religion over those who are more culturally distant (Firth 1981; Adida et al. 2010).

2. See Chapter 3, Endnote 4.

3. I demarcate between individuals who have spent fewer than two years in a host state and those who have spent two or more years residing in a host state. Based on my conversations with the eighty interviewees, two years is the best approximation of the time it takes to become situated in the host state: to learn about neighborhoods, to establish relationships with other nationals from one's home country residing in the host state, to potentially find a job, and to learn both the formal and informal rules of the host state.

4. This can include either refugee or asylum seeker status or a valid residency permit obtained by another means.

5. Specifically, a small group of 5,200 Turkish-speaking Afghans from UNHCR camps in northern Pakistan were accepted by Turkey as "national refugees" (Kirişci 1991).

6. While citizenship as defined by the Turkish Citizenship Law of 2009 (Law No. 5901) is based on *jus sanguinis* or parental citizenship, naturalization is possible through marriage or by working in Turkey for more than five years (with some additional criteria) (Atasü-Topçuoğlu 2018). Citizenship can also be granted to "people who cannot meet the general criteria" via cabinet council decisions, which is the path by which some Syrians were able to acquire citizenship (Atasü-Topçuoğlu 2018).

7 The Domestic Influence of International Actors: UNHCR and IOM's Role in Host State Policy Outcomes

1. The UNHCR and the IOM, both part of the UN system, are examples of intergovernmental organizations – a subgroup of international organizations – that comprise member states.

8 The Post-2015 Migration Paradigm in the Mediterranean

1. For a detailed account of Libya's use of migration diplomacy in negotiations with Europe, see Kelly Greenhill (2010) and Gerasimos Tsourapas (2017).
2. The situation in 2015 was being referred to as a crisis in April by some European officials, leading to the publication of the "European Agenda on Migration" in May 2015, which called for the creation of "hot spot" reception centers in Greece and Italy. However, even following the issuance of the agenda, "there was a sense of complacency [among senior policy circles in Brussels] that the response had been sufficient for what was viewed as a largely localized crisis. The 'crisis situation in the Mediterranean,' many felt, was primarily the responsibility of frontline states, notably Italy, that had [received] increased support from the EU and other Member States. At the highest level of the Commission, there was a desire to swiftly return to business as usual" (Collett and Le Coz 2018, 11).

References

11.11.11. 2018. "Syrian Refugees in Lebanon: Long Road to Return." www .11.be/en/news/item/long-road-to-return.

3RP. 2014. "Overview: 2015 Syria Response Plan and 2015–2016 Regional Refugee and Resilience Plan." Regional Refugee Response & Resilience Plan. www.3rpsyriacrisis.org/wp-content/uploads/2015/01/Overview-of-2015-Response-Plans-for-Syria-Crisis_final.pdf.

——— 2015. "Regional Refugee & Resilience Plan 2015–2016 Regional Strategic Overview." Regional Refugee Response & Resilience Plan. https://relief web.int/sites/reliefweb.int/files/resources/3RP-Report-Overview.pdf.

Abdel-Samad, Mounah. 2014. "Why Reform Not Revolution: A Political Opportunity Analysis of Morocco 2011 Protests Movement." *The Journal of North African Studies* 19 (5): 792–809.

Aboulenein, Ahmed. 2017. "لخناق على المعارضة مصر تصدر قانونا للمنظمات غير الحكومية يضيق ا." Reuters. https://ara.reuters.com/article/idARAKBN18P1O9? pageNumber=1&virtualBrandChannel=0.

Abu-Sahlieh, Sami A. Aldeeb. 1996. "The Islamic Conception of Migration." *International Migration Review* 30 (1): 35–57.

Achilli, Luigi. 2015. "Syrian Refugees in Jordan: A Reality Check." Migration Policy Centre, EUI. http://cadmus.eui.eu/bitstream/handle/1 814/34904/MPC_2015-02_PB.pdf.

Açıkgöz, Meral, and Hakkı Onur Ariner. 2014. "Turkey's New Law on Foreigners and International Protection: An Introduction." Centre on Migration, Policy and Society, Turkish Migration Studies Group (TurkMiS), University of Oxford.

Adamson, Fiona. 2006. "Crossing Borders: International Migration and National Security." *International Security* 31 (1): 165–99.

——— 2019. "Sending States and the Making of Intra-diasporic Politics: Turkey and Its Diaspora(s)." *International Migration Review* 53 (1): 210–36. https://doi.org/10.1177/0197918318767665.

Adida, Claire L. 2014. *Immigrant Exclusion and Insecurity in Africa.* New York: Cambridge University Press.

Adida, Claire L., David D. Laitin, and Marie-Anne Valfort. 2010. "Identifying Barriers to Muslim Integration in France." *Proceedings of* the *National Academy of Sciences of the United States of America* 107 (52): 22384–90.

Agier, Michel, and David Fernbach. 2011. *Managing the Undesirables: Refugee Camps and Humanitarian Government*. Cambridge: Polity Press.

Ahmida, Ali Abdullatif. 2009. "Neither a Divide nor an Empty Space: The Sahara as a Bridge." In *Bridges across the Sahara: Social, Economic and Cultural Impact of the Trans-Sahara Trade during the 19th and 20th Centuries*, 1–12. Newcastle-upon-Tyne: Cambridge Scholars.

Al Jazeera. 2018a. "EU Leaders to Seek 'in-Depth Cooperation' with Egypt on Migration." www.aljazeera.com/news/2018/09/180920184826680.html.

⸻ 2018b. "Fighting in Afrin Displaces Thousands, Says Monitor." Al Jazeera, March 15. www.aljazeera.com/news/2018/03/turkish-led-assault-syria-afrin-displaced-10000-day-180315181847193.html.

Aleinikoff, Alexander. 2007. "International Legal Norms on Migration: Substance without Architecture." In *International Migration Law: Developing Paradigms and Key Challenges*, 467–79. The Hague: TMC Asser Press.

al-Kashef, Muhammed, and Marie Martin. 2019. "EU–Egypt Migration Cooperation: At the Expense of Human Rights." EuroMed Rights. https://euromedrights.org/publication/eu-egypt-migration-cooperation-where-are-human-rights/.

Alpes, Maybritt Jill, Sevda Tunaboylu, Orcun Ulusoy, and Saima Hassan. 2017. "Post-deportation Risks under the EU–Turkey Statement: What Happens after Readmission to Turkey?" Migration Policy Centre (MPC) Issue 2017/30, Robert Schuman Centre for Advanced Studies, San Domen. http://cadmus.eui.eu/bitstream/handle/1814/49005/PB_2017_30_MPC.pdf.

Amnesty International. 2012. "'We Are Foreigners, We Have No Rights': The Plight of Refugees, Asylum-Seekers and Migrants in Libya." Amnesty International. www.amnesty.org/download/Documents/24000/mde190202012en.pdf.

⸻ 2013. "We Cannot Live Here Anymore: Refugees from Syria in Egypt." Amnesty International. www.amnestyusa.org/research/reports/we-cannot-live-here-anymore-refugees-from-syria-in-egypt.

⸻ 2018. "Weathering the Storm: Defending Human Rights in Turkey's Climate of Fear." Amnesty International. www.amnesty.org/download/Documents/EUR4482002018ENGLISH.PDF.

Andersson, Ruben. 2014. *Illeality, Inc.: Clandestine Migration and the Business of Bordering Europe*. Oakland, CA: University of California Press.

Arar, Rawan. 2017. "The New Grand Compromise: How Syrian Refugees Changed the Stakes in the Global Refugee Assistance Regime." *Middle East Law and Governance* 9 (3): 298–312.

Associated Press. 2015. "Morocco Clears Migrant Camps near Spanish Enclave." *Daily Mail*, February 11. www.dailymail.co.uk/wires/ap/arti cle-2949011/Morocco-clearsmigrant-camps-near-Spanish-enclave.html.

Atasü-Topçuoğlu, Reyhan. 2018. "Media Discussion on the Naturalization Policy for Syrians in Turkey." *International Migration*, May. https://doi .org/10.1111/imig.12463.

Aydin, Umut, and Kemal Kirişci. 2013. "With or without the EU: Europeanisation of Asylum and Competition Policies in Turkey." *South European Society and Politics* 18 (3): 375–95.

Ayubi, Nazih N. 1996. *Over-stating the Arab State: Politics and Society in the Middle East*. London: I. B. Tauris.

Babar, Zahra, Michael Ewers, and Nabil Khattab. 2019. "Im/Mobile Highly Skilled Migrants in Qatar." *Journal of Ethnic and Migration Studies* 45 (9): 1553–70. https://doi.org/10.1080/1369183X.2018.1492372.

Babar, Zahra R. 2014. "The Cost of Belonging: Citizenship Construction in the State of Qatar." *The Middle East Journal* 68 (3): 403–20. https://doi .org/10.3751/68.3.14.

Barnett, Michael. 2001. "Humanitarianism with a Sovereign Face: UNHCR in the Global Undertow." *International Migration Review* 35 (1): 244–77.

BBC. 2016. "Four Dead after 'Libyan Coast Guard' Vessel Attacks Migrant Boat." October 21. www.bbc.com/news/world-europe-37731094.

Betts, Alexander. 2008. "North–South Cooperation in the Refugee Regime: The Role of Linkages." *Global Governance* 14 (2): 157–78.

   2009. *Protection by Persuasion: International Cooperation in the Refugee Regime*. Ithaca, NY: Cornell University Press.

   2011. "Introduction: Global Migration Governance." In *Global Migration Governance*, 1–33. Oxford: Oxford University Press.

Betts, Alexander, and Gil Loescher, eds. 2011. *Refugees in International Relations*. Oxford: Oxford University Press.

Biehl, Kristen. 2013. "New Migrations to Istanbul and Emerging Local Practices." In *Countries of Migrants, Cities of Migrants: Italy, Spain, Turkey*. Istanbul: Isis Press.

Bishara, Dina. 2015. "The Politics of Ignoring: Protest Dynamics in Late Mubarak Egypt." *Perspectives on Politics* 13 (4): 958–75.

Bono, Irene. 2010. "L'activisme associatif comme marché du travail: Normalisation sociale et politique par les 'Activités génératrices de revenus' à El Hajeb." *Politique africaine* 120 (4): 25–44.

Boubakri, Hassan. 2013. "Revolution and International Migration in Tunisia." Migration Policy Centre (MPC) Research Report 2013/14, Robert Schuman Centre for Advanced Studies, San Domen. www .migrationpolicycentre.eu/docs/MPC-RR-2013-04.pdf.

Bozonnet, Charlotte. 2018. "Maroc: 'La Seule Politique Migratoire Cohérente de l'Europe, c'est Mettre La Pression Sur Les Pays de Transit.'" *Le Monde Afrique*. www.lemonde.fr/afrique/article/201 8/11/02/maroc-la-seule-politique-migratoire-coherente-de-l-europe-c-est-mettre-la-pression-sur-les-pays-de-transit_5377982_3212. html.

Brand, Laurie A. 2006. *Citizens Abroad: Emigration and the State in the Middle East and North Africa*. Cambridge: Cambridge University Press.

Brewer, Kelly T., and Yükseker Deniz. 2006. "A Survey on African Migrants and Asylum Seekers in Istanbul." Migration Research Program at the Koç Univeristy.

Brown, Nathan J. 2002. *Constitutions in a Nonconstitutional World: Arab Basic Laws and the Prospects for Accountable Government*. SUNY Series in Middle Eastern Studies. Albany: State University of New York Press.

2011. "Dictatorship and Democracy through the Prism of Arab Elections." In *The Dynamics of Democratization: Dictatorship, Development and Diffusion*, 46–63. Baltimore, MD: Johns Hopkins University Press.

Brubaker, Rogers. 1992. *Citizenship and Nationhood in France and Germany*. 6th ed. Cambridge, MA: Harvard University Press.

Buehler, Matt, and Kyung Joon Han. 2019. "Divergent Opposition to Sub-Saharan African and Arab Migrants in Morocco's Casablanca Region: Prejudice from the Pocketbook?" *British Journal of Middle Eastern Studies*, August, 1–23. https://doi.org/10.1080/13530194.2019.1651633.

Buzan, Barry, Ole Wæver, and Jaap de Wilde. 1998. *Security: A New Framework for Analysis*. Boulder, CO: Lynne Rienner.

CARIM. 2004. "The Four Freedoms Agreement between Egypt and Sudan." CARIM-South. http://carim-south.eu/database/legal-module/the-four-freedoms-agreement-between-egypt-and-sudan/.

Carvalho, Cátia de, and Marta Pinto. 2018. "Refugee Camp as an Immediate Solution: Response and Its Psychological Meanings." *Peace and Conflict: Journal of Peace Psychology* 24 (3): 277–82. https://doi.org/10 .1037/pac0000318.

Castle, Stephen. 2006. "EU Freezes Talks on Turkey Membership." *Independent*. www.independent.co.uk/news/world/europe/eu-freezes-talks-on-turkey-membership-428085.html.

Castles, Stephen. 2006. "Guestworkers in Europe: A Resurrection?" *International Migration Review* 40 (4): 741–66.

Castles, Stephen, and Nicholas Van Hear. 2011. "Root Causes." In *Global Migration Governance*, 287–306. Oxford: University of Oxford Press.

CCSM-GADEM. 2015. "Note d'information Conjointe CCSM–GADEM Sur Les Déplacements et Les Détentions Arbitraires de Migrants Au Maroc à La Suite Des Rafles Du 10 Février 2015." www.gadem-asso.org/note-dinformation-conjointe-ccsm-gadem/.

Center for Refugee Solidarity. 2016. "The Sudanese in Egypt: Violence, Negligence, Neglect." www.refugeesolidarity.org/publication/report/e gypt/the-case-of-yehia-zakareyas-torture.

Cetingulec, Mehmet. 2014. "Syrian Refugees Aggravate Turkey's Unemployment Problems." Al-Monitor, July 9. www.al-monitor.com/ pulse/originals/2014/07/cetingulec-syrian-refugees-turkey-unemploy ment-illegal-work.html.

Chan, Kwok B., and David Loveridge. 1987. "Refugees 'in Transit': Vietnamese in a Refugee Camp in Hong Kong." *International Migration Review* 21 (3): 745–59. https://doi.org/10.1177/019791838702100316.

Chatty, Dawn. 2010. *Displacement and Dispossession in the Modern Middle East*. The Contemporary Middle East 5. New York: Cambridge University Press.

———. 2018. *Syria: The Making and Unmaking of a Refuge State*. http://public .eblib.com/choice/publicfullrecord.aspx?p=5313244.

Cherti, Myriam, and Michael Collyer. 2015. "Immigration and Pensée d'Etat: Moroccan Migration Policy Changes as Transformation of 'Geopolitical Culture.'" *Journal of North African Studies* 20 (4): 590–604. https://doi.org/10.1080/13629387.2015.1065043.

CNDH. 2013. "Présentation Du Counseil National Des Droits de l'Homme." www.cndh.org.ma/fr/presentation/presentation-du-conseil-national-des-droits-de-lhomme.

———. 2014. "Report of the National Human Rights Council to Parliament." Human Rights Council Publications. http://cndh.ma/sites/default/ files/report_ofthe_national_human_rights_council_to_the_parliement .pdf.

Collett, Elizabeth, and Camille Le Coz. 2018. "After the Storm: Learning from the EU Response to the Migration Crisis." Migration Policy Institute Europe. https://www.migrationpolicy.org/research/after-stor m-eu-response-migration-crisis.

Cook, Lorne. 2019. "EU, Arab Leaders in First Summit Focus on Security, Migrants." Associated Press. https://apnews.com/853a30a92da64798945e 49b677b8cf60.

Cornelius, Wayne A., and Marc R. Rosenblum. 2005. "Immigration and Politics." *Annual Review of Political Science* 8: 99–119.

Crisp, Jeffrey, and Katy Long. 2016. "Safe and Voluntary Refugee Repatriation: From Principle to Practice." *Journal on Migration and Human Security* 4 (3): 141–74.

Cuéller, Mariano-Florentino. 2006. "Refugee Security and the Organizational Logic of Legal Mandates." Georgetown Journal of International Law Stanford Public Law Working Paper 37 (918320): 1–102.

Daily Sabah. 2015. "CHP's Latest Election Promise of Sending Back Syrian Refugees in Turkey Comes under Criticism." April 23. www.dailysa bah.com/politics/2015/04/23/chps-latest-election-promise-of-sending-b ack-syrian-refugees-in-turkey-comes-under-criticism.

——— 2018. "Turkish Efforts in Afrin, Idlib Will Allow Syrians to Return Home." *Daily Sabah*. www.dailysabah.com/war-on-terror/2018/02/09 /turkish-efforts-in-afrin-idlib-will-allow-syrians-to-return-home.

Dalmasso, Emanuela. 2012. "Surfing the Democratic Tsunami in Morocco: Apolitical Society and the Reconfiguration of a Sustainable Authoritarian Regime." *Mediterranean Politics* 17 (2): 217–32.

Dancygier, Rafaela M., and David D. Laitin. 2014. "Immigration into Europe: Economic Discrimination, Violence, and Public Policy." *Annual Review of Political Science* 17: 43–64.

Danish Refugee Council, Oxfam, and Save the Children. 2017. "Stand and Deliver: Urgent Action Needed on Commitments Made at the London Conference One Year On." www.care.org/sites/default/files/documents/ helsinki_report_stand_and_deliver_digital.pdf.

Davis, Diane E. 2018. "Reflections on 'The Politics of Informality': What We Know, How We Got There, and Where We Might Head Next." *Studies in Comparative International Development* 53 (3): 365–78. https://doi .org/10.1007/s12116-018-9273-2.

Davis, Rochelle. 2012. "Matar ʿAbdelraheem: From a Village in Palestine to a Refugee Camp in Syria." In *Struggle and Survival in Palestine/Israel*, edited by Mark LeVine and Gershon Shafir, 179–95. Berkeley, CA: University of California Press.

Davis, Uri. 2000. "Conceptions of Citizenship in the Middle East: State, Nation, and People." In *Citizenship and the State in the Middle East: Approaches and Applications*, 49–69. Syracuse, NY: Syracuse University Press.

Deane, Shelley. 2013. "Transforming Tunisia: The Role of Civil Society in Tunisia's Transition." International Alert. www.international-alert.org /sites/default/files/publications/Tunisia2013EN.pdf.

Deutsche Welle. 2017. "Turkey Hits Back at Germany over Election 'Interference' Criticism." August 19. www.dw.com/en/turkey-hits-back-at-germany-over-election-interference-criticism/a-40162026.

Dionigi, Filippo. 2017. "Statehood and Refugees: Patterns of Integration and Segregation of Refugee Populations in Lebanon from a Comparative Perspective." *Middle East Law and Governance* 9 (2): 113–46. https://doi.org/10.1163/18763375-00902001.

Dorman, W. Judson. 2007. "The Politics of Neglect: The Egyptian State in Cairo, 1974–98." Unpublished PhD thesis, School of Oriental and African Studies, London.

Dunne, Michelle. 2017. "The United States' Assistance for Egypt." Carnegie Endowment for International Peace. http://carnegieendowment.org/2017/04/25/united-states-assistance-for-egypt-pub-68756.

Durac, Vincent. 2015. "A Flawed Nexus? Civil Society and Democratization in the Middle East and North Africa." Middle East Institute. www.mei.edu/content/map/flawed-nexus-civil-society-and-democratization-middle-east-and-north-africa.

El Abed, Oroub. 2004. "The Forgotten Palestinians: How Palestinian Refugees Survive in Egypt." *Forced Migration Review* 20: 29–30.

2009. *Unprotected: Palestinians in Egypt since 1948*. Washington, DC: Institute for Palestine Studies.

El Amrani, Issandr. 2012. "Morocco's Citizen Subjects." *New York Times*, October 31. http://latitude.blogs.nytimes.com/2012/10/31/moroccos-citizen-subjects/.

El Hamel, Chouki. 2012. *Black Morocco: A History of Slavery, Race, and Islam*. Cambridge: Cambridge University Press. http://dx.doi.org/10.1017/CBO9781139198783.

El Qadim, Nora. 2015. *Le Gouvernement Asymétrique Des Migrations. Maroc/Union Européenne*. Paris: Dalloz.

2019. "The Funding Instruments of the EU's Neogtiation on External Migraton Policy. Incentives for Cooperation?" In *EU External Migration Policies in an Era of Global Mobilities: Intersecting Policy Universes*, edited by Sergio Carrera, Leonhard den Hertog, Marion Panizzon, and Theodora Kostakopoulou, 341–63. Immigration and Asylum Law and Policy in Europe 44. Boston: Brill Nijhoff.

Elbagir, Nima, Raja Razek, Alex Platt, and Bryony Jones. 2017. "People for Sale: Where Lives Are Auctioned for $400." CNN. www.cnn.com/2017/11/14/africa/libya-migrant-auctions/index.html.

Erdoğan, M. Murat. 2017. "Thinking Outside the Camp: Syrian Refugees in Istanbul." Migration Policy Institute. www.migrationpolicy.org/article/thinking-outside-camp-syrian-refugees-istanbul.

Escoffier, Claire, Pierre Tainturier, Ayman Halasa, Naima Baba, and Chadi Sidhom. 2008. "Economic and Social Rights of Migrants and Refugees in the Euro-Med Region: Access to Healthcare and the Labour Market." Euro-Mediterranean Human Rights Network.

https://ec.europa.eu/migrant-integration/librarydoc/economic-and-social-rights-of-migrants-and-refugees-in-the-euro-med-region-access-to-health-care-and-the-labour-market.

European Commission. 2014. "Global Approach to Migration and Mobility." European Commission: Migration and Home Affairs. https://ec.europa.eu/home-affairs/what-we-do/policies/international-affairs/global-approach-to-migration_en.

——— 2016a. "European Neighborhood Policy and Enlargement Negotiations: Egypt." European Commission. https://ec.europa.eu/neighbourhood-enlargement/neighbourhood/countries/egypt_en.

——— 2016b. "European Neighborhood Policy and Enlargement Negotiations: Morocco." European Commission. https://ec.europa.eu/neighbourhood-enlargement/neighbourhood/countries/morocco_en.

——— 2016c. "Joint Action Plan on the Implementation of the EU–Turkey Statement." European Commission. https://ec.europa.eu/commission/sites/beta-political/files/december2016-action-plan-migration-crisis-management_en.pdf.

——— 2017a. "Seventh Report on the Progress Made in the Implementation of the EU–Turkey Statement." Report from the European Commission to the European Parliament. https://ec.europa.eu/neighbourhood-enlargement/sites/near/files/20170906_seventh_report_on_the_progress_in_the_implementation_of_the_eu-turkey_statement_en.pdf.

——— 2017b. "EU Emergency Trust Fund for Africa." European Commission Press Release. https://ec.europa.eu/europeaid/sites/devco/files/factsheet-eu-emergency-trust-fund-africa-2017-09-11_en.pdf.

Fargues, Philippe. 2009. "Work, Refuge, Transit: An Emerging Pattern of Irregular Immigration South and East of the Mediterranean." *International Migration Review* 43 (3): 544–77.

Faris, Mehdi. 2015. "Maroc: Premier Bilan Après Une Régularisation Massive de sans-Papiers." *Le Monde Afrique*. www.lemonde.fr/afrique/article/2015/03/30/maroc-premier-bilan-apres-une-regularisation-massive-de-sans-papiers_4605803_3212.html.

Farooq, Umar. 2018. "Turkish President Erdogan Faces Pushback for Pro-Syrian Refugee Stance ahead of June Election." *Los Angeles Times*, May 28. www.latimes.com/world/la-fg-turkey-election-syrians-2018-story.html.

Feldman, Ilana. 2015. "Looking for Humanitarian Purpose: Endurance and the Value of Lives in a Palestinian Refugee Camp." *Public Culture* 27 (377): 427–47. https://doi.org/10.1215/08992363-2896171.

——— 2017. "Humanitarian Care and the Ends of Life: The Politics of Aging and Dying in a Palestinian Refugee Camp." *Cultural Anthropology* 32 (1): 42–67. https://doi.org/10.14506/ca32.1.06.

Firth, Raymond. 1981. "Engagement and Detachment: Reflections on Applying Social Anthropology to Social Affairs." *Human Organization* 40 (3): 193–201.

FitzGerald, David. 2019. *Refuge beyond Reach: How Rich Democracies Repel Asylum Seekers.* New York: Oxford University Press.

Foley, Michael W., and Bob Edwards. 1996. "The Paradox of Civil Society." *Journal of Democracy* 7 (3): 38–52.

Freeman, Gary. 1995. "Modes of Immigration Politics in Liberal Democracies." *International Migration Review* 29 (4): 881–902.

Fujii, Lee Ann. 2015. "Five Stories of Accidental Ethnography: Turning Unplanned Moments in the Field into Data." *Qualitative Research* 15 (4): 525–39. https://doi.org/10.1177/1468794114548945.

Gabiam, Nell. 2016. *The Politics of Suffering: Syria's Palestinian Refugee Camps.* Public Cultures of the Middle East and North Africa. Bloomington: Indiana University Press.

GADEM. 2013. "Rapport Sur l'Application Au Maroc de La Convention Internationale Sur La Protection Des Droits de Tous Les Travailleurs Migrants et Des Membres de Leur Famille." www.gadem-asso.org/IMG/pdf/201308285_-_Rapport_CMW_a_imprimer.pdf.

Gall, Carlotta. 2019. "Turkey's Radical Plan: Send a Million Refugees Back to Syria." *New York Times*, September 10. www.nytimes.com/2019/09/10/world/middleeast/turkey-syria-refugees-erdogan.html.

Gallien, Max. 2020. "Informal Institutions and the Regulation of Smuggling in North Africa." Perspectives on Politics 18(2): 492–508.

Gamlen, Alan. 2014. "Diaspora Institutions and Diaspora Governance." *International Migration Review* 48 (1): 180–217.

Gammeltoft-Hansen, Thomas. 2011. *Access to Asylum: International Refugee Law and the Globalisation of Migration Control.* Cambridge Studies in International and Comparative Law. Cambridge: Cambridge University Press.

Geddes, Andrew. 2005. "Europeanisation Goes South: The External Dimension of EU Migration and Asylum Policy." *Zeitschrift Für Staats- Und Europawissenschaften (ZSE) / Journal for Comparative Government and European Policy* 3 (2): 275–93.

Geiger, Martin, and Antoine Pécoud. 2010. "The Politics of International Migration Management." In *The Politics of International Migration Management*, 1–21. Basingstoke: Palgrave Macmillan.

George, Alexander L., and Andrew Bennett. 2005. *Case Studies and Theory Development in the Social Sciences.* BCSIA Studies in International Security. Cambridge, MA: Massachusetts Institute of Technology Press.

Georgi, Fabian. 2010. "For the Benefit of Some: The International Organization for Migration and Its Global Migration Management." In *The Politics of International Migration Management*, 45–72. Basingstoke: Palgrave Macmillan.

Gerring, John. 2006. *Case Study Research Principles and Practices*. Leiden: Cambridge University Press.

Global Compact for Migration. 2018. "Global Compact for Safe, Orderly and Regular Migration: Final Draft." https://refugeesmigrants.un.org/sites/default/files/180711_final_draft_0.pdf.

Goldschmidt, Elie. 2006. "Storming the Fences: Morocco and Europe's Anti-migration Policy." Middle East Research and Information Project. www.merip.org/mer/mer239/storming-fences.

Grabska, Katarzyna. 2006. "Marginalization in Urban Spaces of the Global South: Urban Refugees in Cairo." *Journal of Refugee Studies* 19 (3): 287–307.

Greenhill, Kelly M. 2010. *Weapons of Mass Migration: Forced Displacement, Coercion, and Foreign Policy*. Cornell Studies in Security Affairs. Ithaca, NY: Cornell University Press.

Guiraudon, Virginie. 2000. "European Integration and Migration Policy: Vertical Policy-making as Venue Shopping." *JCMS: Journal of Common Market Studies* 38 (2): 251–71. https://doi.org/10.1111/1468-5965.00219.

Haas, Hein de. 2005. "Morocco: From Emigration Country to Africa's Migration Passage to Europe." Migration Policy Institute. www.migrationpolicy.org/article/morocco-emigration-country-africas-migration-passage-europe.

——— 2007. "Turning the Tide? Why Development Will Not Stop Migration." *Development and Change* 38 (5): 819–41.

Hall, John A., and G. John Ikenberry. 1989. *The State*. Stratford: Open University Press.

Hamdan, Hanan. 2018. "Lebanon–UNHCR Feuding over Syrian Refugees." Al-Monitor, July 6. www.al-monitor.com/pulse/originals/2018/07/lebanon-syrian-displaced-voluntary-return-unhcr.html.

Hamzawy, Amr. 2017. "Legislating Authoritarianism: Egypt's New Era of Repression." https://carnegieendowment.org/2017/03/16/legislating-authoritarianism-egypt-s-new-era-of-repression-pub-68285.

Hanafi, S., and T. Long. 2010. "Governance, Governmentalities, and the State of Exception in the Palestinian Refugee Camps of Lebanon." *Journal of Refugee Studies* 23 (2): 134–59. https://doi.org/10.1093/jrs/feq014.

Hansen, Randall, Jobst Koehler, and Jeannette Money, eds. 2011. *Migration, Nation States, and International Cooperation*. Routledge Research in Transnationalism 23. New York: Routledge.

Hargrave, Karen, Sara Pantuilano, and Ahmed Idris. 2016. "Closing Borders: The Ripple Effects of Australian and European Refugee Policy: Case Studies from Indonesia, Kenya and Jordan." HPG Working Paper. www.odi.org/sites/odi.org.uk/files/resource-docu ments/11147.pdf.

Hassan, Hamdy A. 2011. "Introduction." In *Regional Integration in Africa: Bridging the North–Sub-Saharan Divide*, ix–xiii. Africa: Institute of South Africa.

Hassan, Lisa. 2000. "Deterrence Measures and the Preservation of Asylum in the United Kingdom and United States." *Journal of Refugee Studies* 13 (2): 184–204.

Hathaway, James C., and Michael Foster. 2014. *The Law of Refugee Status*. 2nd ed. Cambridge: Cambridge University Press.

Hawthorne, Amy. 2004. "Middle Eastern Democracy: Is Civil Society the Answer?" Carnegie Endowment for International Peace. http://carne gieendowment.org/files/CarnegiePaper44.pdf.

Helmke, Gretchen, and Steven Levitsky. 2004. "Informal Institutions and Comparative Politics: A Research Agenda." *Perspectives on Politics* 2 (4): 725–40. https://doi.org/10.1017/S1537592704040472.

Helton, Arthur C. 2007. *The Price of Indifference: Refugees and Humanitarian Action in the New Century*. Reprint. A Council on Foreign Relations Book. Oxford: Oxford University Press.

Hintz, Lisel. 2019. *Identity Politics Inside Out: National Identity Contestation and Foreign Policy in Turkey*. New York: Oxford University Press.

Hintz, Lisel, and Caroline Feehan. 2017. "Burden or Boon? Turkey's Tactical Treatment of the Syrian Refugee Crisis." Middle East Institute. www.mei.edu/content/map/burden-or-boon-turkey-s-tacti cal-treatment-syrian-refugee-crisis.

Hirschl, Ran. 2010. *Constitutional Theocracy*. Cambridge, MA: Harvard University Press.

Hirschon, Renee. 2003. "'Unmixing Peoples' in the Aegean Region." In *Crossing the Aegean: An Appraisal of the 1923 Compulsory Population Exchange between Greece and Turkey*, 3–12. Studies in Forced Migration 12. New York: Berghahn Books.

Hochschild, Jennifer L., and John H. Mollenkopf. 2009. "Modeling Immigrant Political Incorporation." In *Bringing Outsiders In: Transatlantic Perspectives on Immigrant Political Incorporation*, 15–30. Ithaca, NY: Cornell University Press.

Hoeffler, Anke. 2013. "Out of the Frying Pan into the Fire? Migration from Fragile States to Fragile States." OECD Development Co-operation Working Paper.

Hoffmann, Sophia. 2016. *Iraqi Migrants in Syria: The Crisis before the Storm*. 1st ed. Contemporary Issues in the Middle East. Syracuse, NY: Syracuse University Press.

Holland, Alisha C. 2017. *Forbearance as Redistribution: The Politics of Informal Welfare in Latin America*. Cambridge Studies in Comparative Politics. Cambridge: Cambridge University Press.

Holland, Hereward. 2015. "Over One Million Sea Arrivals Reach Europe in 2015." UNHCR. www.unhcr.org/afr/news/latest/2015/12/5683d0b56/ million-sea-arrivals-reach-europe-2015.html.

Hollifield, James Frank. 1992. *Immigrants, Markets and States: The Political Economy of Postwar Europe*. Cambridge, MA: Harvard University Press.

——— 2004. "The Emerging Migration State." *International Migration Review* 38 (3): 885–912.

Hollifield, James Frank, Philip L. Martin, and Pia M. Orrenius, eds. 2014. *Controlling Immigration: A Global Perspective*. 3rd ed. Stanford, CA: Stanford University Press.

Hopper, Kate. 2017. "European Leaders Pursue Migration Deals with North African Countries, Sparking Concerns about Human Costs." Migration Policy Institute. www.migrationpolicy.org/article/top-10–2017-issue-3-european-leaders-pursue-migration-deals-north-african-countries.

Hovil, Lucy. 2014. "Local Integration." In *The Oxford Handbook of Refugee and Forced Migration Studies*, edited by Elena Fiddian-Qasmiyeh, Gil Loescher, Katy Long, and Nando Sigona, 488–98. Oxford: Oxford University Press. https://doi.org/10.1093/oxfordhb/97 80199652433.013.0042.

Human Rights Watch. 2013. "Egypt: Syria Refugees Detained: Coerced to Return." www.hrw.org/news/2013/11/10/egypt-syria-refugees-detaine d-coerced-return.

——— 2014. "All According to Plan: The Rab'a Massacre and Mass Killings of Protesters in Egypt." www.hrw.org/report/2014/08/12/all-according-plan/raba-massacre-and-mass-killings-protesters-egypt.

——— 2017. "'I Have No Idea Why They Sent Us Back': Jordanian Deportations and Expulsions of Syrian Refugees." www.hrw.org/report/2017/10/02/ i-have-no-idea-why-they-sent-us-back/jordanian-deportations-and-exp ulsions-syrian.

Hyndman, Jennifer. 2000. *Managing Displacement: Refugees and the Politics of Humanitarianism*. Borderlines 16. Minneapolis: University of Minnesota Press.

İçduygu, Ahmet. 2007. "EU-Ization Matters: Changes in Immigration and Asylum Practices in Turkey." In *The Europeanization of National*

Policies and Politics of Immigration: Between Autonomy and the European Union, 201–22. London: Palgrave Macmillan.

2009. "International Migration and Human Development in Turkey." Human Development Research Paper, United Nations Development Program.

İçduygu, Ahmet, and Damla B. Aksel. 2012. "Irregular Migration in Turkey." International Organization for Migration. https://mirekoc.ku .edu.tr/wp-content/uploads/sites/22/2017/01/Irregular-Migration-in-T urkey.pdf

İçduygu, Ahmet, and Kirişçi Kirisci. 2009. *Land of Diverse Migrations: Challenges of Emigration and Immigration in Turkey*. Istanbul: Istanbul Bilgi University Press.

ICG. 2017. "Time to Reset African Union–European Union Relations." International Crisis Group No. 255. www.crisisgroup.org/africa/255-time-reset-african-union-european-union-relations.

ICMPD. 2018. "Migration Dialogues." International Centre for Migration Policy Development. www.icmpd.org/our-work/migration-dialogues/.

Iskander, Natasha N. 2010. *Creative State: Forty Years of Migration and Development Policy in Morocco and Mexico*. Ithaca, NY: ILR Press.

Jacobsen, Karen. 2001. "The Forgotten Solution: Local Integration for Refugees in Developing Countries." UNHCR Working Paper No. 45.

Jeune Afrique. 2013a. "Macky Sall Entame Sa Première Visite Officielle Au Maroc." www.jeuneafrique.com/169509/politique/macky-sall-entame-sa-premi-re-visite-officielle-au-maroc/.

2013b. "Maroc: Affrontements Entre Policiers et Clandestins à l'ambassade Du Sénégal." www.jeuneafrique.com/170527/politique/maroc-affrontements-entre-policiers-et-clandestins-l-ambassade-du-s-n-gal/.

Jones, Reece. 2016. *Violent Borders: Refugees and the Right to Move*. London: Verso.

Joppke, Christian. 1998a. "Why Liberal States Accept Unwanted Immigration." *World Politics* 50 (2): 266–93.

1999a. "How Immigration Is Changing Citizenship: A Comparative View." *Ethnic and Racial Studies* 22 (4): 629–52.

1999b. *Immigration and the Nation-State: The United States, Germany and Great-Britain*. Oxford: Oxford University Press.

Judell, Alice, and Pauline Brücker. 2015. "Israel and Its 'Infiltrators': Reflecting upon a Political Crisis." Network of Researchers in International Affairs. www.noria-research.com/israel-and-its-infiltrators-reflecting-upon-a-political-crisis/.

Kagan, Michael. 2002. "Assessment of Refugee Status Determination Procedures at UNHCR's Cairo Office 2001–2002." Forced Migration and Refugee Studies Program, Working Paper 1, American University in Cairo.

2011. "Shared Responsibility in a New Egypt: A Strategy for Refugee Protection." School of Global Affairs and Public Policy, American University in Cairo.

2012. "The UN 'Surrogate State' and the Foundation of Refugee Policy in the Middle East." *UC Davis International Journal of Law & Policy* 18 (2): 307–42.

Kale, Başak. 2014. "Transforming an Empire: The Ottoman Empire's Immigration and Settlement Policies in the Nineteenth and Early Twentieth Centuries." *Middle Eastern Studies* 50 (2): 252–71.

Karasapan, Omer. 2016. "Who Are the 5 Million Refugees and Immigrants in Egypt?" Brookings Institution. www.brookings.edu/blog/future-development/2016/10/04/who-are-the-5-million-refugees-and-immigrants-in-egypt/.

Kaymaz, Timur, and Omar Kadkoy. 2016. "Syrians in Turkey: The Economics of Integration." Al Sharq Forum. www.sharqforum.org/2016/09/06/syrians-in-turkey-the-economics-of-integration/.

Keck, Margaret E., and Kathryn Sikkink. 1998. *Activists beyond Border: Advocacy Networks in International Politics.* Cornell, NY: Cornell University Press.

Khachani, Mohamed. 2010. "Le Tissu Associatif et Le Traitement de La Question Migratoire." Federation Internationale des Societes de la Croix Rouge et des Croissants Rouges. http://amerm.ma/wp-content/uploads/2014/05/Le-tissu-associatif-et-le-traitement-de-la-question-migratoire-au-Maroc.pdf

Khakee, Anna. 2017. "Democracy Aid or Autocracy Aid: Unintended Effects of Democracy Assistance in Morocco." *Journal of North African Studies* 22 (2): 238–58.

Kilberg, Rebecca. 2014. "Turkey's Evolving Migration Identity." Migration Policy Institute. www.migrationpolicy.org/article/turkeys-evolving-migration-identity.

Kirişci, Kemal. 1991. "Refugee Movements and Turkey." *International Migration* 29 (4): 545–59.

2012. "Turkey's New Draft Law on Asylum: What to Make of It?" Hamburg Institute of International Economics, Series Edition HWWI 5.

2018. "How to Read Turkey's Election Results." Brookings Institution. www.brookings.edu/blog/order-from-chaos/2018/06/25/how-to-read-turkeys-election-results/.

Kirisci, Kirişçi. 2003. "Turkey: A Transformation from Emigration to Immigration." Migration Policy Institute. www.migrationpolicy.org/article/turkey-transformation-emigration-immigration.

Kituo Cha Sheria: Legal Advice Centre. 2017. "Judgement on Closure of Dadaab Refugee Camp and DRA." Kituo Cha Sheria: Legal Advice Centre. http://kituochasheria.or.ke/wp-content/uploads/2017/02/Dada ab-Closure-Judgment-1.pdf.

Klotz, Audie. 2013. *Migration and National Identity in South Africa, 1860–2010.* New York: Cambridge University Press.

Kymlicka, Will, and W. J. Norman, eds. 2000. *Citizenship in Diverse Societies.* Oxford: Oxford University Press.

Kymlicka, Will, and Eva Pföstl. 2014. "Introduction." In *Multiculturalism and Minority Rights in the Arab World,* 1–26. Oxford: Oxford University Press.

La Cimade. 2017. "Coopération UE-Afrique Sur Les Migrations: Chronique d'un Chantage Décryptage Des Instruments Financiers et Politiques de l'Union Européenne." www.migreurop.org/IMG/pdf/cimade_coopera tion_ue_afrique.pdf.

Lake, David A. 2011. *Hierarchy in International Relations.* Cornell Studies in Political Economy. Ithaca, NY: Cornell University Press.

Lavenex, Sandra. 2007. "The External Face of Europeanization: Third Countries and International Organizations." In *The Europeanization of National Policies and Politics of Immigration: Between Autonomy and the European Union,* 246–64. London: Palgrave Macmillan.

——— 2008. "Beyond Conditionality: International Institutions in Postcommunist Europe after Enlargement." *Journal of European Public Policy* 15 (6): 938–55.

Lavenex, Sandra, and Frank Schimmelfennig. 2009. "EU Rules beyond EU Borders: Theorizing External Governance in European Politics." *Journal of European Public Policy* 16 (6): 791–812.

Lenner, Katharina, and Lewis Turner. 2018. "Learning from the Jordan Compact." *Forced Migration Review* 57: 48–51.

Levitan, Rachel, Esra Kaytaz, and Oktay Durukan. 2009. "Unwelcome Guests: The Detention of Refugees in Turkey's "Foreigners' Guesthouses." *Refuge* 26 (1): 77–90.

Levitsky, Steven, and Lucan A. Way. 2002. "The Rise of Competitive Authoritarianism." *Journal of Democracy* 13 (2): 51–65.

——— 2010. *Competitive Authoritarianism: Hybrid Regimes after the Cold War.* Cambridge: Cambridge University Press.

Lewis, Bernard. 1992. *Race and Slavery in the Middle East.* Oxford: Oxford University Press. https://doi.org/10.1093/acprof:oso/9780195053265 .001.0001.

Loescher, Gil. 2003. "UNHCR at Fifty: Refugee Protection and World Politics." In *Problems of Protection: The UNHCR, Refugees, and*

Human Rights, edited by Niklaus Steiner, Mark Gibney, and Gil Loescher, 3–18. New York: Routledge.

Lombardi, Clark B., and Nathan J. Brown. 2006. "Do Constitutions Requiring Adherence to Sharia Threaten Human Rights? How Egypt's Constitutional Court Reconciles Islamic Law with the Liberal Rule of Law." *American University International Law Review* 21: 379–435.

Lori, Noora. 2019. *Offshore Citizens: Permanent Temporary Status in the Gulf.* Cambridge: Cambridge University Press.

Loveluck, Louisa. 2018. "Syria Offers Amnesty to Military Deserters, but Exiles Are Cautious." *Washington Post*, October 9. www .washingtonpost.com/world/syria-offers-amnesty-to-military-deserters -but-exiles-are-cautious/2018/10/09/8dcdec26-cbcc-11e8-ad0a-0e01ef ba3cc1_story.html.

MACP. 2013. "King Mohammed VI Deepens Morocco's Economic, Security Ties with African Countries, Gains Support for W. Sahara Initiative." Moroccan American Center for Policy. www.prnewswire.com/news-releases/king-mohammed-vi-deepens-moroccos-economic-security-ties -with-african-countries-gains-support-for-w-sahara-initiative-1995904 01.html.

Magra, Iliana. 2018. "Greece's Island of Despair." *New York Times*, March 29. www.nytimes.com/2018/03/29/world/europe/greece-lesbos-migrant-crisis-moria.html.

Malka, Haim, and Jon B. Alterman. 2006. *Arab Reform and Foreign Aid: Lessons from Morocco.* Significant Issues Series 28, no. 4. Washington, DC: CSIS Press, Center for Strategic and International Studies.

Mann, Michael. 1988. *States, War and Capitalism.* Oxford: Basil Blackwell.

Manna, Haytham. 2012. "Syria's Opposition Has Been Led Astray by Violence." *Guardian*, June 22. www.theguardian.com/commentisfree/ 2012/jun/22/syria-opposition-led-astray-by-violence.

MAP. 2015. "Morocco Regularizes Status of around 18,000 Migrants in 2014." Ministry of Culture and Communication. www.maroc.ma/en/ node/20197.

Marshall, Monty G. 2017. "Polity IV Annual Time-Series, 1800–2016." Polity IV Project, Center for Systemic Peace. www.systemicpeace.org/i nscr/p4manualv2016.pdf.

Marshall, Monty G., and Gabrielle Elzinga-Marshall. 2017. "Global Report 2017: Conflict, Governance, and State Fragility." Center for Systemic Peace. www.systemicpeace.org/vlibrary/GlobalReport2017.pdf.

Martin, Lisa L., and Beth A. Simmons. 1998. "Theories and Empirical Studies of International Institutions." *International Organization* 52 (4): 729–57.

Masters, James, and Nadine Schmidt. 2018. "Stranded Ship with More than 230 Migrants Finally Docks in Malta." CNN, June 28. https://edition

.cnn.com/2018/06/27/europe/lifeline-migrant-boat-docks-malta-intl/in dex.html.

Mattern, Janice Bially, and Ayşe Zarakol. 2016. "Hierarchies in World Politics." *International Organization* 70 (3): 623–54.

McAdam, Jane. 2019. "The Global Compacts on Refugees and Migration: A New Era for International Protection?" *International Journal of Refugee Law* 30 (4): 571–4. https://doi.org/10.1093/ijrl/eez004.

McConnell, Alan, and Paul 't Hart. 2019. "Inaction and Public Policy: Understanding Why Policymakers 'Do Nothing.'" *Policy Sciences* 52: 645–61.

Mearsheimer, John J. 1994. "The False Promise of International Institutions." *International Security* 19 (3): 5–49.

MEO. 2013. "Côte d'Ivoire Reiterates Its Support to Morocco's Western Sahara Initiative." *Middle East Online*. https://middle-east-online.com /en/c%C3%B4te-divoire-reiterates-its-support-morocco%E2%80%99 s-western-sahara-initiative.

Miller, Mark. 1981. *Foreign Workers in Western Europe: An Emerging Political Force*. New York: Praeger.

Milner, James. 2009. *Refugees, the State and the Politics of Asylum in Africa*. Basingstoke: Palgrave Macmillan.

Minderhound, Paul E. 1999. "Asylum Seekers and Access to Society Security: Recent Developments in the Netherlands, United Kingdom, Germany and Belgium." In *Refugees, Citizenship and Social Policy in Europe*, 132–48. London: Macmillan.

Modood, Tariq. 2009. "The State and Ethno-Religious Mobilization in Britain." In *Bringing Outsiders In: Transatlantic Perspectives on Immigrant Political Incorporation*, 233–49. Ithaca, NY: Cornell University Press.

Morris, Lydia. 1998. "Governing at a Distance: The Elaboration of Controls in British Immigration." *International Migration Review* 32 (4): 949–73.

Moss, Dana. 2014. "Repression, Response, and Contained Escalation under 'Liberalized' Authoritarianism in Jordan." *Mobilization: An International Quarterly* 19 (3): 261–86.

2016. "Transnational Repression, Diaspora Mobilization, and the Case of the Arab Spring." *Social Problems* 63 (4): 480–98. https://doi.org/10 .1093/socpro/spw019.

Mourad, Lama. 2017a. "Inaction as Policy-Making: Understanding Lebanon's Early Response to the Refugee Influx." *Project on Middle East Political Science (POMEPS) Studies*, Vol. 25.

2017b. "'Standoffish' Policy-Making: Inaction and Change in the Lebanese Response to the Syrian Displacement Crisis." *Middle East Law and Governance* 9 (3): 249–66. https://doi.org/10.1163 /18763375–00903005.

Mourji, Fouzi, Jean-Noël Ferrié, Saadia Radi, and Mehdi Alioua. 2016. "Les Migrants Subsahariens Au Maroc: Enjeux d'une Migration de Résidence." Konrad Adenauer Stiftung, Bureau du Maroc. www .kas.de/wf/doc/kas_47249-1522-3-30.pdf.

MSF. 2013. "Violence, Vulnerability and Migration: A Report on the Situation of Sub-Saharan Migrants in an Irregular Situation in Morocco." Médecins Sans Frontières.

Mutiga, Murithi, and Emma Graham-Harrison. 2016. "Kenya Says It Will Shut World's Biggest Refugee Camp at Dadaab." *Guardian*, May 11. www.theguardian.com/world/2016/may/11/kenya-close-worlds-big gest-refugee-camp-dadaab.

Mylona, Eftychia. 2018. "A Presence without a Narrative: The Greeks in Egypt, 1961–1976/Une présence sans récit: la communauté grecque en Égypte, 1961–1976." *Revue des Mondes Musulmans et de la Méditerranée*, November, no. 144: 175–90.

Mylonas, Harris. 2012. *The Politics of Nation-Building: Making Co-nationals, Refugees, and Minorities*. Problems of International Politics. New York: Cambridge University Press.

Naceur, Sofian Philip, and Tom Rollins. 2017. "Europe's Migration Trade with Egypt." *Mada Masr*, February 1. www.madamasr.com/en/2017/0 2/01/feature/politics/europes-migration-trade-with-egypt/.

Naib, Fatima. 2018. "Slavery in Libya: Life inside a Container." Al Jazeera, January 26. www.aljazeera.com/news/2018/01/slavery-libya-life-container-180121084314393.html.

Nasr, Kameel B. 1997. *Arab and Israeli Terrorism: The Causes and Effects of Political Violence, 1936–1993*. Jefferson, NC: McFarland.

Natter, Katharina. 2015. "Almost Home? Morocco's Incomplete Migration Reforms." *World Politics Review*. www.worldpoliticsre view.com/articles/15691/almost-home-morocco-s-incomplete-migra tion-reforms.

——— 2018. "Rethinking Immigration Policy Theory beyond 'Western Liberal Democracies'." *Comparative Migration Studies* 6 (1): 1–21. https://doi .org/10.1186/s40878-018-0071-9.

New Arab. 2018. "Returning Syrian Refugees Face Death and Disappearance." November 7. www.alaraby.co.uk/english/indepth/20 18/11/7/returning-syrian-refugees-face-death-and-disappearance.

News Abidjan. 2015. "L'Ambassadeur de La Côte d'Ivoire Auprès de l'ONU Démis de Ses Fonctions." March 13. http://news.abidjan.net/h/528615 .html.

Niang, Bocar. 2017. "Maghreb-Afrique Noire: Derrière Le Drame Des Migrants, Le Poids Des Préjugés Raciaux." http://histoireengagee.ca/ca tegory/collaborateurs/bocar-niang/.

Nielsen, Nikolaj. 2016. "People Leaving Egypt to Italy Doubled in Past Year." *EU Observer*, July 1. https://euobserver.com/migration/134163.

Nkrumah, Gamal. 2013. "The Golden Age of Arab-African Relations." Research on Islam and Muslims in Africa. https://muslimsinafrica.wordpress.com/2013/06/28/the-golden-age-of-arab-african-relations-2/.

Norman, Kelsey P. 2014. "Turkey's New Migration Policy: Control through Bureaucratization." *Jadaliyya*. www.jadaliyya.com/pages/index/19384/turkey%E2%80%99s-new-migration-policy_control-through-bure.

2016a. "Access to Legal Residency for Refugees in the Middle East: Bureaucracy, Deterrence, and Prolonged Impermanence." Middle East Institute. www.mei.edu/content/map/access-legal-residency-refugees-middle-east.

2016b. "Between Europe and Africa: Morocco as a Country of Immigration." *Journal of the Middle East and Africa* 7 (4): 421–39.

2016c. "Migrants, Refugees and the Egyptian Security State." *International Journal of Migration and Border Studies* 2 (4): 345–64.

2019. "Inclusion, Exclusion or Indifference? Redefining Migrant and Refugee Host State Engagement Options in Mediterranean 'Transit' Countries." *Journal of Ethnic and Migration Studies* 45 (1): 42–60. https://doi.org/10.1080/1369183X.2018.1482201.

2020. "Migration Diplomacy and Policy Liberalization in Morocco and Turkey." *International Migration Review*. https://doi.org/10.1177/0197918319895271.

OECD. 2010. "Tackling the Policy Challenges of Migration." Organization for Economic Co-operation and Development.

Ogata, Sadako. 2005. *The Turbulent Decade: Confronting the Refugee Crises of the 1990s*. New York: W. W. Norton.

OHCHR. 2017. "EU 'Trying to Move Border to Libya' Using Policy That Breaches Rights – UN Experts." United Nations Human Rights, Office of the High Commissioner. www.ohchr.org/EN/NewsEvents/Pages/DisplayNews.aspx?LangID=E%23pq%3DineCjE&NewsID=21978.

Olcot, Martha Brill, and Marina Ottaway. 1999. "Challenge of Semi-Authoritarianism." Carnegie Papers, Carnegie Endowment for International Peace. http://carnegieendowment.org/1999/10/01/challenge-of-semi-authoritarianism/cm8.

Onoma, Ato Kwamena. 2013. *Anti-refugee Violence and African Politics*. Cambridge: Cambridge University Press. https://doi.org/10.1017/CBO9781139568135.

Orchard, Phil. 2014. *A Right to Flee: Refugees, States, and the Construction of International Cooperation*. Cambridge: Cambridge University Press. https://doi.org/10.1017/CBO9781139923293.

Ottaway, Marina, and Meredith Riley. 2008. "Morocco: Top-Down Reform without Democratic Transition." In *Beyond the Façade: Political Reform in the Arab World*, 161–86. Washington, DC: Carnegie Endowment for International Peace.

Oyen, Meredith. 2015. *The Diplomacy of Migration: Transnational Lives and the Making of US–Chinese Relations in the Cold War*. Ithaca, NY: Cornell University Press.

Palm, Anja. 2017. "EU Immigration and Asylum Law and Policy/Droit et Politique de l'Immigration et de l'Asile de l'UE." http://eumigrationlaw blog.eu/the-italy-libya-memorandum-of-understanding-the-baseline-of -a-policy-approach-aimed-at-closing-all-doors-to-europe/.

Parolin, Gianluca Paolo. 2009. *Citizenship in the Arab World: Kin, Religion and Nation-State*. IMISCOE Research. Amsterdam: Amsterdam University Press.

Pearlman, Wendy. 2014. "Competing for Lebanon's Diaspora: Trans-nationalism and Domestic Struggles in a Weak State." *International Migration Review* 48 (1): 34–75. https://doi.org/10.1111/imre.12070.

Peraldi, Michel. 2011. *D'une Afrique à l'autre, Migrations Subsahariennes Au Maroc*. Paris: Karthala Editions.

Perry, Tom. 2018. "Russian Envoy Urges Syrian Refugee Return." Reuters, July 26. www.reuters.com/article/us-mideast-crisis-russia-syria-refu gees/russian-envoy-urges-syrian-refugee-return-idUSKBN1KG2C8.

Pierini, Marc. 2018. "The 2018 Turkey Progress Report." Carnegie Europe. http://carnegieeurope.eu/2018/03/14/2018-turkey-regress-report-pub -75794.

Plumer, Brad. 2013. "The US Gives Egypt $1.5 Billion a Year in Aid: Here's What It Does." *Washington Post*, July 9. www.washingtonpost.com/n ews/wonk/wp/2013/07/09/the-u-s-gives-egypt-1-5-billion-a-year-in-aid -heres-what-it-does/.

Putnam, Robert D. 1988. "Diplomacy and Domestic Politics: The Logic of Two-Level Games." *International Organization* 42 (3): 427–60. https://doi.org/10.1017/S0020818300027697.

Ragazzi, Francesco. 2009. "Governing Diasporas." *International Political Sociology* 3: 378–97.

Ramadan, Adam, and Sara Fregonese. 2017. "Hybrid Sovereignty and the State of Exception in the Palestinian Refugee Camps in Lebanon." *Annals of the American Association of Geographers* 107 (4): 949–63. https://doi.org/10.1080/24694452.2016.1270189.

Rankin, Jennifer. 2018. "EU Leaders Hail Summit Victory on Migration but Details Scant." *Guardian*, June 29. www.theguardian.com/world/2018/ jun/29/eu-leaders-summit-migration-doubts.

Reidy, Eric. 2017. "Special Report: The Libyan Migrant 'Prisons' of Europe's Making." *IRIN News*, November 1. www.irinnews.org/spe cial-report/2017/11/01/libyan-migrant-prisons-europe-s-making.

Rosenblum, Marc R. 2004. "Beyond the Policy of No-Policy: Emigration from Mexico and Central America." *Latin American Political Science* 4 (1): 91–125.

Roxström, Erik, and Mark Gibney. 2003. "The Legal and Ethical Obligations of UNHCR: The Case of Temporary Protection in Western Europe." In *Problems of Protection: The UNHCR, Refugees, and Human Rights*, edited by Niklaus Steiner, Mark Gibney, and Gil Loescher, 61–78. New York: Routledge.

Rudolph, Christopher. 2003. "Security and the Political Economy of International Migration." *American Political Science Review* 97 (4): 603–20.

Ruhs, Martin. 2013. *The Price of Rights: Regulating International Labor Migration*. Princeton, NJ: Princeton University Press.

Sadiq, Kamal. 2009. *Paper Citizens: How Illegal Immigrants Acquire Citizenship in Developing Countries*. Oxford: Oxford University Press.

Salih, Assad Khalid. 2006. "Sudanese Demonstration in Cairo: Different Stands and Different Opinions." Presented at the Fourth Annual Forced Migration Postgraduate Student Conference, University of East London, London, March 18.

Sassen, Saskia. 2002. "Towards Post-national and Denationalized Citizenship." In *Handbook of Citizenship Studies*, 277–91. London: Sage.

Sassoon, Joseph. 2009. *The Iraqi Refugees: The New Crisis in the Middle East*. International Library of Migration Studies 3. London: I. B. Tauris.

Sater, James N. 2010. *Morocco: Challenges to Tradition and Modernity*. The Contemporary Middle East. Milton Park: Routledge.

Scheel, Stephan, and Philipp Ratfisch. 2014. "Refugee Protection Meets Migration Management: UNHCR as a Global Police of Populations." *Journal of Ethnic and Migration Studies* 40 (6): 924–41. https://doi.org /10.1080/1369183X.2013.855074.

Schuettler, Kirsten. 2017. "A Second Regularization Campaign for Irregular Immigrants in Morocco: When Emigration Countries Become Immigration Countries." World Bank Blogs. https://blogs .worldbank.org/peoplemove/second-regularization-campaign-irregular -immigrants-morocco-when-emigration-countries-become.

Schwenk, Katya. 2019. "Despite Accelerated Growth, Unemployment Persists in Morocco." *Morocco World News*, June 5. www.morocco worldnews.com/2019/06/275140/acceleration-growth-unemployment- morocco-industries/.

Segura, Natalia. 2018. "EU–Egypt: Toward a New Migration Agreement?" https://euranetplus-inside.eu/eu-egypt-towards-a-new-migration-agree ment/.

Sly, Liz. 2015. "8 Reasons Europe's Refugee Crisis Is Happening Now." *Washington Post*, September 18. www.washingtonpost.com/news/wor ldviews/wp/2015/09/18/8-reasons-why-europes-refugee-crisis-is-hap pening-now/.

Soysal, Yasmine Nuhoglu. 1994. *The Limits of Citizenship: Migrants and Postnational Membership in Europe.* Chicago: University of Chicago Press.

Sperl, Stefan. 2001. "Evaluation of UNHCR's Policy on Refugees in Urban Areas: A Case Study Review of Cairo." United Nations High Commissioner for Refugees Evaluation and Policy Analysis Unit.

Stern, Rachel E., and Kevin J. O'Brien. 2012. "Politics at the Boundary: Mixed Signals and the Chinese State." *Modern China* 38 (2): 174–98.

Strickland, Patrick. 2018. "Concern as 300 Refugees and Migrants Reach Greek Island of Lesbos." Al Jazeera, March 28. www.aljazeera.com/ne ws/2018/03/concern-300-refugees-migrants-reach-greek-island-lesbos-180328115153014.html.

Su, Yang, and Xin He. 2010. "Street as Courtroom: State Accommodation of Labor Protest in South China." *Law and Society Review* 44 (1): 157–84.

Sunderland, Judith. 2018. "Europe Is Losing Its Moral Compass in the Mediterranean: EU Should Support, Not Obstruct, Rescue at Sea." Human Rights Watch. www.hrw.org/news/2018/07/03/europe-losing-its-moral-compass-mediterranean.

Suzan, Benedicte. 2002. "The Barcelona Process and the European Approach to Fighting Terrorism." Center on the US and France, Brookings Institution. www.brookings.edu/wp-content/uploads/2016/06/suzan .pdf.

Teevan, Chloe. 2018. "Morocco, the EU, and the Migration Dilemma." European Council on Foreign Relations. www.ecfr.eu/article/comm entary_morocco_the_eu_and_the_migration_dilemma.

Teitelbaum, Michael S. 1984. "Immigration, Refugees, and Foreign Policy." *International Organization* 38 (3): 429–50. https://doi.org/10.1017 /S0020818300026801.

Theofilopoulou, Anna. 2010. "Western Sahara: The Failure of 'Negotiations without Preconditions'." United States Institute of Peace (USIP) Peace Brief 22.

Thiolett, Helene. 2011. "Migration as Diplomacy: Labor Migrants, Refugees, and Arab Regional Politics in the Oil-Rich Countries." *International Labor and Working-Class History* 79: 103–21.

TIMEP. 2019. "Draft NGO Law of 2019." Tahrir Institute for Middle East Policy. https://timep.org/reports-briefings/draft-ngo-law-of-2019/.

Toaldo, Mattia. 2017. "The EU Deal with Libya on Migration: A Question of Fairness and Effectiveness." European Council on Foreign Relations. www.ecfr.eu/article/commentary_the_eu_deal_with_libya_on_migra tion_a_question_of_fairness_a.

Toksöz, Gülay, Seyhan Erdoğdu, and Selmin Kaşka. 2012. "Irregular Labour Migration in Turkey and Situation of Migrant Workers in the Labour Market." Swedish International Development Cooperation Agency and the International Organization for Migration. http://lastra dainternational.org/lsidocs/3072-IOM_irregular_labour_migration%2 0Turkey.pdf.

Tokuzlu, Lami Bertan. 2010. "Burden-Sharing Games for Asylum Seekers between Turkey and the European Union." EUI Working Papers, Robert Schuman Centre for Advanced Studies. www.eui.eu/RSCAS/Pu blications/.

Trew, Bel, Oshah Abdullah, and Tom Kington. 2017. "Libyan Militia Chief Admits Deal with Tripoli to Stem Migrant Flow." *Times*, September 1. www.thetimes.co.uk/article/libyan-militia-chief-admits-deal-with-tri poli-to-stem-migrant-flow-ahmed-dabbashi-brigade-migrant-crisis-ital y-538lwtgf5.

Tsourapas, Gerasimos. 2017. "Migration Diplomacy in the Global South: Cooperation, Coercion and Issue Linkage in Gaddafi's Libya." *Third World Quarterly* 38 (10): 2367–85.

———. 2019a. *The Politics of Migration in Modern Egypt: Strategies for Regime Survival in Autocracies*. Cambridge: Cambridge University Press. http s://doi.org/10.1017/9781108630313.

———. 2019b. "The Syrian Refugee Crisis and Foreign Policy Decision-Making in Jordan, Lebanon, and Turkey." Preprint. SocArXiv. https://doi.org/10 .31235/osf.io/a6s58.

Turkey Purge. 2018. "Turkey Purge: Turkey's Post-Coup Crackdown." July 12. https://turkeypurge.com/.

UN General Assembly. 2017. "Address by H.E. General Michael Aoun, President of the Republic of Lebanon, at the Seventy-Second Session of the United Nations General Assembly." https://gadebate.un.org/sites/d efault/files/gastatements/72/lb_en.pdf.

———. 2018. "Press Release: United Nations Finalized First Ever Global Compact for Migration." www.un.org/pga/72/2018/07/13/press-release-united- nations-finalizes-first-ever-global-compact-for-migration/.

UN Population Division. 2013. "The Number of International Migrants Worldwide Reaches 232 Million." United Nations Department of Economic and Social Affairs, Population Division No. 2013/2.

2017. "The World Counted 258 Million International Migrants in 2017, Representing 3.4 Per Cent of the Global Population." www.un.org/en/development/desa/population/publications/pdf/popfacts/PopFacts_2017-5.pdf.

UNHCR. 2013. "UNHCR Urges Countries to Enable Safe Passage, Keep Borders Open for Syrian Refugees." www.unhcr.org/526108d89.html.

2015. "The Sea Route to Europe: The Mediterranean Passage in the Age of Refugees." www.unhcr.org/5592bd059.html#11.

2016. "UNHCR Chief Pledges More Support for Turkey Refugee Response." www.unhcr.org/en-us/news/latest/2016/9/57c856484/unhcr-chief-pledges-support-turkey-refugee-response.html.

2018. "UNHCR Urges Hungary to Withdraw Draft Law Impacting Refugees." www.unhcr.org/en-us/news/press/2018/5/5b0d71684/unhcr-urges-hungary-withdraw-draft-law-impacting-refugees.html.

2019. "UN Refugee Chief in Egypt on First Official Visit in 2019." www.unhcr.org/eg/12488-un-refugee-chief-in-egypt-on-first-official-visit-in-2019.html.

UNHCR Turkey. 2016. "UNHCR Turkey: Key Facts and Figures December 2016." https://reliefweb.int/sites/reliefweb.int/files/resources/UNHCRTurkeyKeyfactsandfiguresExternal.December.pdf.

UNICEF. 2017. "A Deadly Journey for Children: The Central Mediterranean Route." www.unicef.de/blob/135970/6178f12582223da6980ee1974a772c14/a-deadl-journey-for-children–unicef-report-data.pdf.

UNOCHA. 2018. "Syria Humanitarian Response Plan 2018." https://fts.unocha.org/appeals/629/summary.

Vairel, Frederic. 2013. "Protesting in Authoritarian Situations: Egypt and Morocco in Comparative Perspective." In *Social Movements, Mobilization, and Contestation in the Middle East and North Africa*, 33–48. Stanford, CA: Stanford University Press.

Vammen, Ida Marie, and Hans Lucht. 2017. "Refugees in Turkey Struggle as Border Walls Grow Higher." Danish Institute for International Studies. www.diis.dk/en/research/refugees-in-turkey-struggle-as-border-walls-grow-higher.

Vora, Neha. 2013. *Impossible Citizens: Dubai's Indian Diaspora*. Durham, NC: Duke University Press.

Ward, Patricia. 2014. "Refugee Cities: Reflections on the Development and Impact of UNHCR Urban Refugee Policy in the Middle East." *Refugee Survey Quarterly* 33 (1): 77–93. https://doi.org/10.1093/rsq/hdt024.

Weber, Bobo. 2016. "Time for a Plan B: The European Refugee Crisis, the Balkan Route and the EU–Turkey Deal." Democratization Policy

Council. www.democratizationpolicy.org/pdf/DPC_Policy_Paper_Eur op_refugee_crisis_EU_Turkey_deal.pdf.

Wedeen, Lisa. 2010. "Reflections on Ethnographic Work in Political Science." *Annual Review of Political Science* 13 (1): 255–72. https://doi .org/10.1146/annurev.polisci.11.052706.123951.

Weiner, Myron. 1985. "On International Migration and International Relations." *Population and Development Review* 11 (3): 441. https:// doi.org/10.2307/1973247.

Willis, Michael J. 1999. "Between *Alternance* and the *Makhzen: At-Tawhid Wa Al-Islah's* Entry into Moroccan Politics." *Journal of North African Studies* 4 (3): 45–80. https://doi.org/10.1080/13629389908718373.

Witte, Grif. 2013. "Egypt Sees Ethiopian Dam as Risk to Water Supply." *Guardian*, June 18. www.theguardian.com/world/2013/jun/18/egypt-ethiopia-dam-blue-nile.

Woldemariam, Yohannes. 2017. "Morocco's New Tango with the African Union." LSE Centre for Africa. http://blogs.lse.ac.uk/africaatlse/2017/01/20/moroccos-new-tango-with-the-african-union/.

Wolff, Sarah. 2014. "The Politics of Negotiating Readmission Agreements: Insights from Morocco and Turkey." *European Journal of Migration and Law* 16(1): 69–95.

——— 2015. "Migration and Refugee Governance in the Mediterranean: Europe and International Organisations at a Crossroads." IAI Working Papers. www.iai.it/en/pubblicazioni/migration-and-refugee-governance-mediterranean.

Zohry, Ayman. 2003. "The Place of Egypt in the Regional Migration System as a Receiving Country." *Revue Européenne Des Migrations Internationales* 19 (3): 129–49.

Zohry, Ayman, and Barbara Harrell-Bond. 2003. "Contemporary Egyptian Migration: An Overview of Voluntary and Forced Migration." Forced Migration and Refugee Studies Program, Working Paper C3, American University in Cairo.

Zolberg, Aristide, Astri Suhrke, and Aguayo Sergio. 1989. *Escape from Violence: Conflict and the Refugee Crisis in the Developing World.* Oxford: Oxford University Press.

Zunes, Stephen, and Jacob Mundy. 2010. *Western Sahara: War, Nationalism, and Conflict Irresolution.* 1st ed. Syracuse Studies on Peace and Conflict Resolution. Syracuse, NY: Syracuse University Press.

Index

248

CPSIA information can be obtained
at www.ICGtesting.com
Printed in the USA
LVHW041543230822
726649LV00003B/130